AF572046

INDUSTRIAL EYE

Photographs by Jet Lowe
from the Historic American
Engineering Record

Essays by David Weitzman
and Michael Leccese

Preface by Robert J. Kapsch

Text by Gray Fitzsimons

Edited by Diane Maddex

THE PRESERVATION PRESS

EARTH

AIR

FIRE

WATER

LIBERTY

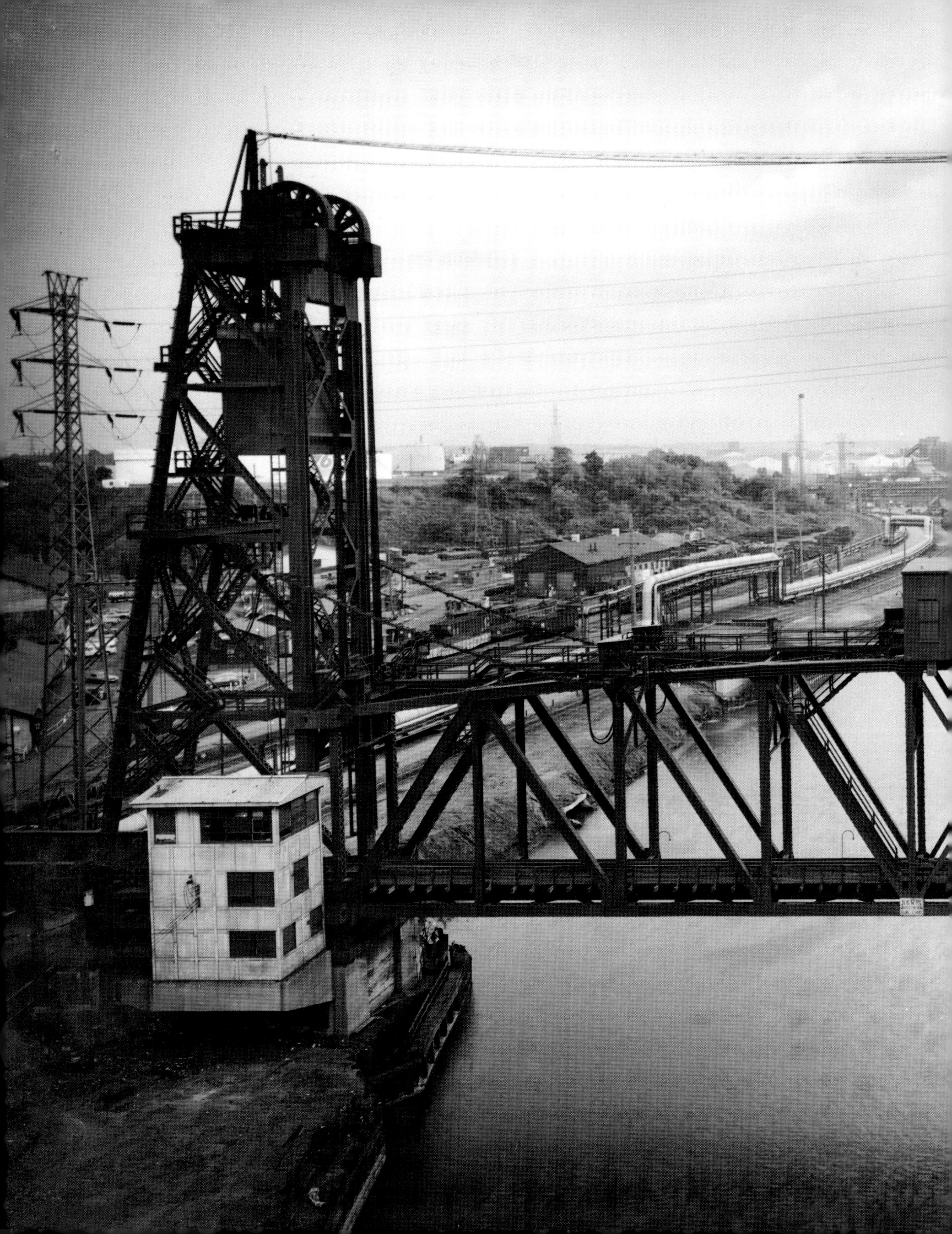

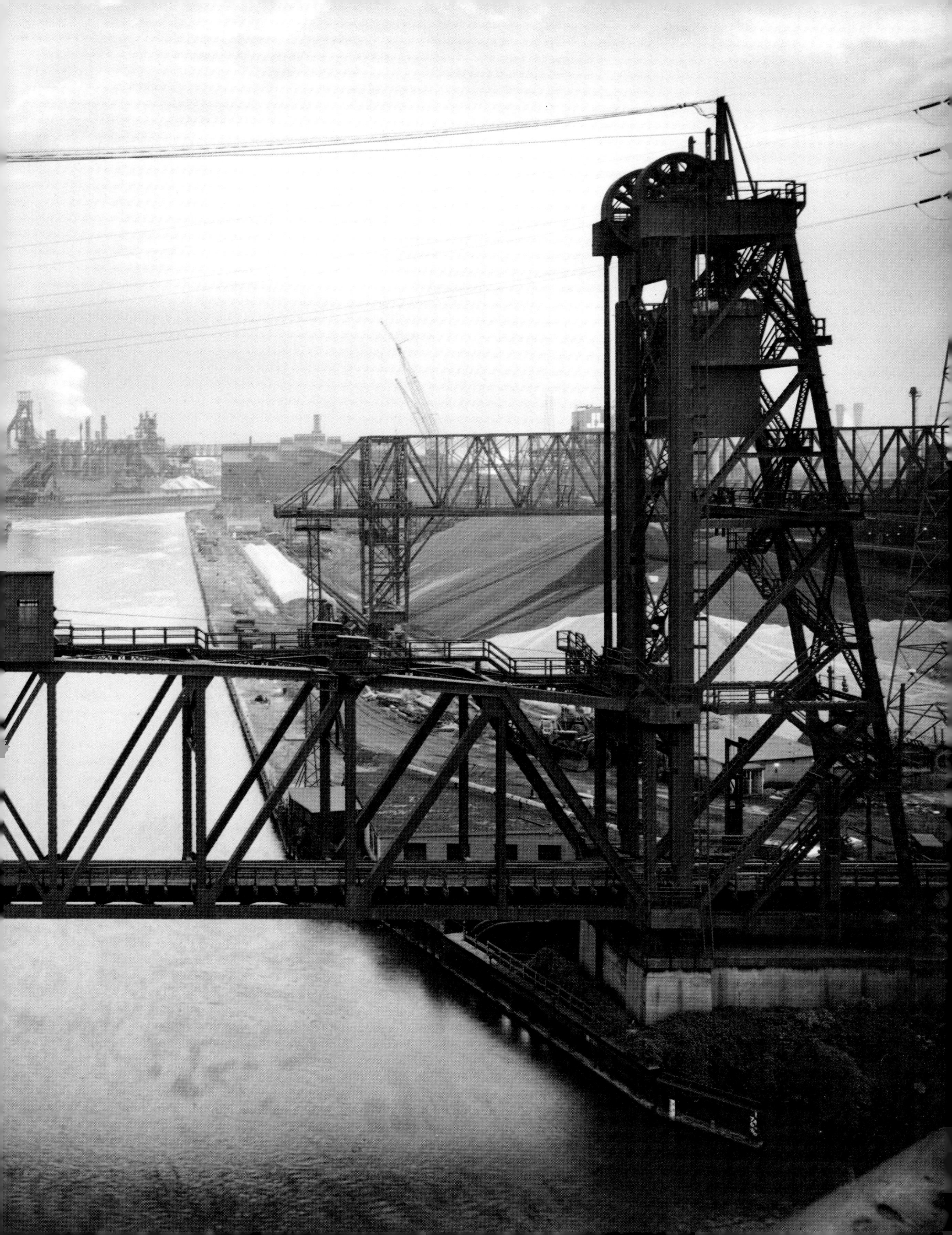

PREFACE

ROBERT J. KAPSCH

This is a book of beautiful photographs. But it is also much more. To understand these photographs, it is necessary to understand the conditions under which Jet Lowe works and the purpose these photographs are meant to serve.

Lowe is one of the few field photographers in the United States who still work in large format. Large-format photography is heavy, grueling work, and it is also slow and tedious. His work produces not just photographs but archivally processed documents intended to last 500 years and, together with measured drawings and histories, to provide an accurate record of the nation's industrial and engineering landmarks for generations of scholars. These scholars represent varied fields of historical inquiry, including the history of engineering and technology, industrial archeology, and labor and social history. Unlike some older interpretations of American history, these fields are united in their view that the economic basis of American life, and particularly the industrial revolution, has been the prime shaper of this country. As American society continues to evolve rapidly from industrial production toward service production, the need to record America's industrial past becomes more pressing. Jet Lowe's photographs thus are not merely beautiful photographs, but documents that reveal something to us about America's past and perhaps its future.

Across America's industrial landscape, his camera's eye encounters a fascinating range of technological images, old and new. From small wood-frame grist mills to hulking, iron-columned and brick textile mills, these images capture the human attempt to shape and control nature's elements, the earth, air, fire and water. The photographs here bear witness to our endeavors to harness raw power for useful work and to transform natural resources into finished products. In Butte, Mont., abandoned mineyards now stand where the earth one yielded a rich lode of copper. From Brooklyn to San Francisco, suspension bridges — among the most striking of technological feats — soar through the air, linking together communities and commerce. Along the Cuyahoga River in Cleveland, blast furnaces still glow with fire from an ore smelting operation. And in California's Sierra Nevadas, four turn-of-the-century hydroelectric plants continue to draw water from Battle Creek and generate electricity for surrounding farms and towns.

A careful examination of Jet Lowe's work shows us industrial processes and changes in American technology. At the same time, one cannot help but feel that these images are the product of an extraordinary artist. I have had the pleasure of working with Jet for seven years. This book is testimony to the many long and hard hours of work that he has undertaken in remote, and sometimes hazardous, locations. But it cannot fully portray the character of the man, an affable Georgian who takes great intellectual interest in the technological subjects he photographs. I invite you to sample these photographs selected from the thousands that reside in the Library of Congress. This work makes a rich contribution to the understanding of a vital part of American history.

INTRODUCTION

DAVID WEITZMAN

Page through this book, and what do you see? Red-brick factories. Lattice truss bridges, all rivets and girders. Rusted train tracks. Canals no longer busy with packet boats, shingled windmills whose sails have been furled for generations now, tumbledown corn cribs and warehouses. Romantic places, with names such as United Waste Company, Burnsville Natural Gas Pumping Station, Quincy Mining, Picatinny Arsenal and the Cleveland Breakwater. Why do a book about them? Cast-iron buildings in SoHo. Yes. Victorian row houses in San Francisco. Sure. But a blast furnace?

Yes, a blast furnace, and a steam plant and as many old textile mills as you can find. To most of us, it takes considerable imagination to see what is intriguing about an ore loader or a dilapidated sawmill. The steam engine in the Quincy Mining Company is . . . interesting. And the Goodyear Airdock is . . . big, yes, very big. (It's hard to find words to describe things we've not noticed before, never thought much about.) But take a second look. Try to escape, for the moment, your computer age perspective. Try to feel the excitement and fascination of another generation, for whom these things were as modern and futuristic, surely, as supersonic swept-wing aircraft and antenna-studded orbiters. Remember that steam engines did our work for more than a century. We once regarded them as magnificent machines, the symbols of a modern industrial nation. Our fathers took us on walks to the pumping station or powerhouse to peer inside at the big engine, steam chest and flywheel painted bright green and yellow and red, striped and ornamented. And remember when dirigibles once excited another generation of Americans who did not know sleek airliners and rockets? We are still awed by these massive airships and a structure huge enough to house one. They required, even by current standards, spectacular engineering.

Today we have become more aware of the value of saving all types of old structures — even blast furnaces and airdocks. There is now a preservation consciousness that reaches into the neighborhoods and small towns of America. Many of us have our own preservation stories to tell, about the locomotive works becoming a museum, the schoolhouse turned into a library, the cast-iron fountain and lamp posts that have been returned to the park. Similar stories are now being told about communities rising up to save historic bridges slated for demolition, the 19th-century iron foundry that continues to provide skilled jobs and old New England textile mills being converted into roomy, airy housing for the elderly.

But awareness doesn't just happen. Someone had to point out to us what was there that we weren't seeing. We had to learn to see and then to acknowledge the values and tastes of another age. We came to appreciate buildings as part of our roots, our lives, a diversity of styles arising from a diversity of people. The skills of their architects and builders began showing through checked and peeling paint. They became old friends again. If for no other reason, we valued them as interesting and useful spaces. And then we acted, to save and to preserve them.

Looking at industrial structures, though, will be a new experience for many people. Even those who consider themselves sensitive to old buildings may have trouble with splintered wooden trusses and the rubble that was once a canal lock chamber. But we've found a new book, *Industrial Eye*, filled with images of working places from the collection of the Historic American Engineering Record. The photographs here rouse us to confront our feelings about machines and industrial structures just as we once had to acknowledge how we felt about old buildings. That's important, because these feelings affect how we see them — indeed, whether we see them at all.

Americans have some unfinished business with their industrial past. I remember first discovering the industrial object as a child, during the 1930s and 1940s, in the form of the steam locomotive. As a young art student, my attention was constantly being drawn to natural subjects, to the green landscape, the flowers and bowls of fruit thoughtfully set up before me by my teachers. Still, whenever I had the chance, I sat for hours in the tall grasses and wildflowers on a prairie hillside but with eyes only for the locomotives that steamed by. It was a secret I kept from others. I was embarrassed, I suppose, that I alone preferred the aesthetic of machinery (a concept I neither knew nor understood then). By the early 1950s, though, I was out of step with the new age. Streamlined diesels made steam locomotives, machines and work old fashioned, dirty. I skipped, and skipped again, to try and get into step but the new gait never felt comfortable to me. Later I realized that my life had spanned a curious turn of events. I was born and spent my early childhood in an America fascinated by machines and industry, girders and black smoke, among people who valued good workmanship. Here was where my attitudes were formed. But, then, I grew up and became an adult in a society that relegated machinery to some mossy, gritty past. What had been the pride of generations before me became, in a very few years, an embarrassment to mine. Proud symbols became eyesores. Not only didn't we gaze upon them, we no longer saw them, wished them gone. Your first response to Jet Lowe's photographs, I suspect, will have a lot to do with which side of that turn you grew up on.

I think Americans encounter some blind spots when they try to look at work and working places. We don't see industrial structures because we've learned to filter them out. If we are aware of them at all, we probably see them as junk. But it's not enough just to remind ourselves we once felt that way about iron-front buildings too, that appreciating a mine hoist house just takes a little more concentration. It's more complicated than that. When we look at an old working place we may not be seeing at all, but instead hearing disgruntled voices.

We've become disenchanted with machinery, with the rational order it once symbolized. The promise that machines and automation would free workers from a life of toil and give them endless leisure has turned out to be a bitter, hollow one. Far from freeing workers, new technologies have devalued personal skill, developed often over a lifetime of devoted practice, and deprived even skilled workers of the satisfaction of their craft. Few Americans today could accept Le Corbusier's declaration of 1923 that American engineering and industries "make the work of man ring in unison with universal orders." Having read about the lives of the jobless in America, it would be hard to keep a straight face were an industrialist to proclaim today as Henry Ford once did that "Machinery is the new Messiah."

There's not only disappointment, there's

also anger. Some blame industry for having wrought havoc on the environment. For others industrial structures are bitter monuments to the exploitation of generations of workers. Pollution, conflicts between labor and management, the cynicism of workers who have discovered that the "leisure" promised by machines is actually unemployment have dulled the bright, heroic colors with which industry and workers were once painted.

So the task faced by a HAER photographer is a difficult one. Often staff arrives just ahead of the wrecking crews. Sometimes owners are hesitant to admit them to old factories and mills, because the equipment is outdated or because they just want privacy to dispose of it as they see fit — which is why HAER needs to be there. The value of the structures to be recorded on film is no longer self-evident. Neither are their purpose and workings. The lines and forms of industrial structures no longer attract the eye as they once did — indeed, they may repel us. Jet Lowe wants us to look at what we no longer see, don't want to see. What he records to be remembered, many people want to forget. Because we do not readily accept the premise of his work, Lowe must lead us, perhaps trick us, into seeing a new way. A web of suspension bridge cables, a derelict mine hoist, an overgrown canal lock must be recorded in such a way that we learn something about what it does, how it works. But before he can awaken our curiosity, Lowe knows, he must compel our attention.

Jet Lowe is not the first to record historic American working places on film. Before him were other HABS and HAER photographers, most notably Jack E. Boucher and Wm. Edmund Barrett, whose work set standards for photographing architectural, industrial and engineering sites. The images Jack, Bill and Jet caught on film were my introduction to industrial archeology. I remember my first visit to the HAER office, discovering all the wonderful things there and having to choose from among thousands of photographs to illustrate my own books. I wanted them all, and always came home from HAER with dozens more photographs than I needed. These three made me aware, too, of how other photographers, especially Margaret Bourke-White, Lewis W. Hine and Ansel Adams, had also focused their talents on American industry.

Lowe continues an American tradition of artists setting down images of workers and working places. His medium, photography, puts him in the most recent chapters of that tradition. But the care with which he approaches his subject, his viewpoints, the textures and contours he renders, his spirit, echo the work of America's earliest limners. His images in color and black and white tantalize us to touch the surface of the print, expecting to feel the cold iron, the rough, weathered wood, the grit of the masonry. He goes beyond documentation to re-create a place and time in the past. He is an artist, to be sure, a master of technique with a firm control over his medium and an eye for fascinating detail. But he is also an industrial archeologist and a preservationist. Much of what he records will survive only on the delicate surfaces of his negatives and in his images of silver.

Work has always attracted the artist's eye. Those who know work know also its rhythms, powerful movements, its drama, colors and sounds, the flexing and uncoiling of hard working bodies, the careful movements of deft hands. They know the feeling of muscle worked to its limit and seemingly impossible tasks accomplished with great energy. They know, too, the tiredness and the satisfactions at the end of the day. At the very least work accomplishes tasks that must be done. So painters and photographers have sought out Americans wherever they work, plowing in the fields, hewing cabins and ships from timbers, husking corn, logging, sowing cotton, fishing, digging subways and mining coal.

Among Lowe's predecessors and mentors are American artists who have left us the only glimpses we have into the life of working Americans generations ago. The interior and tools of an early smithy, techniques for casting Civil War cannon, the furniture and presses of an early American print shop and the work of shipwrights are kept alive for us in paintings such as John Ferguson Wir's *The Gun Foundry* and Winslow Homer's *Shipbuilding at Gloucester.* The first iron truss bridges across the Ohio River might have remained unknown to us were it not for the paintings of Thomas P. Anshutz.

The tradition continued into the 20th century. Precisionist painters Charles Sheeler, Elsie Driggs and Charles Demuth, among others, are Jet Lowe's closest antecedents. The dominant elements in their paintings were the dominant structures on America's rural and urban skyline — blast furnaces, smokestacks, cranes, gas tanks, grain elevators, bridges, conveyors and factory buildings. I wish that I had been introduced to their work when I was young, because to these artists there was nothing inconsistent about an aesthetic of industry, about painting images of functional forms made of concrete, glass and steel. Sheeler's steam locomotive, turbine and River Rouge series are rendered with the clarity and precision of the objects themselves. He saw them as honest, straightforward, functional forms. "Forms created by industry to meet its needs," he wrote, "also carry conviction and claim the attention of the artist for the same reason."

From the very beginnings of the American experience up to the 1930s and 1940s, industry glowed in the American gaze. Factories and the work that went on inside and around them were perceived and depicted on canvas and film as positive symbols, emphasizing the dynamism of new technology. The lines, the forms and patterns of towering furnaces, sawtooth factories gleaming with myriad panes of glass and massive clusters of silos seemed to point into the future.

America was once proud of its factories and machines. We boasted of their feats. "Thy knitted frame, thy springs and valves, the tremulous twinkle of thy wheels," Walt Whitman wrote "To a Locomotive in Winter." "Type of the modern — emblem of motion and power — pulse of the continent." The products of American industry, particularly farm machinery, won gold medals at expositions all over Europe. With their power, effortless spinning and mirrorlike finished parts sliding smoothly, silently over each other along mathematical paths, machines became to Americans a metaphor for order and harmony, symbols of a futuristic society.

But if there is continuity in the tradition of which the HAER photographers are a part, there has also been a considerable change in American attitudes toward machinery and industry. Those attitudes have altered our perceptions of historic machines and industrial structures in the landscape. They have led us into an uncomfortable ambivalence. The work has become disjointed from the worker and the factory. We admire the flowing lines of an iron bridge in Central Park and marvel at the thousands of precisely hewn blocks laid one upon the other to form the towers of the Brooklyn Bridge, but without thinking of the foundrymen and stonecutters. We've abandoned the places where our fathers and mothers worked and so, without thinking, may be denying present and future generations places to work as well. Our lives are filled with truly wonderful machines, yet the faces of those who made them are invisible. Ben Shahn's painting of *Welders*, black and white together facing the task of winning a war, was done more than 40 years ago. It was the last heroic portrait of an American worker.

Still, industrial sites are vital parts of American history, although most of us have grown up without really understanding that. Given that most Americans worked on farms, in factories and workshops, on ships and in mines deep below the ground, the elitist history taught in our schools, which ignores the vast subject of work and the role of work in shaping American values, is dishonest. It is American history streamlined, like the shiny candy-colored diesels that replaced hard-working, grimy, oily steam locomotives. Most of us don't know that iron was as great an issue in the American Revolution as stamps and that American ironmasters who defied the British ban on making finished iron products in the colonies were revolutionaries as surely as those who threw tea into Boston's harbor. This has always been a nation of workers. Erecting mills and factories, harnessing water power with dams and canals, spanning rivers and gorges with bridges, cutting tunnels through mountains, linking cities with highways, railroads, waterways and power lines. This is what we do. This is what we've always done. The work and working places of the nation need to be recorded, studied and preserved with the same care as the artifacts and town sites of traditional archeology. In these forgotten structures is the history of most of us, of working Americans.

Even closer to us than the abstractions of a long-ago revolution are the things we might learn from a surviving working place. The origins of the place in which we live is one example. An old industrial site can tell us something about the history of our community, perhaps its beginnings. Industries once provided entire communities with generations of livelihoods and names such as Irondale, Wash., Petrolia, Pa., Irontown, Minn., and Carbondale, Ill. Hercules, Calif., grew out of the manufacture of blasting powder. Coalinga, on the railroad, derived somehow from Coaling Station No. 1. I live in a town called Point Reyes Station. It's not immediately obvious where the name came from; the railroad tracks were torn up long ago and built over. But the station still stands in the middle of town, disguised as a post office. The Wharf Streets, Railroad Avenues, Power House Roads and Sawmill Ponds to be found in cities and towns all over the country remind us again just how closely communities once identified with working places.

What Jet Lowe has discovered in his search for America's discarded industrial past and has seen countless times on the ground glass of his camera, we will soon know too. Industrial artifacts and structures may not be attractive in the conventional sense of beauty. But beauty has other moods, and utilitarian things have a voice of their own. It is because they were to be functional that these things of wood and metal and stone speak to us in other tones. The machines and structures in Lowe's photographs make straightforward, honest statements about work. A massive hydroelectric turbine, the delicate iron filigree ornamenting a bridge portal, the soaring, airy members of a roof truss and the courses of cut stone around a carefully turned arch, all reveal aspects of the American character. Today they remain as symbols of their times. In the sometimes subtle, sometimes striking differences in their form and line and color and textures may be read, as vividly as in any painting or novel, the aspirations and ideals, the dreams, the exhilaration and fascination of generations of Americans long ago.

PROFILE: JET LOWE

MICHAEL LECCESE

One gusty May day, Jet Lowe scaled scaffolding nearly 300 feet high to look the Statue of Liberty straight in her copper eye. Scores of photographers scrambled over the statue before the $64 million dollar restoration was completed, but no one did it quite like Lowe. Most photographers used lightweight, 35-millimeter cameras. Lowe's standard equipment, which he carries strapped to his back on a pack frame, includes a view camera that looks like something Mathew Brady would have carted onto a Civil War battlefield. For each shot, Lowe must set up and level his tripod, then drape himself with a black cloth to see the upside-down and reversed image in the viewfinder. Typically working in dim surroundings without electricity, Lowe usually makes long exposures (up to eight minutes) coupled with enormous old-fashioned flash bulbs to fill in the dark spots. The equipment weighs 30 pounds at the beginning of a day — but it seems like 150 pounds by the end.

The photographer was at the Statue of Liberty to help the National Park Service ensure that the landmark's restoration, unlike its original construction, would be fully recorded with documentation available in a public archive. Lowe, the sole staff photographer for the Park Service's Historic American Engineering Record, was the natural choice to produce the record. His object was to capture on film a visual understanding of how the statue was put together and restored, an exceptional assignment he regarded as a melding of art, engineering and architecture. Economy as well as Lowe's experience and ability entered into his selection. Teams of draftsmen can create accurate measured drawings of structures such as the statue — but at a cost of about $1,500, versus $30 to $70 for a photograph.

To shoot inside the colossal 225-ton figure before restoration, Lowe sometimes had to balance on two-inch-wide angled iron supports. He photographed the inside of the toes, the inside of the lips, the shackle at the statue's feet and other details that most people do not usually see. Then he packed up his gear and caught the same features from the outside scaffolding. Over two and a half years, he took 250 color and black-and-white photographs of the statue as it looked before, during and after restoration.

Lowe's work at the Statue of Liberty was his most difficult assignment for HAER, for whom he has taken more than 10,000 photographs. The HAER archives documenting 1,500 buildings and structures includes close to 20,000 photographs, 1,500 measured drawings and 16,000 pages of written data, all deposited in the Library of Congress. To keep up with the demand for such records — often because of impending demolition — Lowe spends as much as four months of the year on the road. During thousands of miles traveled he has probed old natural gas plants, textile mills, windmills, steel plants, mines, canals, even abandoned military bases in the Aleutians. The journeys often bristle with adventure. Lowe has hopped into helicopters, tiny shuttle planes and jeeps. For two weeks he lived out of a station wagon during a 4,500-mile survey of Montana's old iron-and-wood bridges.

Lowe sees beauty where others find decay:

Among his favorite spots are Butte, Mont., and Cleveland. His uncluttered images of gears, bridge trusses, smelter stacks, iron frames and hydroelectric turbines create a record for future historians. For many of the structures documented by HAER, the sole amount of preservation is a Jet Lowe photograph. HAER, founded in 1969 by the National Park Service, the American Society of Civil Engineers and the Library of Congress, is patterned after the Historic American Buildings Survey, another Park Service program that was initiated in 1933 both to employ architects and to make records of vanishing buildings. Together, the HABS-HAER archives in the Library of Congress embraces 115,000 black-and-white photographs, 45,000 architectural drawings, 62,000 pages of written documentation, plus maps and films of industrial processes. Accounting for only about two percent of the almost 12 million items in the library's Prints and Photographs Division, HABS-HAER makes up approximately 25 percent of the collection's use. HABS photographs and drawings often inspire architects working on new buildings or show them how to do accurate restorations. HAER researchers range from tourists hoping to find traces of a family business to entrepreneurs renovating 19th-century windmills. For a project such as the Statue of Liberty, the photographs may help restorers preparing for the 200th anniversary in 2086.

The difference between HABS and HAER, Lowe says, is that HABS tries to show how things looked while HAER shows how they worked in a "Germanically thorough" fashion. Because HAER cannot record every important structure, it has developed criteria and priorities to determine which sites are documented. First in line are National Historic Landmarks, structures recognized as nationally significant by engineering societies and historic properties owned by the National Park Service. HAER also strives to document structures facing imminent demolition that are listed in or eligible for the National Register of Historic Places. Often these structures are bridges, which are perhaps the most frequently threatened engineering milestones and thus make up a correspondingly large segment of the HAER collection. But bridges constitute just a portion of more than 100 categories of structures that HAER documents to create a picture of industrial America. Major groupings include extractive industries, from coal and oil to gold mines; bulk product processors involving food, metals, textiles and lumber; manufacturing concerns of all types; utilities; power sources, from animals to wind, water and steam; transportation, by road, rail, canals, air and sea; communications facilities; examples of building technology; dams; tunnels; hydraulic works; thermal structures; specialized construction such as underground structures, forts, towers, observatories, rocket launch sites and reactors; materials storage, from silos and gas holders to warehouses; power and energy transmission facilities; workers' housing; adaptively used sites; museums of technology; land surveying landmarks; even amusements — and more than 30 types of bridges, aqueducts and viaducts.

Documentation can come in the form of donated records — architectural drawings and large-format photographs that meet HAER standards for quality, accuracy, endurance and scale — or the task may fall to a HAER recording team consisting of a historian, an engineer and a draftsman or photographer. Cosponsorship from private sources, engineering societies and other federal agencies helps extend HAER's small federal appropriation. Since the early 1970s some 450 teachers and summer interns also have helped expand the HAER archives. Funded by parks, state historic preservation offices, historical societies and private foundations, these teams of architecture students, historians and photographers have documented hundreds of historic sites to meet HAER and Library of Congress standards.

The library sets a firm admission test for materials to be included in its archives: The documents are expected to last 500 years. Drawings must be produced on archivally stable sheets. Black-and-white photographs are printed on traditional fiber, not resin-coated, paper. Because color fades after five or 10 years, no color photographs or transparencies have been admitted to the library's collection yet, although Lowe has taken hundreds of them. A new preservation process is expected to allow HABS-HAER to transmit several thousand color transparencies to the library soon.

Before each assignment, Lowe reads anything relevant he can find. For a shoot at the George Washington Bridge, for example, he checked out *The Bridge*, by Gay Talese, an account of the building of the Verrazzano Narrows Bridge between Brooklyn and Staten Island in the 1950s and 1960s. He often scans voluminous reports prepared by HAER historians or delves into files at the Smithsonian Institution or Library of Congress. For Alaskan journeys, John McPhee's *Coming into the Country* proved immeasurably helpful. Lowe spent a nervous week boning up for a challenging climb up the towers of the Brooklyn Bridge in 1982. He seeks to record the idiosyncracies, he says: "What makes this factory or mill or bridge different from all the rest? That's where historians help."

Lowe's six-pound camera looks like one of the historic artifacts he sets out to record. A collapsible leather bellows connects a movable lens to the metal body. He loads by hand each 5-by-7-inch negative into a filmholder that must be changed after every shot. (Lowe sometimes spends hours preparing these negatives while locked in motel rooms with tape over the door jambs to prevent light leaks.) The camera allows no roll of film that can be advanced with a flip of a lever or a motor drive. Lowe considers 200 shots high productivity for a week's work. With a 35-millimeter camera, a photographer can work much faster but can also overlook the details, he says. Once on location, Lowe takes about 15 minutes to set up each shot — measuring the light, loading the negative and arranging the tripod. Like many fashion and advertising photographers, he uses a large-format view camera because it eliminates distortion and creates a deep field of focus that makes the smallest details bright and crisp — a crucial aspect of Lowe's work. He stays with a subject much longer than most photographers, analyzing the situation all the more carefully because it takes so long to prepare each shot.

Lowe makes an art out of an honest record. In the process, he often risks his life. Assignments such as the Statue of Liberty — and countless bridges across the country — prompt Lowe's fans to call him a daredevil. He tackles his subjects from eye level, not ground level. He gets up in the girders. But the soft-spoken, 6-foot 3-inch photographer plays down the danger, although his usual garb does nothing to dispel the adventurer mystique: well-worn parka, khaki pants studded with pockets and buttons, aviator glasses and a crumpled felt hat, the brim buckled into a jaunty curl. Lowe admits, however, that he lost a night's sleep before recording cable anchorages and tower-top saddles that guide cables along the 3,455-foot-long Brooklyn Bridge. He has developed a healthy respect for height, he says: "It forces you to concentrate on what you're doing."

He invariably climbs with the bright yellow safety belt that California highway workers gave him when he was scaling the San Francisco-Oakland Bay Bridge. Lowe's closest call came in Montana on a railroad bridge over the Flathead River near Glacier National Park. He and a colleague were standing in the middle of the bridge when a freight train came charging at 60 miles an hour. The two escaped by jumping onto a safety platform built only recently to comply with federal standards.

John T. Lowe III did not set out to be a documentary photographer. Born in 1946, the son of a Navy flier (who gave him the nickname Jet "because they were new when I was new"), he went to college in the late 1960s to study history. As part of an independent study project, he traveled to Haiti to write an essay on its people. At the last minute someone loaned him a camera. He wound up exploring the country outside Cap Haitien, sometimes to the dismay of the forces of "Papa Doc" Duvalier. He produced 20 rolls of street scenes, portraits and buildings and returned to the United States to win praise and encouragement from his professors. In 1970 Lowe received a degree in art history from Emory University. Only later, when he sought a master's degree in fine arts at Georgia State University, was he steered towards architectural photography. Lowe got his first break in both photography and preservation in 1970. Working for the Georgia Historical Commission, he helped document buildings nominated to the National Register of Historic Places. But his career hit a lull after he left the commission and his photography equipment was stolen. For years he filled in with odd jobs, working as a courier and construction worker. Then came time as a "pan" carpenter, when he worked high up on the frame of new buildings, before the concrete was poured and the girders really knit together. "That's where I developed my feeling for heights," he says. Finally he was encouraged to leap back into photography by Richard Avedon, whom Lowe met while working as a courier. Avedon had not seen any of Lowe's photographs, but he looked at Lowe and said, "You'll probably make your mark with structures."

Lowe moved to Washington, D.C., in 1974 and joined HAER in 1978. Since then he has captured thousands of scenes of industrial America, from Cleveland's waterfront and a vast iron-and-steel complex of old automobile plants to intricate bridges and massive ore loaders. His favorites include the Million Dollar Bridge spanning two glaciers in Alaska (and partially destroyed in the 1964 earthquake), the Holland Tunnel and a Massachusetts shoddy mill used to manufacture reprocessed wool and mixed-fiber shoddies and batting as sound insulation for new cars. Although his interest in engineering runs deep, he considers himself an outsider, an observer of that professional community. Nonetheless, Lowe's associates say he possesses an intuitive ability to show technology in a way that someone 50 or 100 years from now will be able to understand it. His engineering acumen is more than just handy. At the heights he scales, he cannot have a historian or engineer looking over his shoulder.

The collection here of almost a decade of his work reminds Lowe that about one-third of what he has documented has been destroyed. "This can be a melancholy business. Sometimes I feel like an undertaker." Some day he would like to take a break from photographing ruins and obsolete equipment to follow the creation of something new — the assemblage of a jet plane, for example.

EARTH

Give me a place to stand,
and I will move the earth.

ARCHIMEDES

Pappus of Alexandria

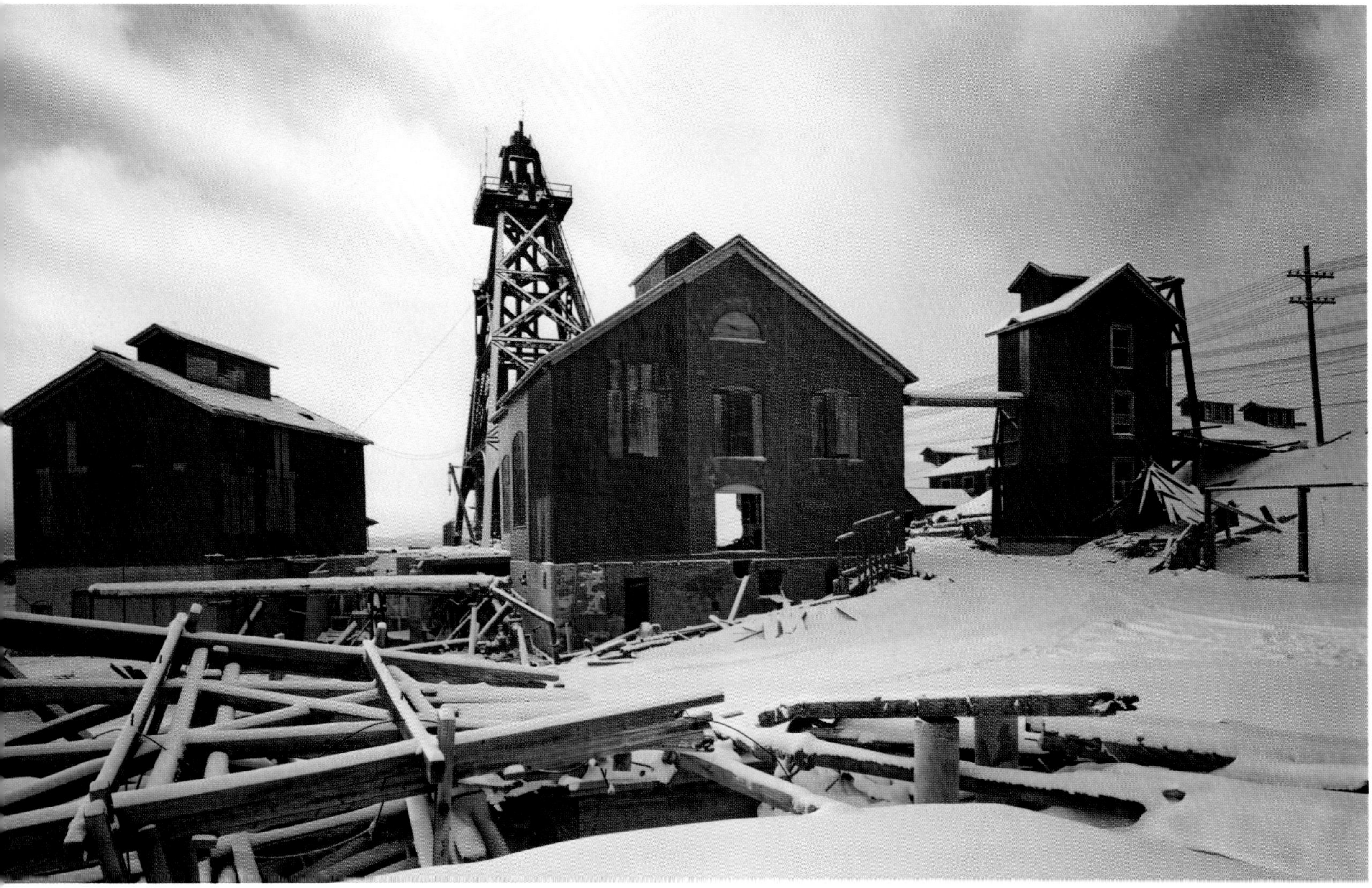

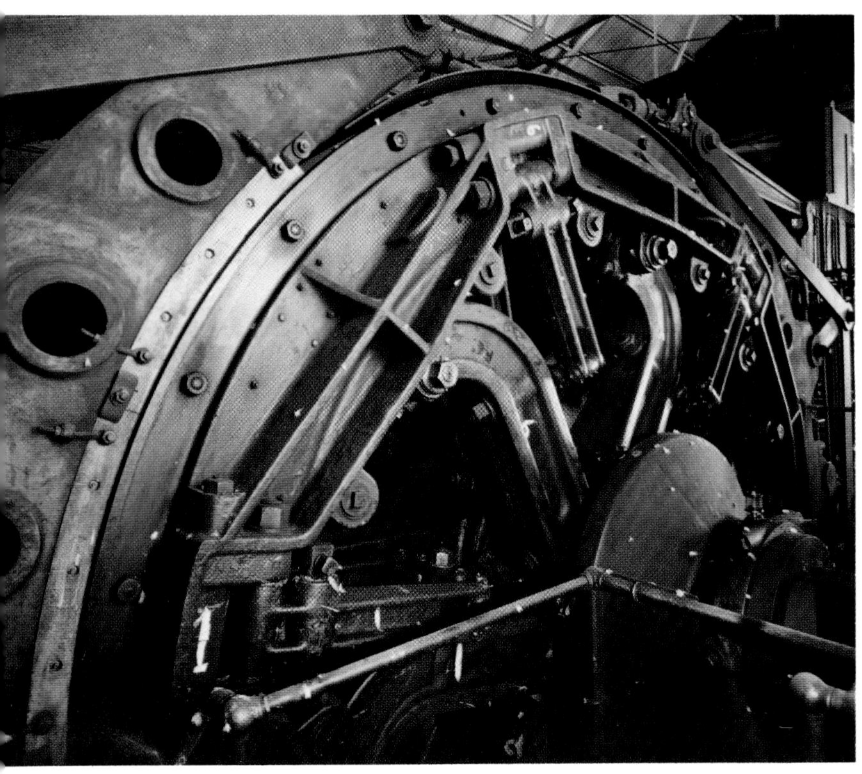

ANACONDA COMPANY

Above. *Headframe and hoist houses in the Diamond mineyard, Butte, Mont., built about 1898. In the 1880s copper replaced silver as Butte's most lucrative resource, and the Anaconda Company soon reigned supreme.*

Left. *Brakeshoe installed about 1900 on a drum of the Steward Mine in Butte. Such drums helped transport miners and ore cars up and down the deep-shaft mines, which closed in the 1970s.*

Opposite. *Breaker House, Anaconda, Mont. This corrugated steel building was constructed about 1900 to recycle scrap iron, which was melted in the nearby foundry where Anaconda's street lamps and cast-iron storefronts also were made.*

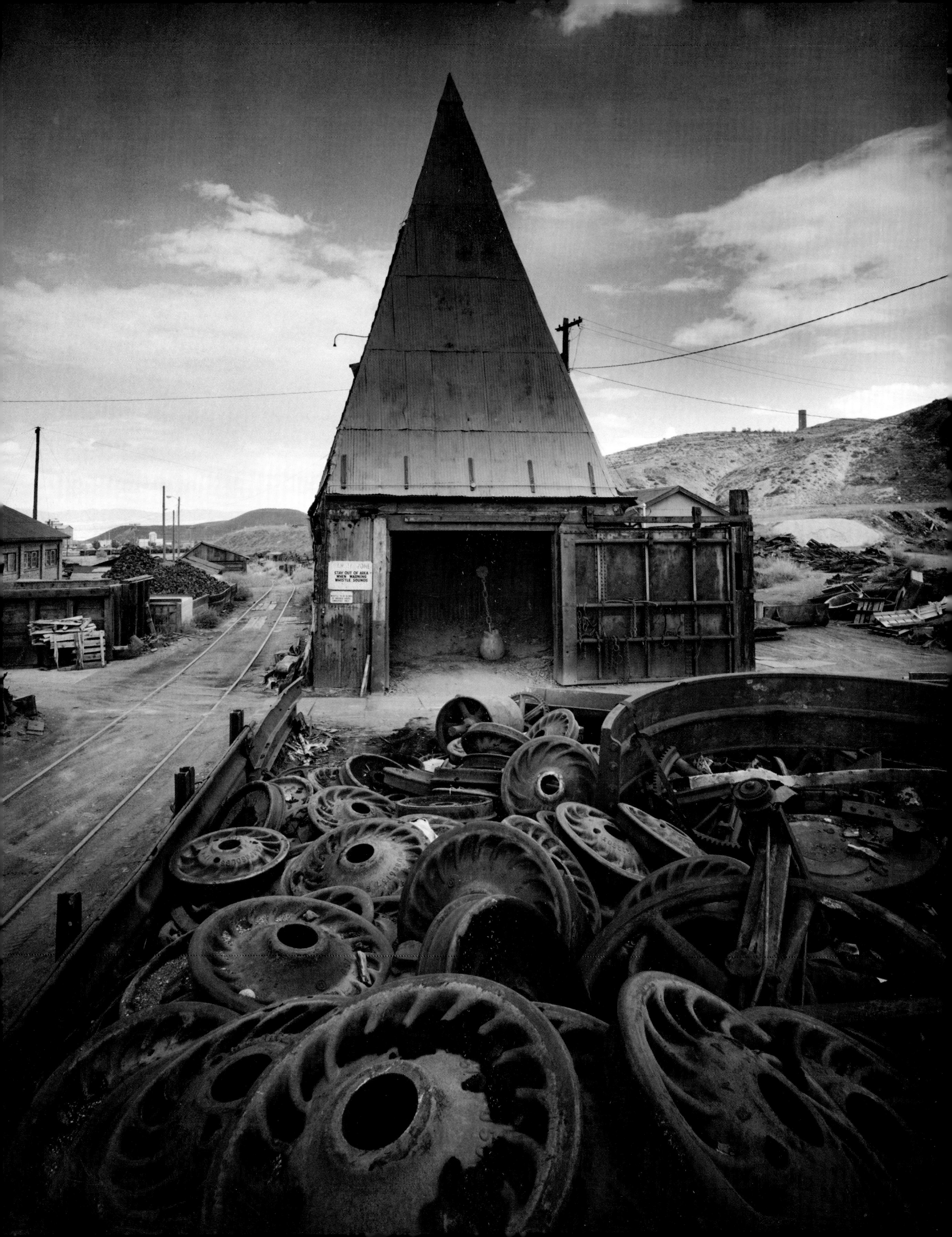
STAY OUT OF AREA
WHEN WARNING
WHISTLE SOUNDS

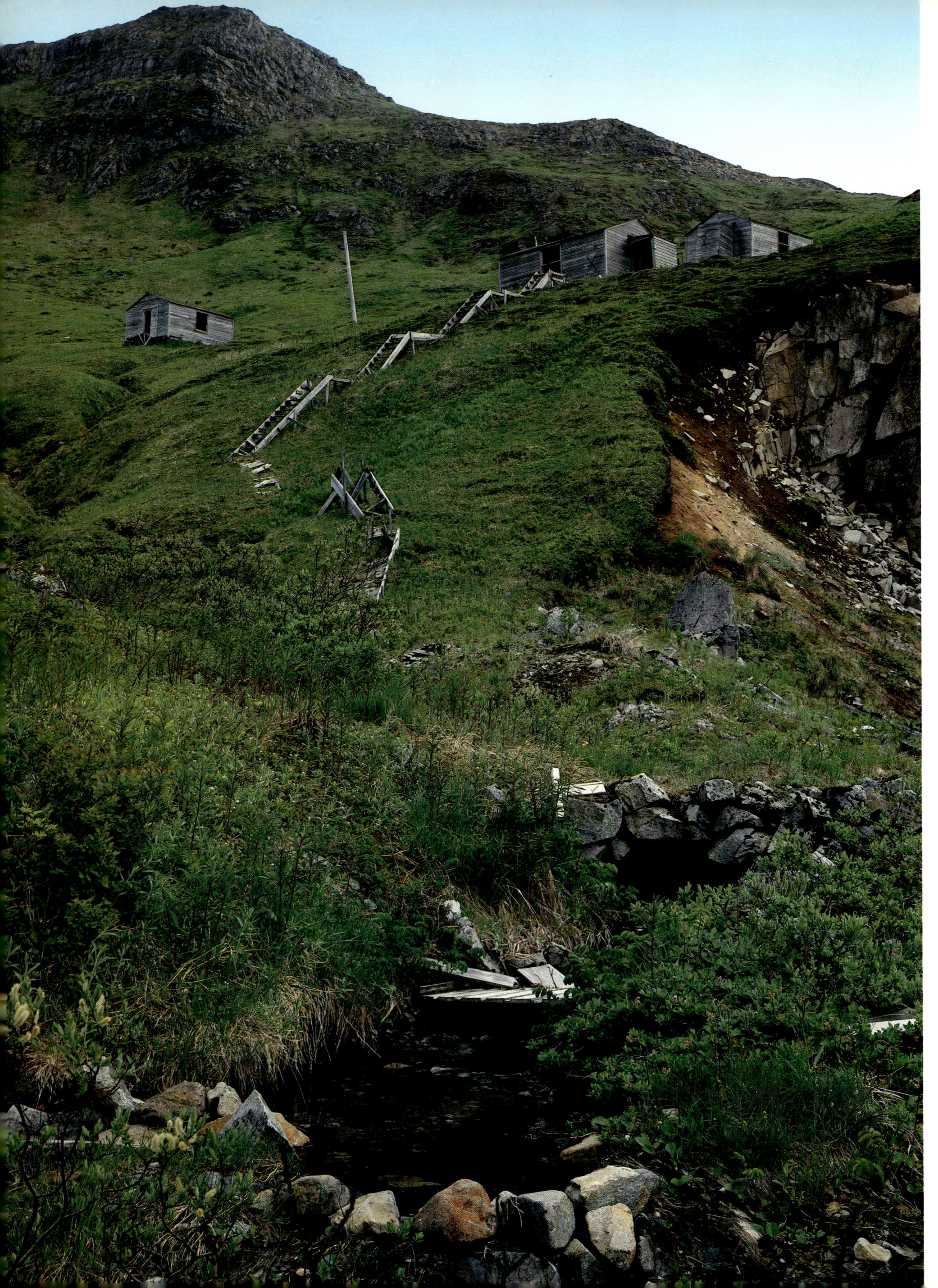

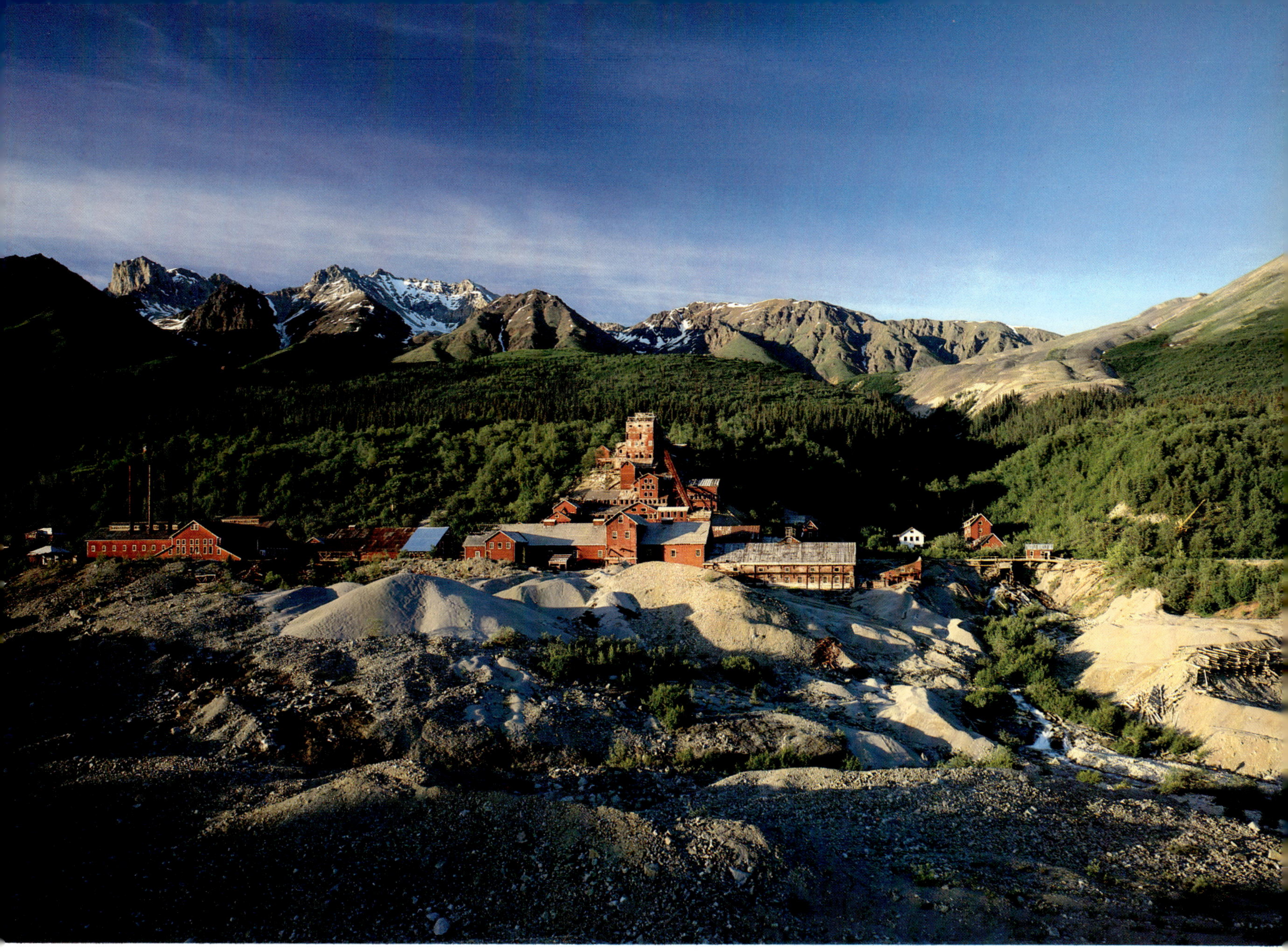

KENNECOTT MINING COMPANY

Above. *Mill complex and mining camp, built on a glacial moraine at Kennicott, Alaska, 1905–23. Ore was moved from the mines by a gravity rail system originating 3,400 feet above the plant.*

Right. *Concentration mill, a massive timber-frame structure built 1910–11. The mines closed in 1938.*

DUTCH HARBOR

Opposite. *Army cabannas at Garrison No. 2, built on Unalaska Island, Alaska, in 1942 as part of a U.S. military base.*

Overleaf. *Naval base at Unalaska's Dutch Harbor. Bombed by the Japanese in 1942 but only slightly damaged, the base was deactivated after the war.*

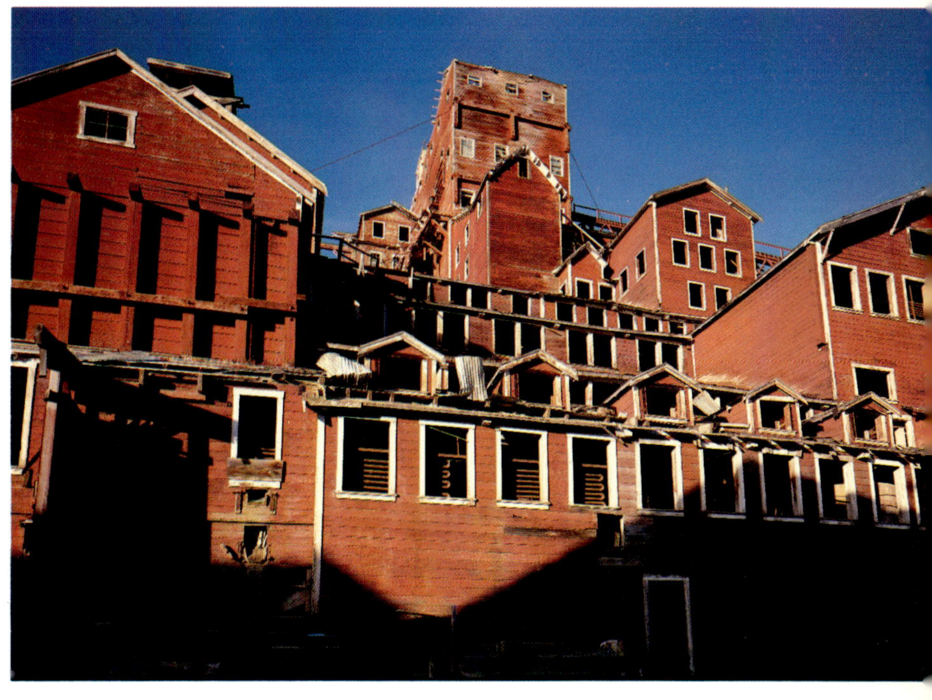

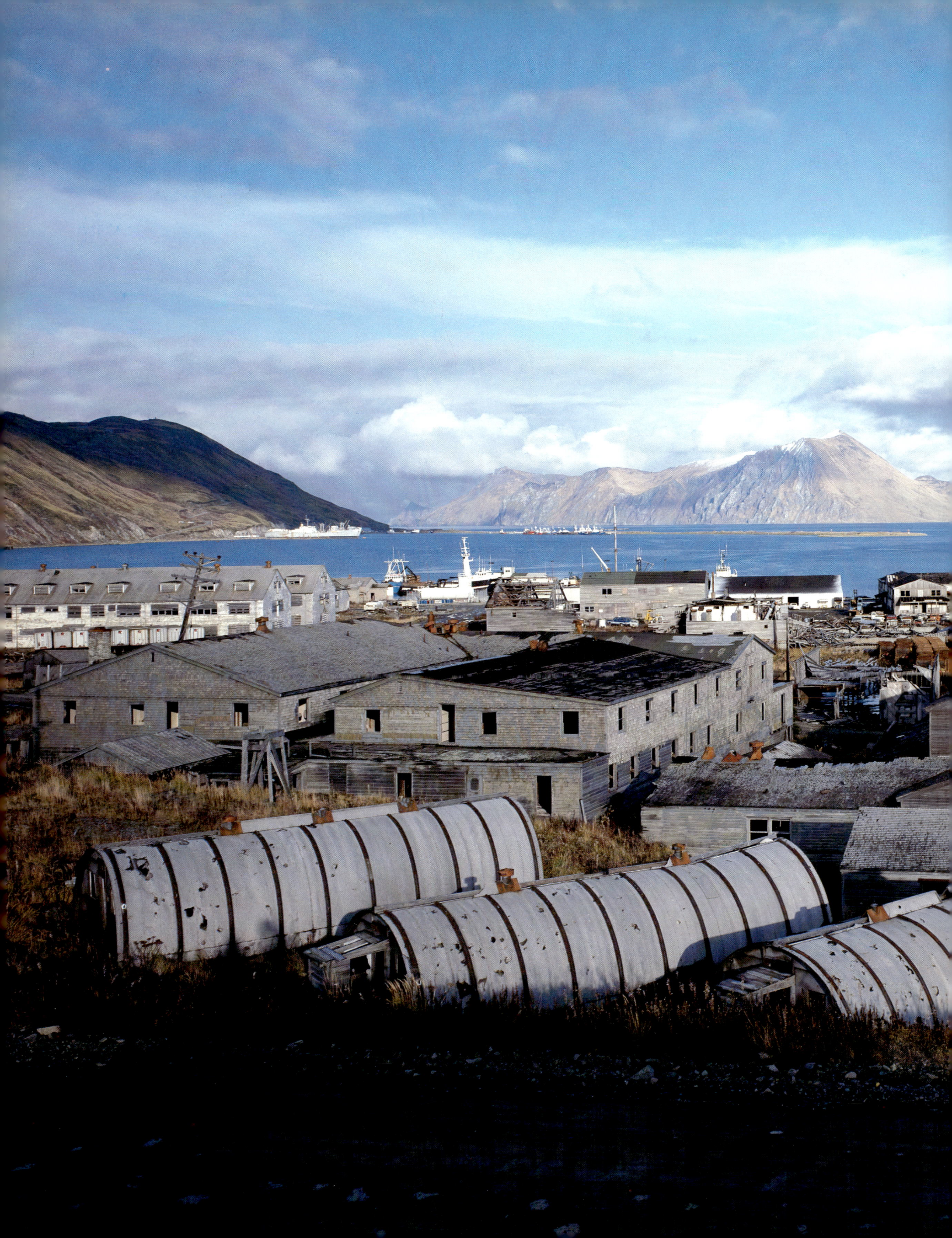

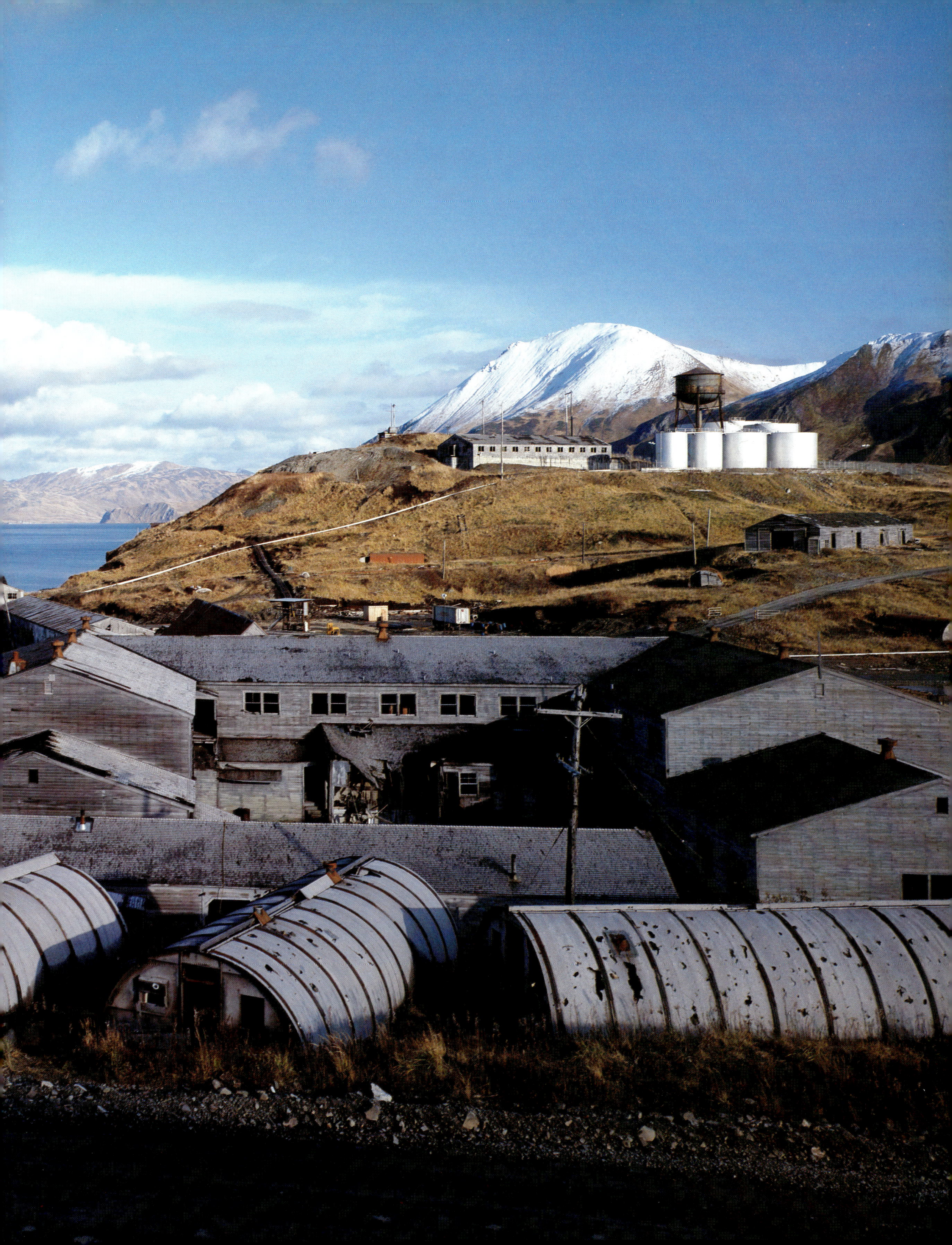

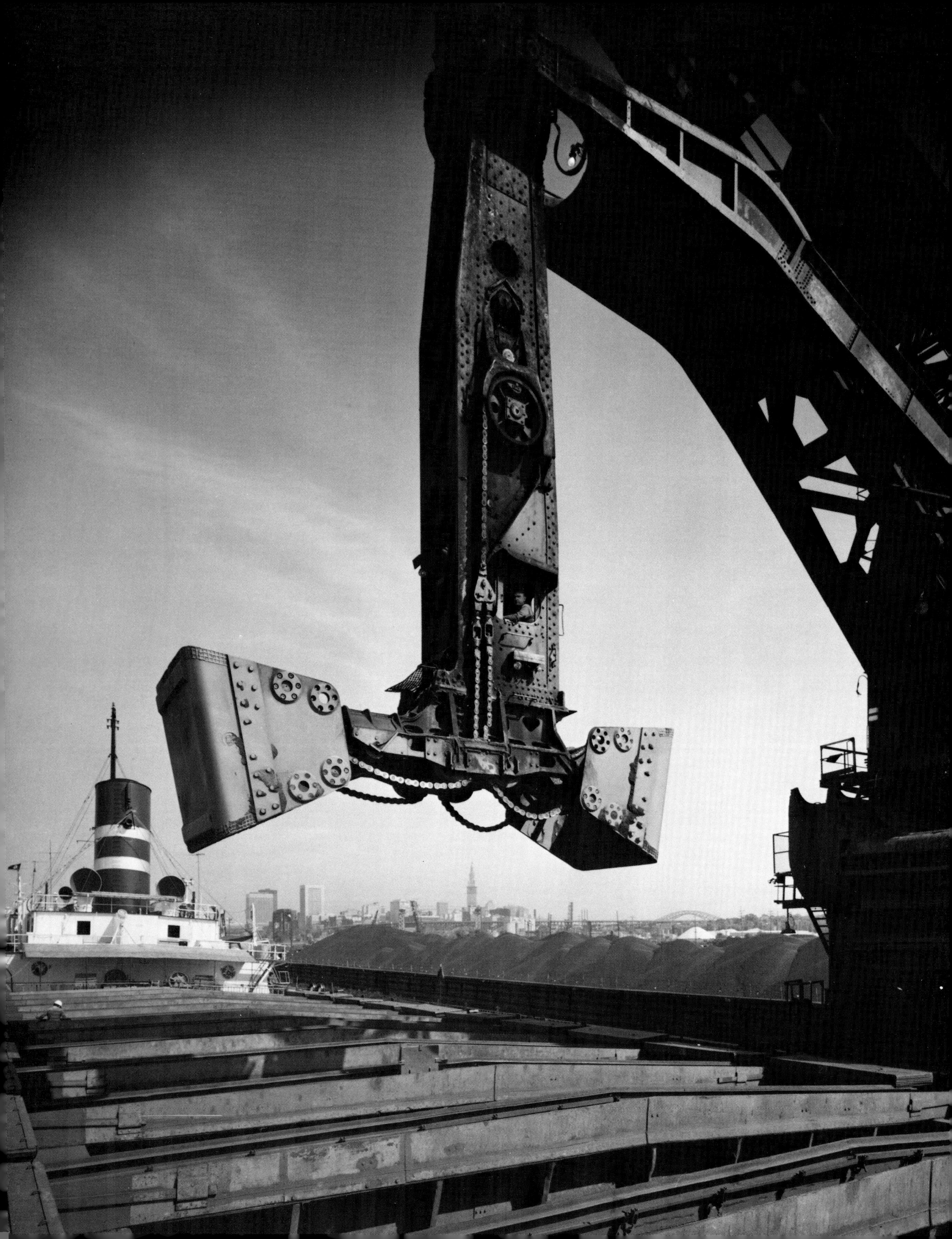

PENNSYLVANIA RAILROAD ORE DOCK

Opposite. *Hulett Ore Unloader No. 1 on the Cleveland waterfront. With a capacity of 17 tons, it has been off-loading coal and iron ore on Lake Erie ever since its installation in 1912.*

Below. *Pennsylvania Railroad shunt car serving the ore dock, used to position rail cars beneath the gigantic Hulett Unloaders.*

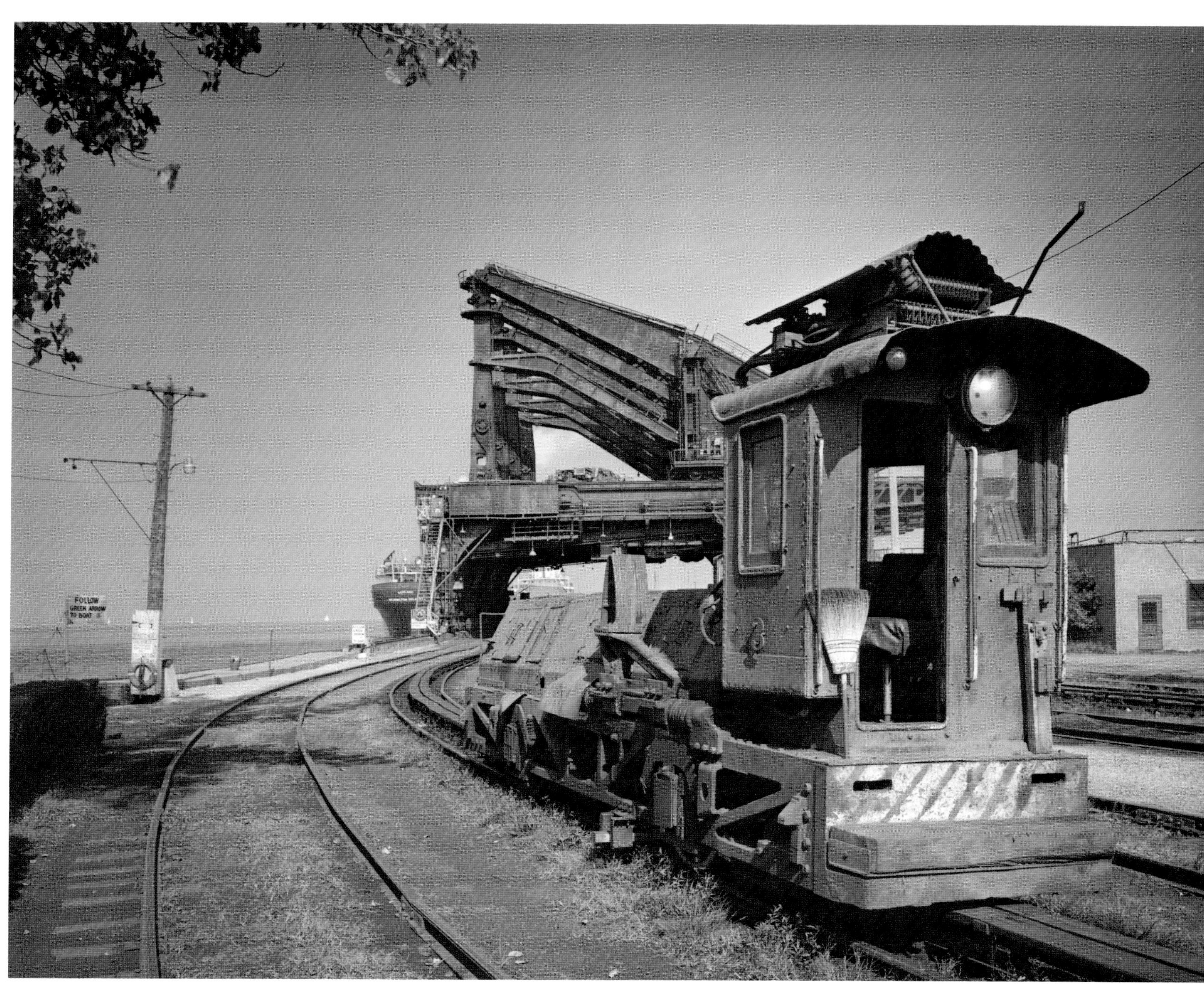

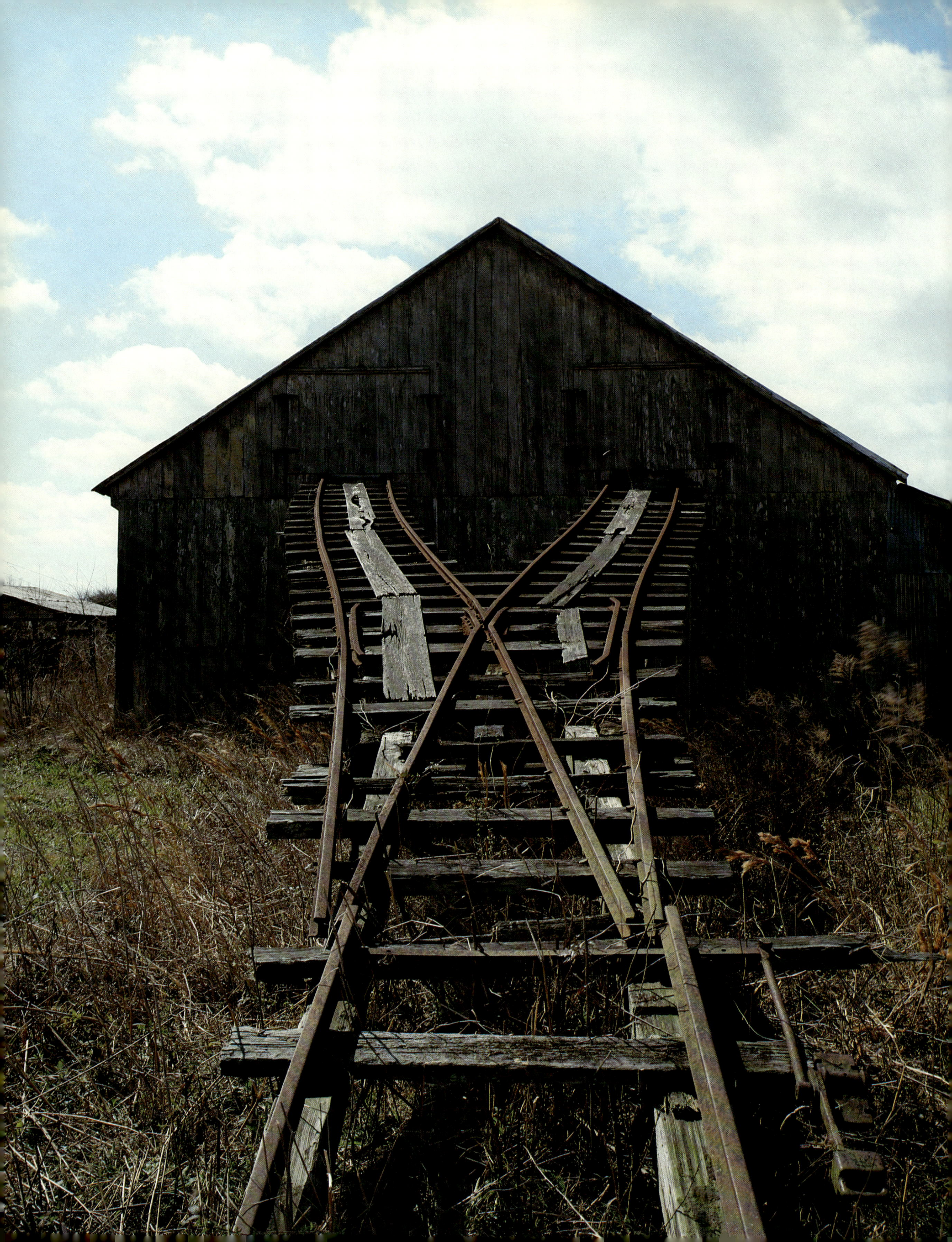

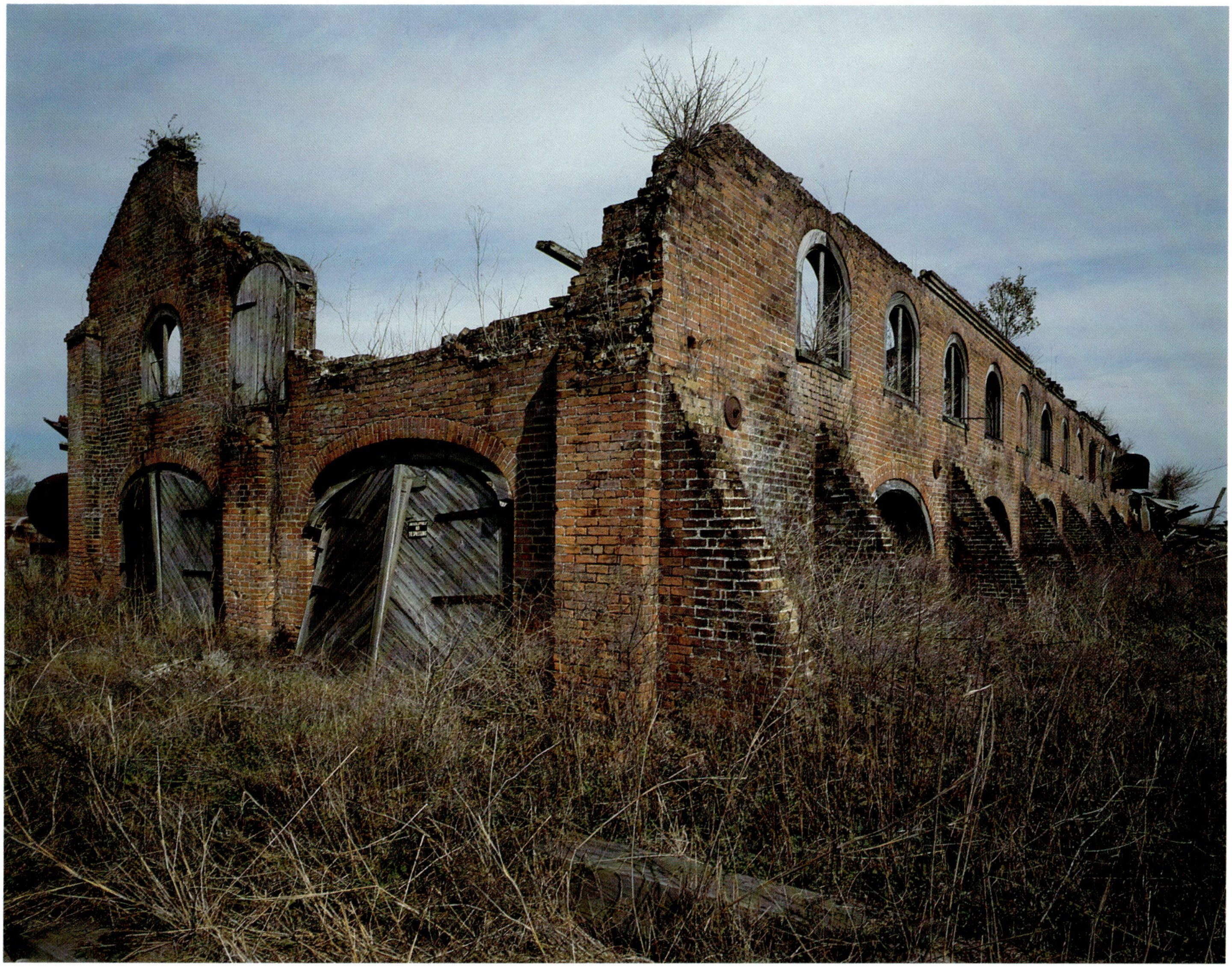

LAUREL VALLEY SUGAR PLANTATION

Opposite. *Corn crib, erected about 1880 at the Thibodaux, La., plantation. Its hoist system for handling corn, installed in 1905, included a double-track rail and rail car.*

Above. *Ruins of the sugar mill, built about 1845 and rebuilt about 1897. Its capacity for grinding 800 tons of sugar cane daily made it among the area's largest sugar manufacturers until it closed in 1926.*

Right. *One-room, wood-frame schoolhouse on the plantation grounds. Built about 1906, it served as a school for the plantation workers' children until 1952.*

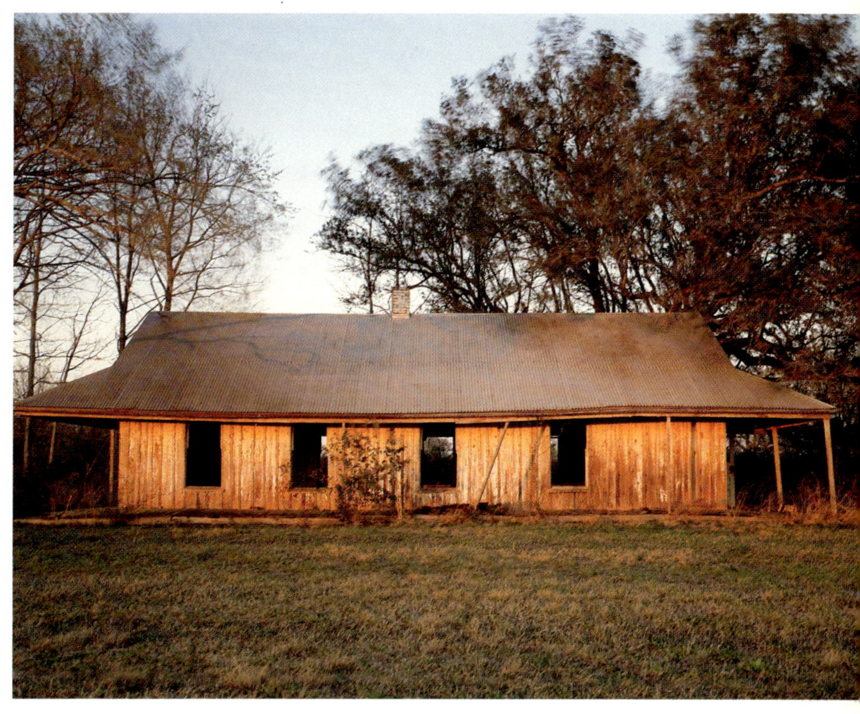

AUDITORIUM BUILDING

Right. *Hand-operated winch, originally used to open and close the upper gallery's cove ceiling. The Auditorium Building in Chicago was designed by the renowned firm of Adler and Sullivan in 1890 and has been carefully restored.*

Below. *Control lever and platform for the star lifter. Located on the floor directly below the stage, the lifter propelled performers up onto the stage.*

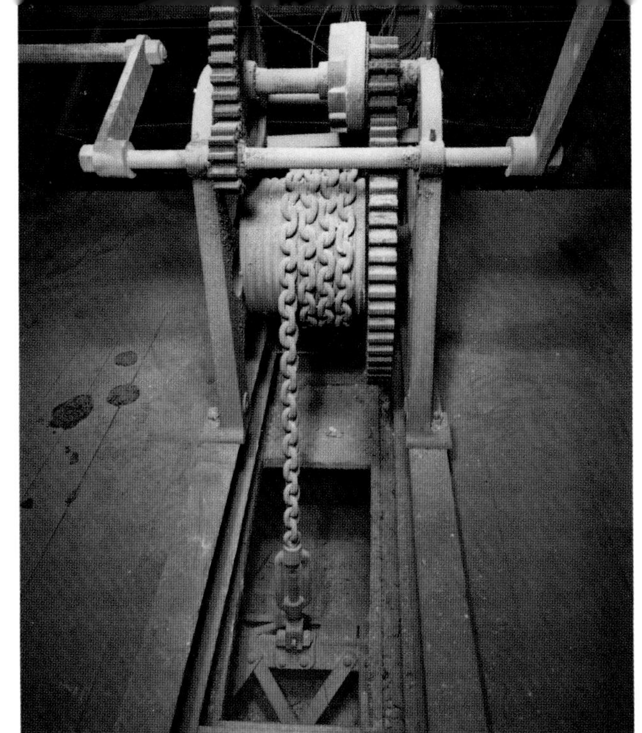

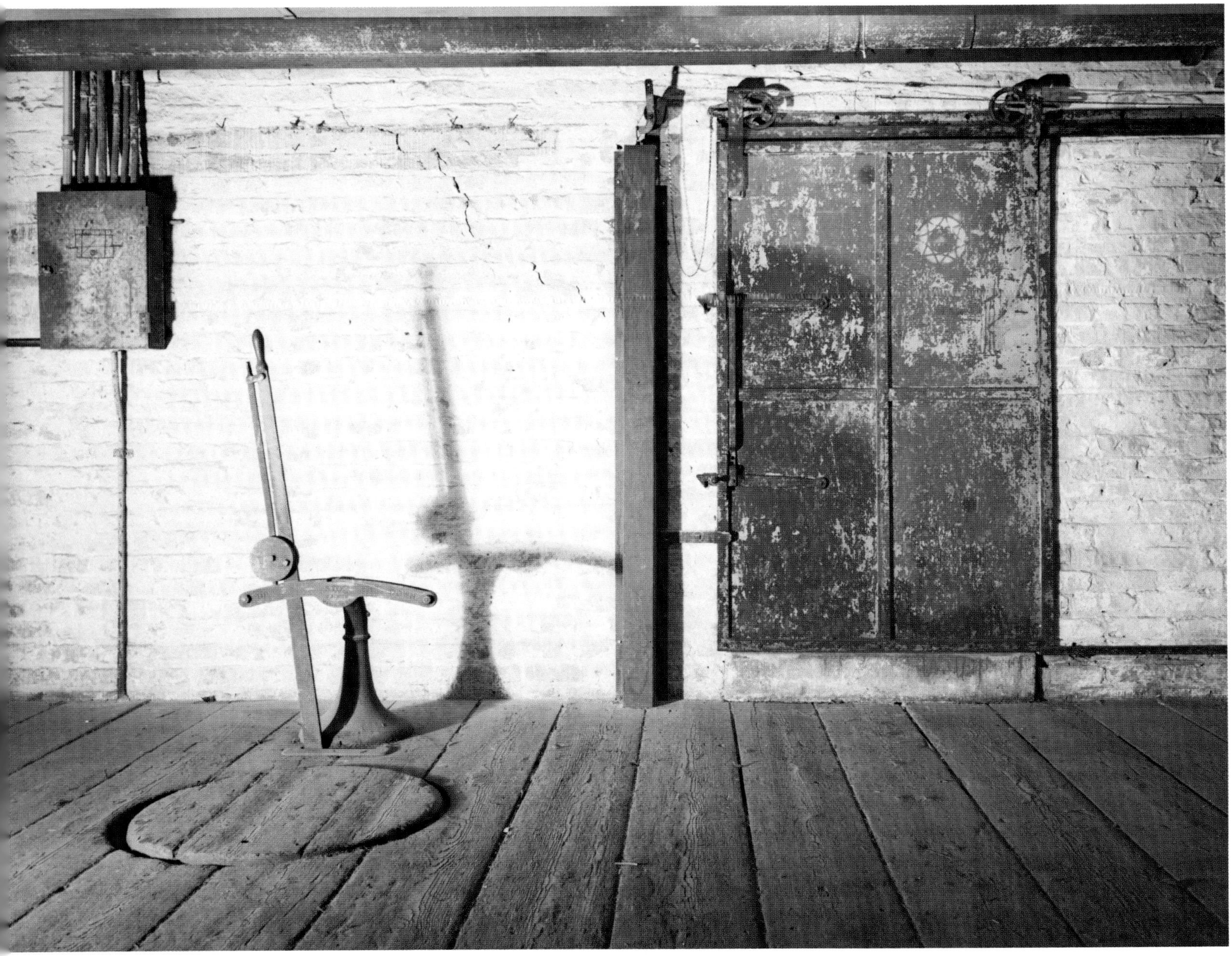

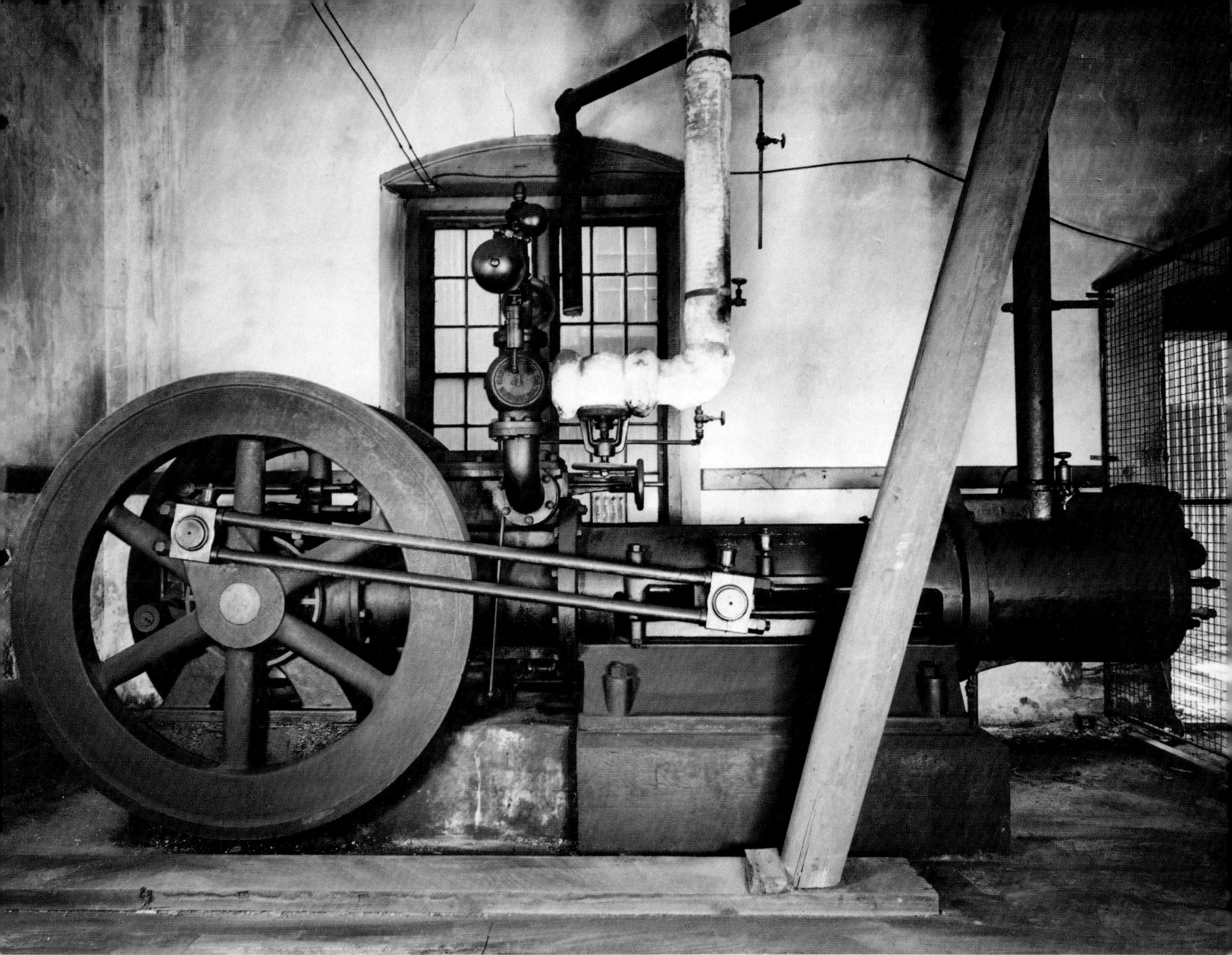

QUINCY MINING COMPANY

Steam-powered air compressor installed in the Hancock, Mich., company about 1900. Quincy Mining smelted its ore, using this compressor to blow air into an adjacent blast furnace.

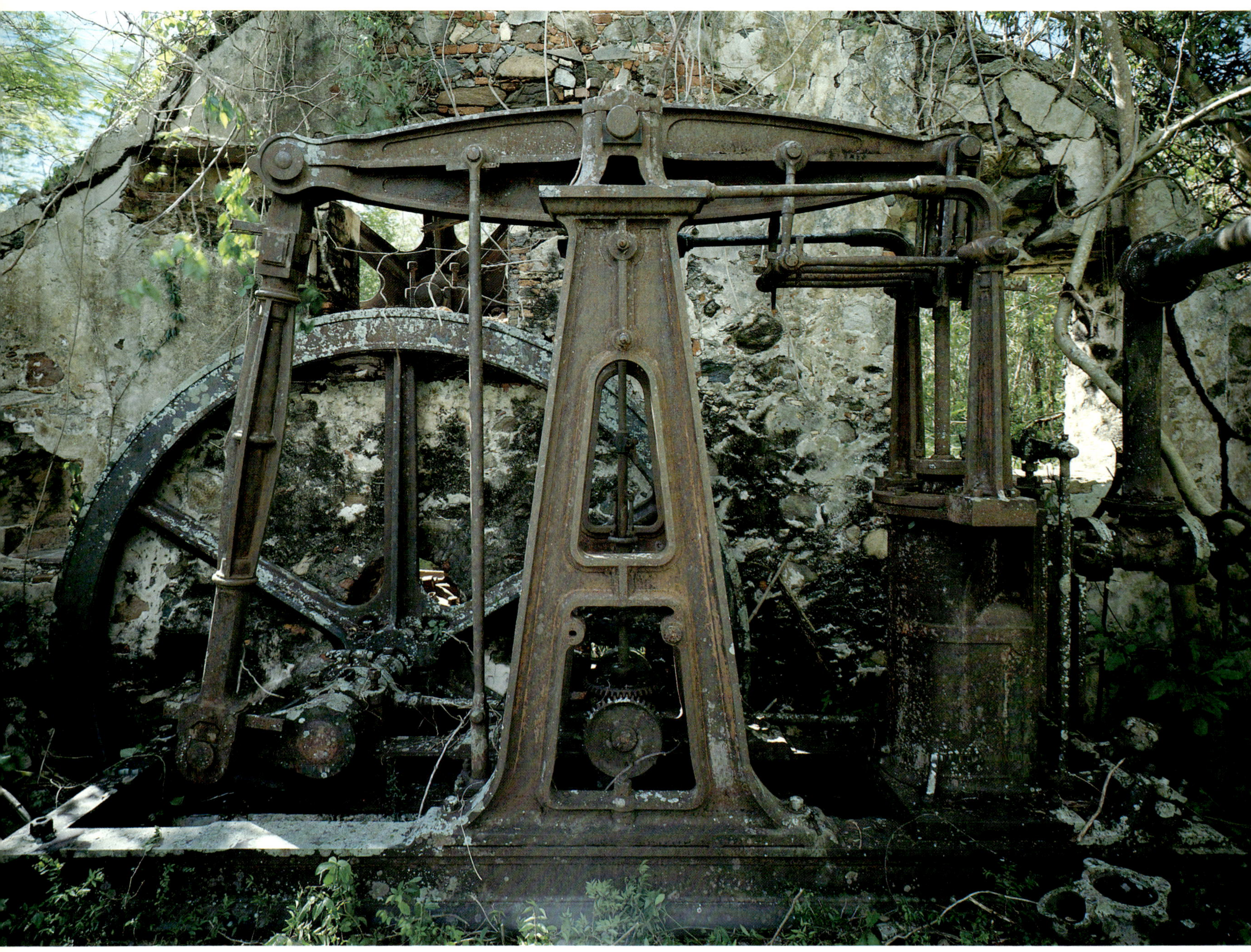

ESTATE ADRIAN SUGAR MILL

Above. *Beam engine once used to power a cane crusher. Installed about 1860, it is among the ruins found on this plantation at St. John, Virgin Islands.*

BROOKLYN TO NOME

Opposite. *Remains of steam locomotives abandoned east of Nome, Alaska. Originally used on one of the elevated rail lines in Brooklyn in the 1880s, the locomotives eventually found their way to the gold fields of Alaska for use on the Council City and Solomon River Railroad.*

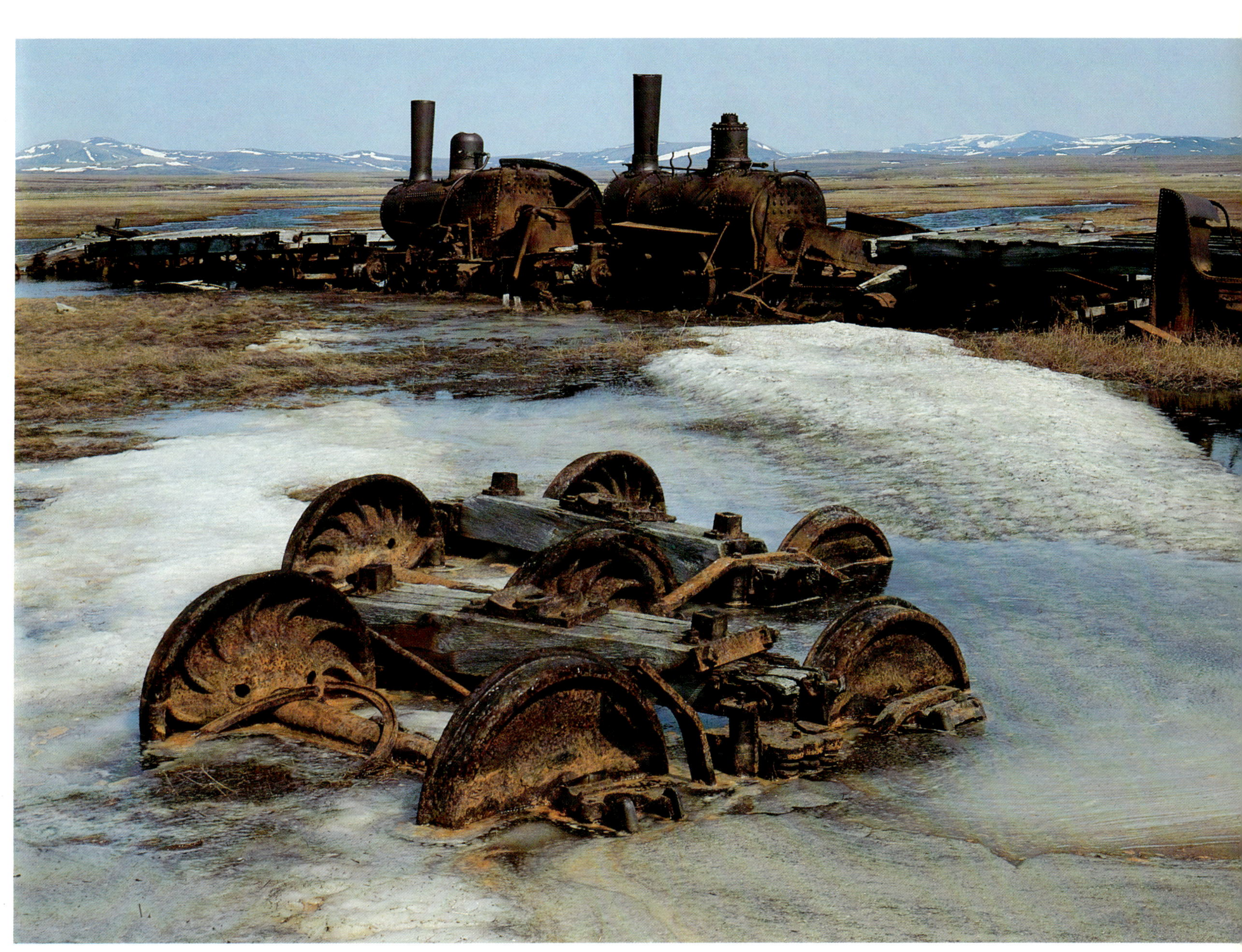

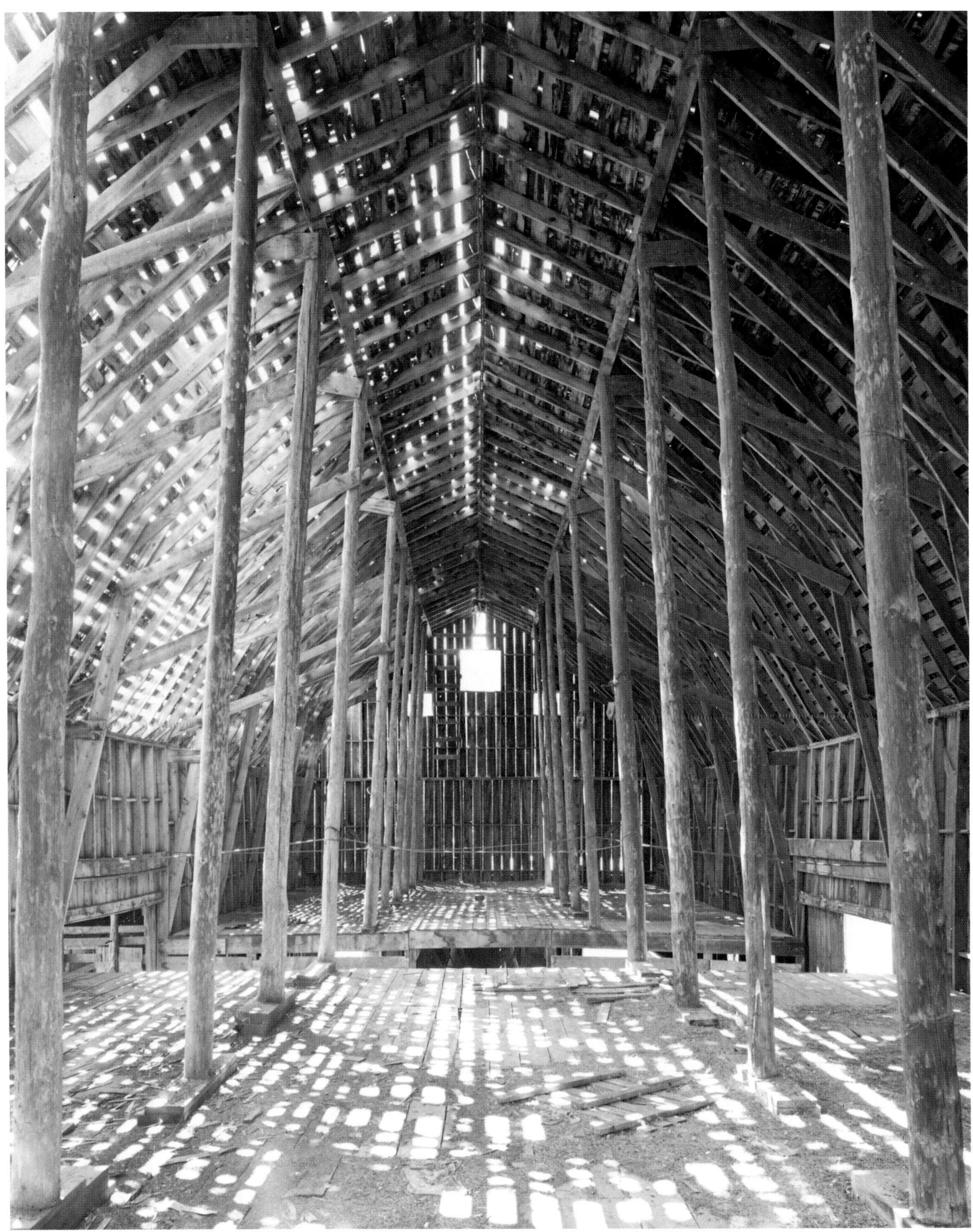

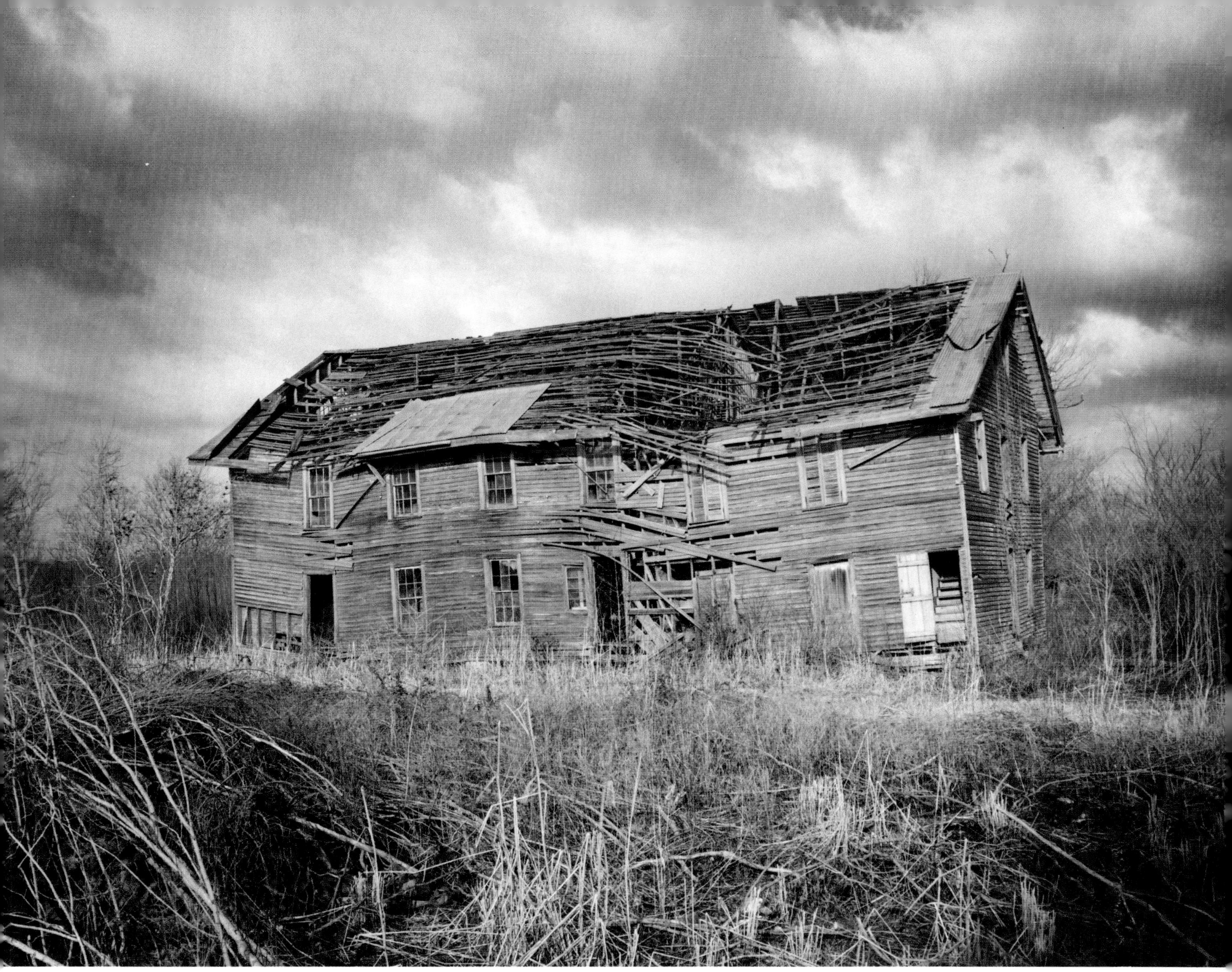

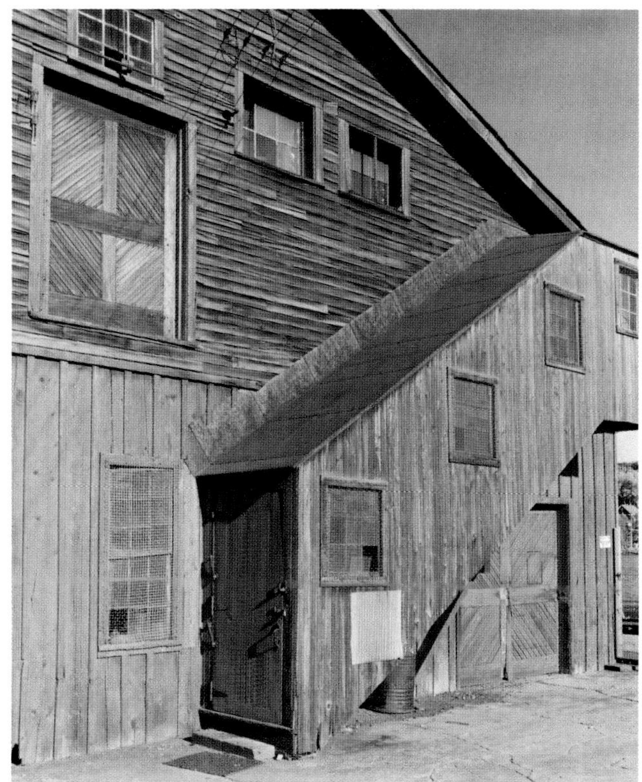

RITTER BARN

Opposite. *Dairy barn built about 1910 in the Delores River Valley of Colorado, operated by the Ritter family from 1908 to 1947.*

LAUREL VALLEY SUGAR PLANTATION

Above. *Decayed boarding house built about 1880 for workers on the Thibodaux, La., plantation.*

QUINCY MINING COMPANY

Left. *Stairway leading into an 1898 warehouse building in Hancock, Mich., where the company stored copper ingots before shipping them out. Founded in 1845, Quincy Mining was among the nation's most profitable copper companies by 1900.*

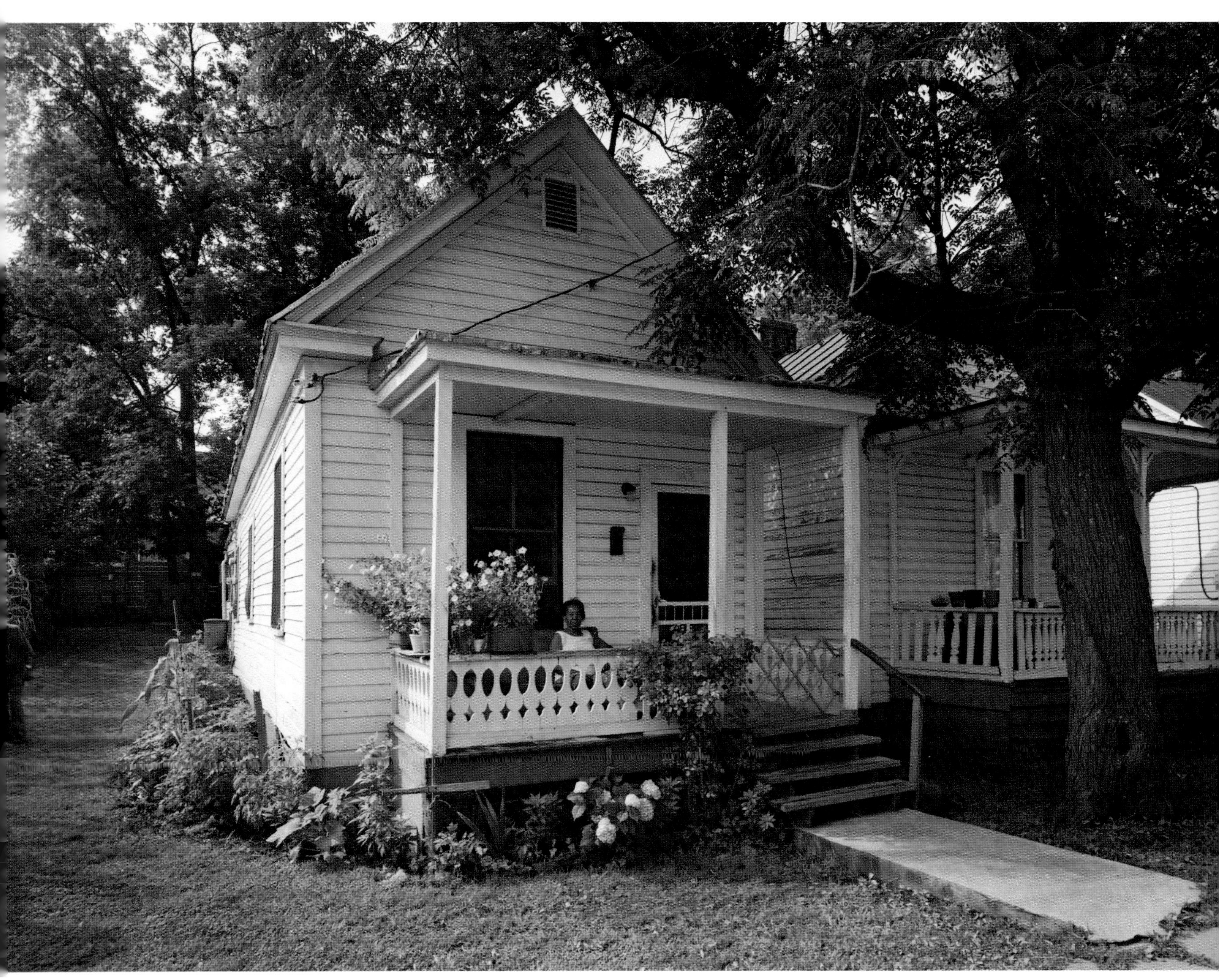

TOBACCO DISTRICT

Opposite. *Workers' housing, Danville, Va., dating from 1880 to 1910. Many of Danville's tobacco workers lived in small, three- to six-room frame houses such as this with tin roofs and lightly ornamented front porches.*

Below. *Late 19th-century warehouses located in the heart of Danville's tobacco district on Craghead Street.*

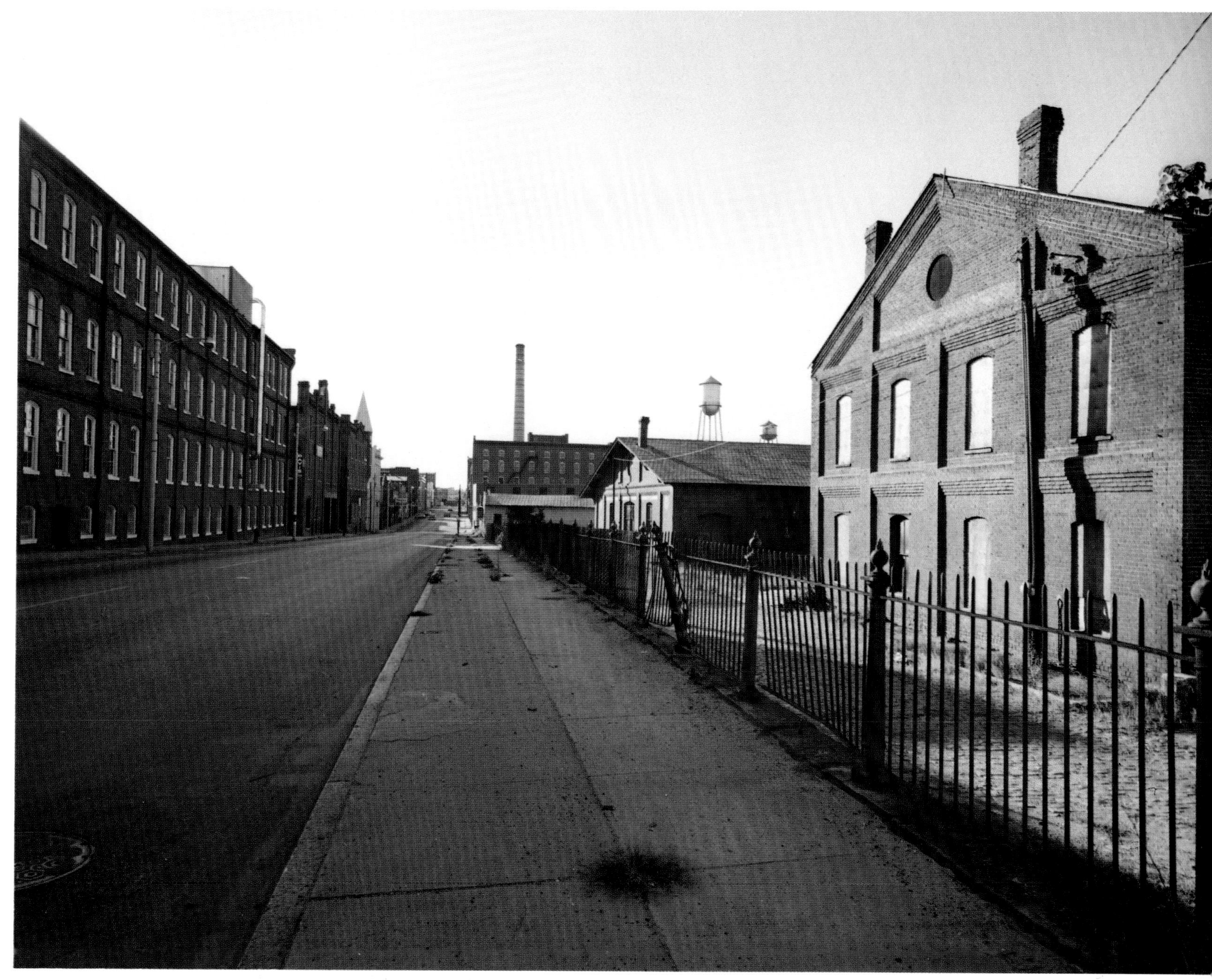

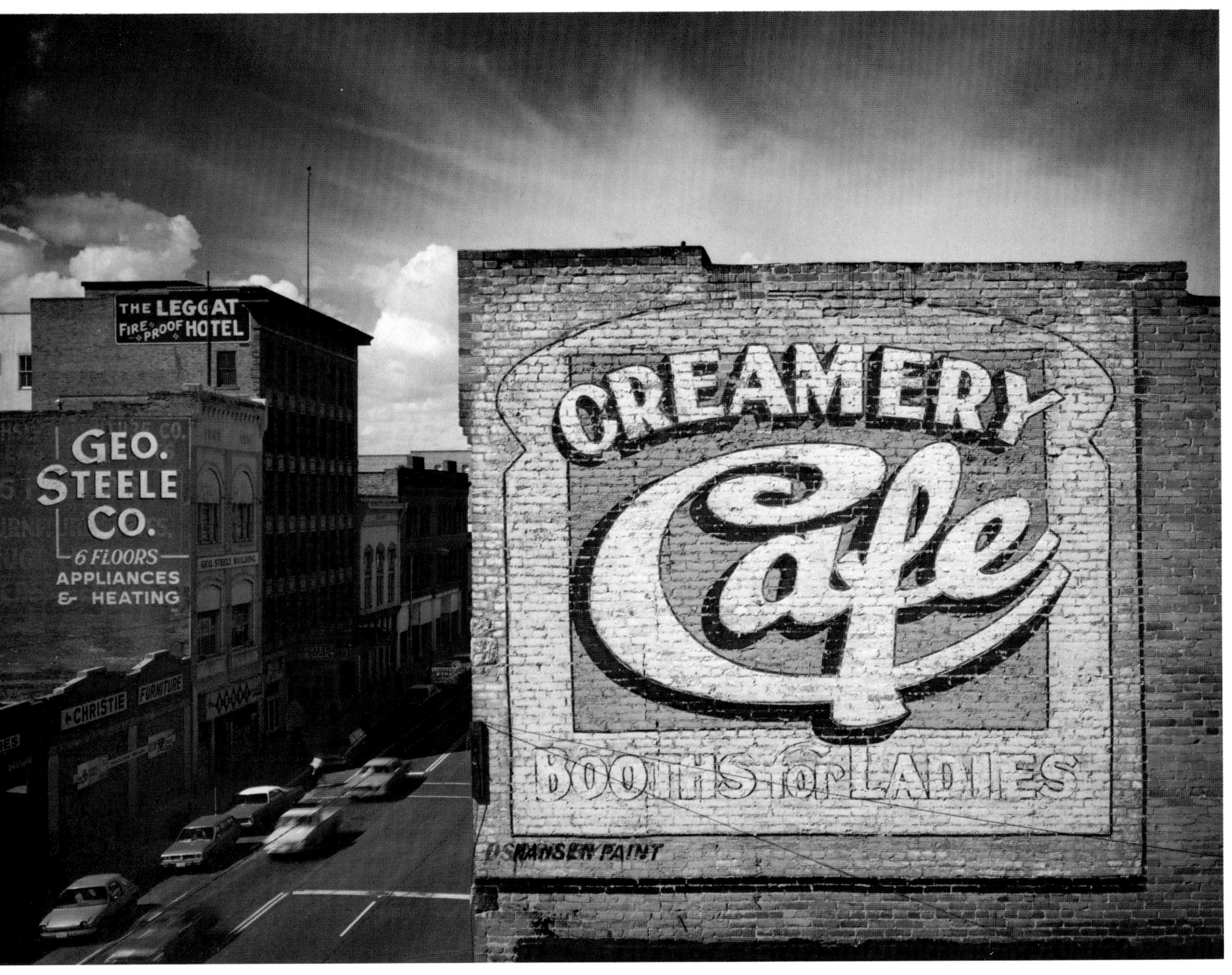

BUTTE WALLS

Above. *Commercial signs painted on buildings in uptown Butte, Mont., about 1910. Known as "the richest hill on earth," Butte with its wealthy copper industry helped support a bustling commercial district, particularly from the 1890s through the 1920s.*

Opposite. *Mural depicting Butte's mining industry as well as the city's rich ethnic heritage. Montana artist Niki Glen designed the mural, dedicated to the people of Butte in 1979.*

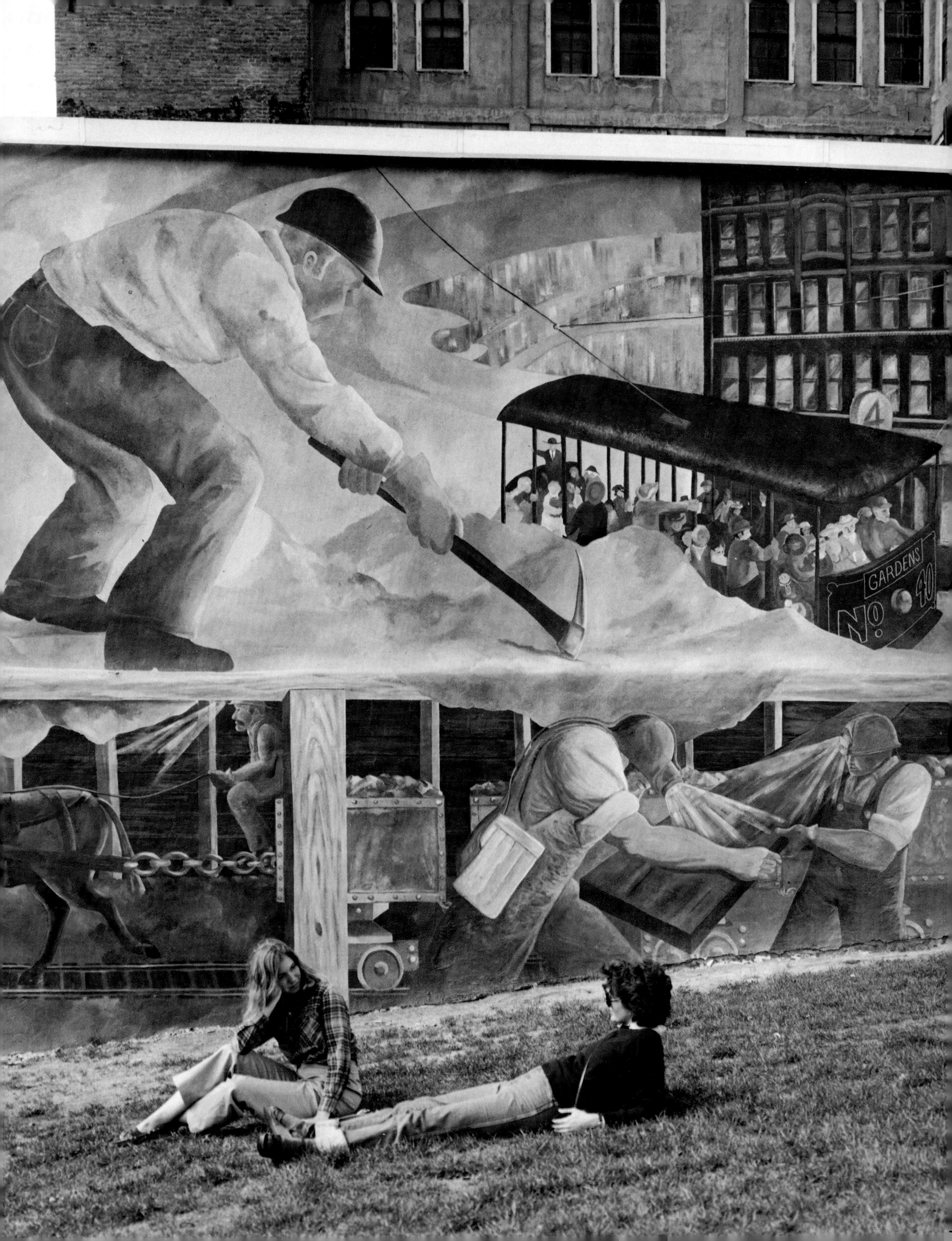
4
GARDENS
No 40

AIR

I have merged,
like the bird,
with the bright air.

THEODORE ROETHKE
The Abyss

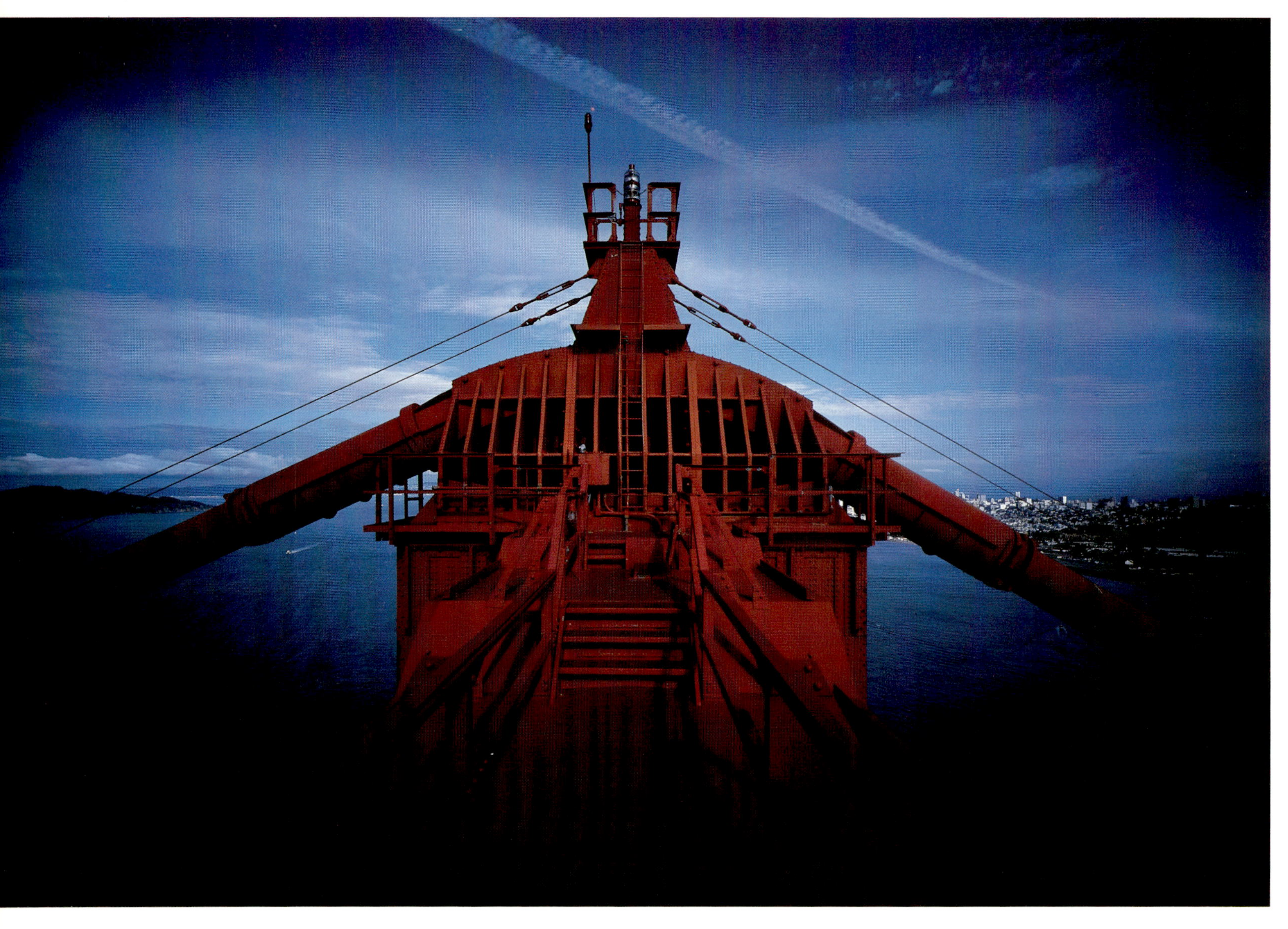

GOLDEN GATE BRIDGE

Above. *Saddle of the main cables on top of the south tower. San Francisco's most famous bridge, begun in 1933 and opened in 1937, was designed by engineer Joseph B. Strauss with Irving F. Morrow serving as consulting engineer.*

Opposite. *View toward Marin County from the south tower. The towers are masterpieces of engineering and architecture, rising nearly 750 feet above San Francisco Bay and supporting a main span of 4,200 feet.*

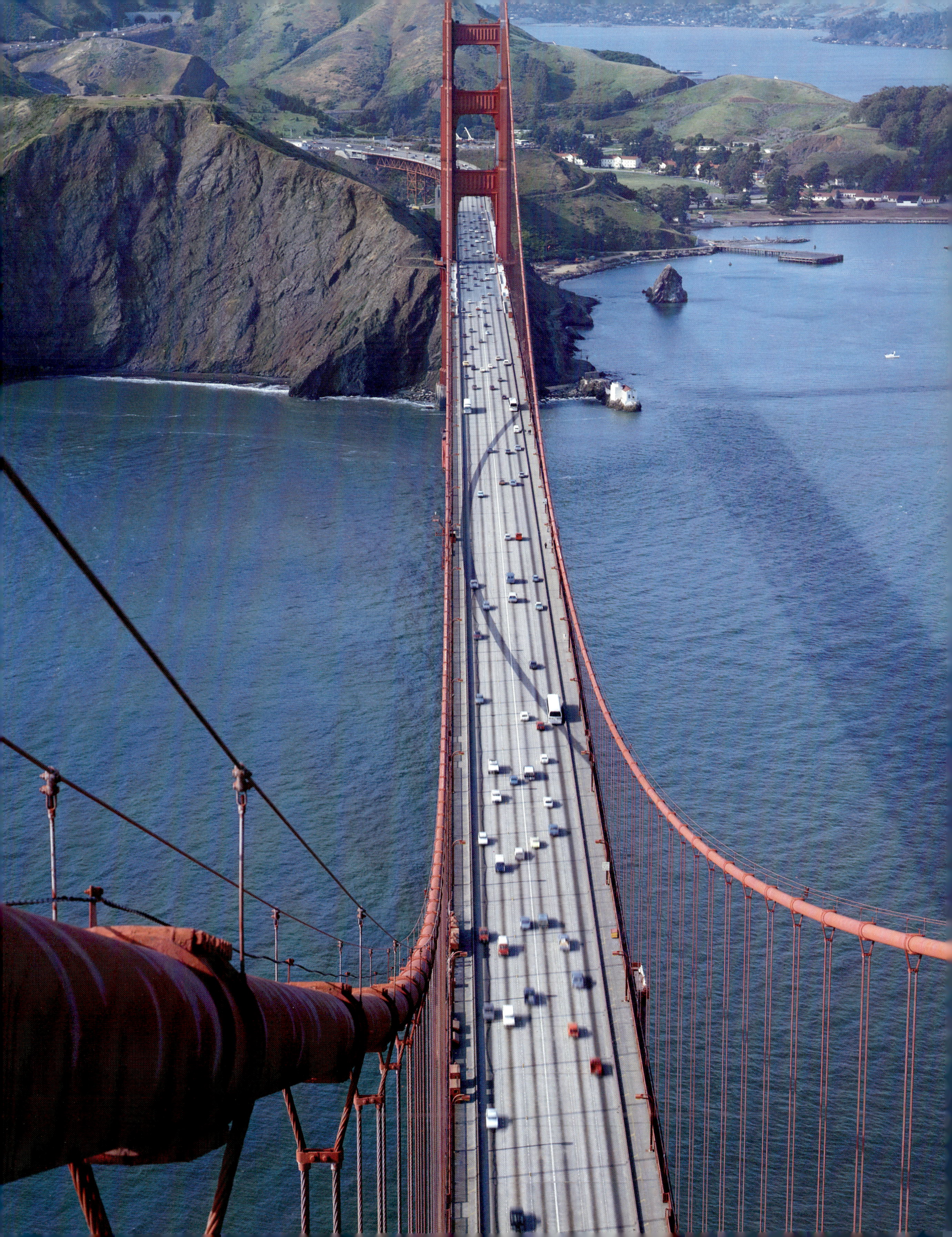

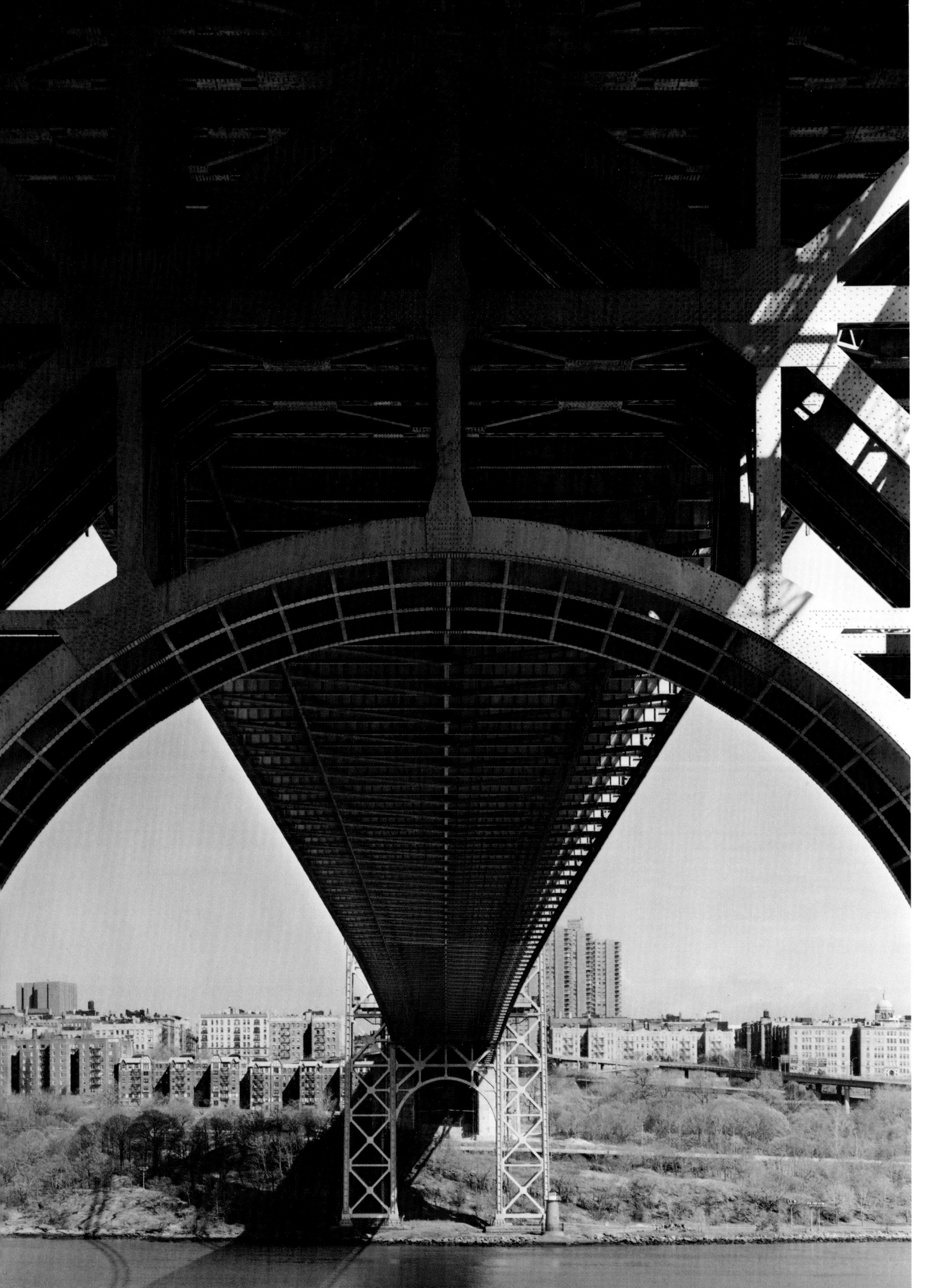

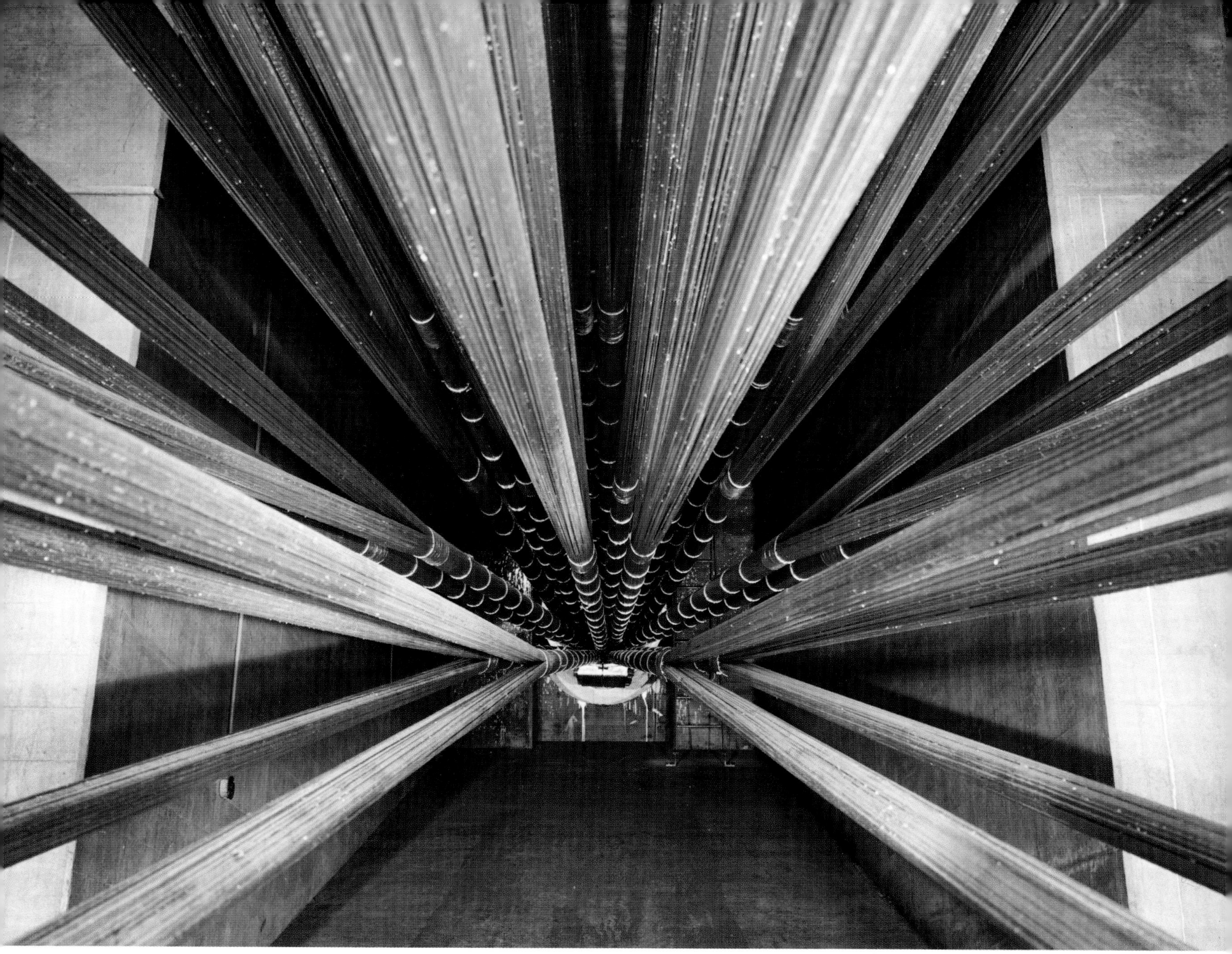

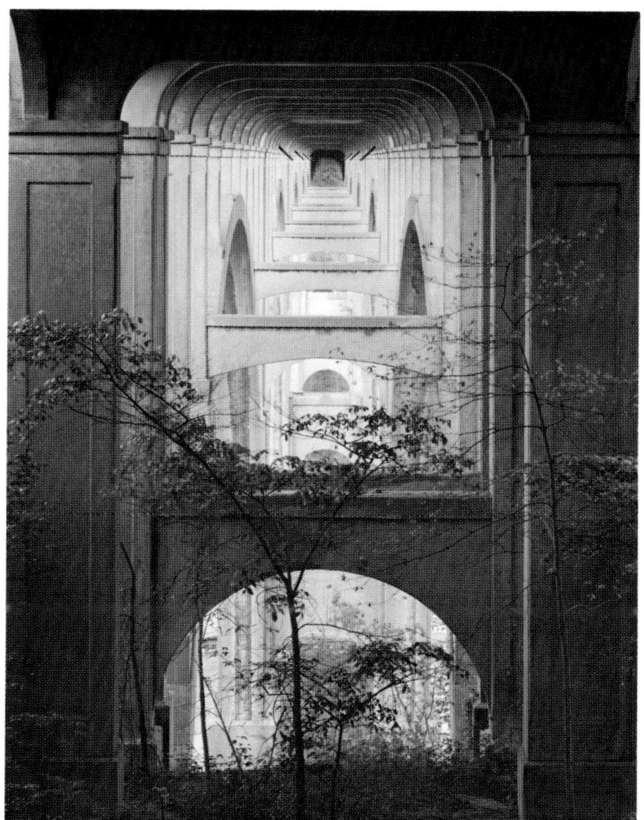

GEORGE WASHINGTON BRIDGE

Opposite. *Looking east to New York from New Jersey. Designed to be clad in stone, the steelwork of the 1931 towers was so impressive that it was left uncovered.*

SAN FRANCISCO-OAKLAND BAY BRIDGE

Above. *San Francisco anchorage of the 1936 bridge, where the main cable splays into individual strands that connect with steel eyebars anchored in concrete.*

BRECKSVILLE-NORTHFIELD BRIDGE

Left. *Below the roadway, Brecksville, Ohio. Massive concrete arches and spandrels support this 1931 bridge.*

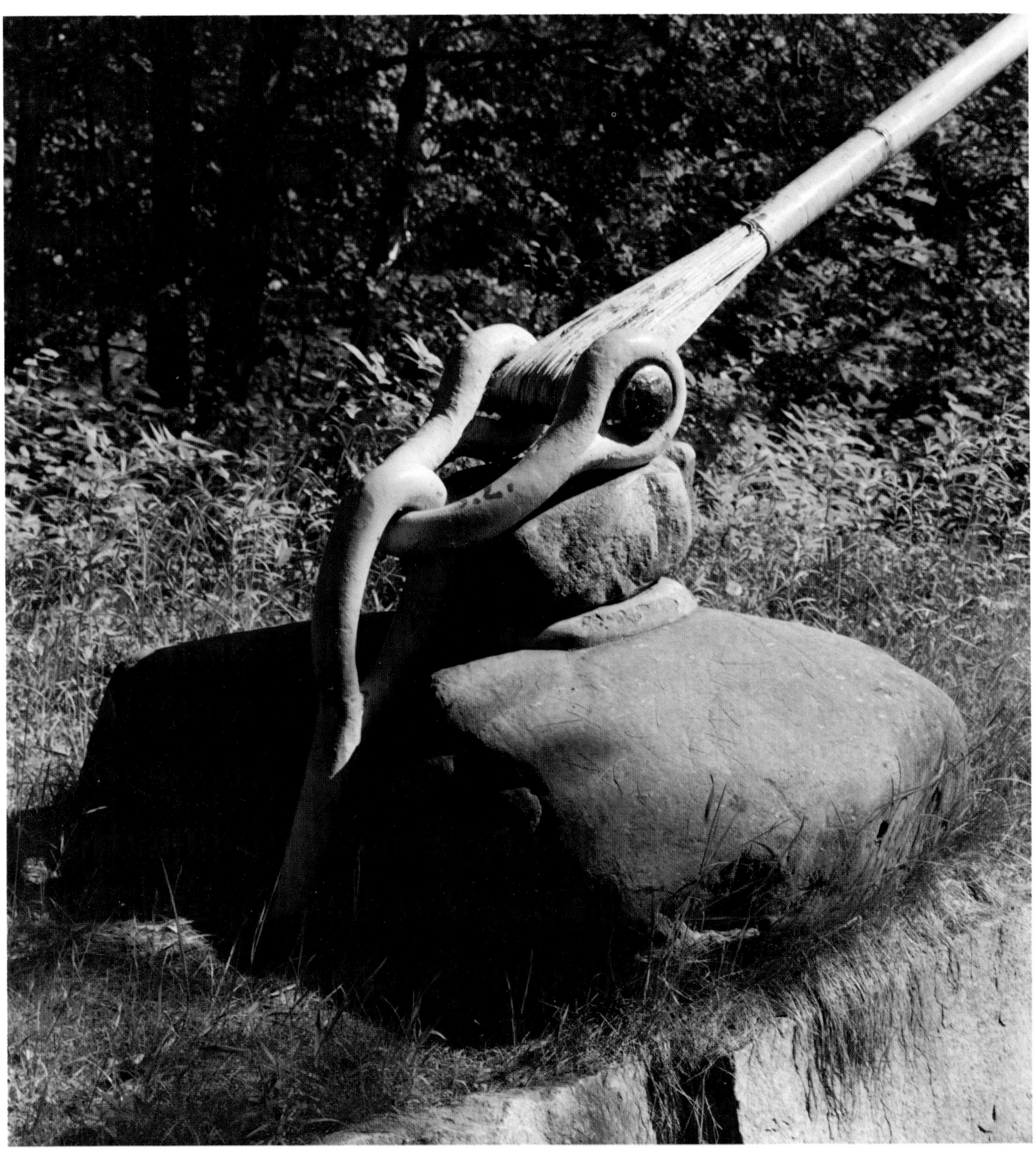

WIRE BRIDGE

Above. *Stone anchorage of Maine's oldest suspension bridge, built at New Portland about 1866.*

DETROIT-SUPERIOR VIADUCT

Opposite. *Supports of the three-hinged, steel-arch main span of the Cleveland bridge, constructed in 1918.*

BELLOWS FALLS BRIDGE

Overleaf. *Main span, Bellows Falls, Vt. Now demolished, the 540-foot parabolic-arch landmark was the longest American steel-arch bridge when it was built in 1905.*

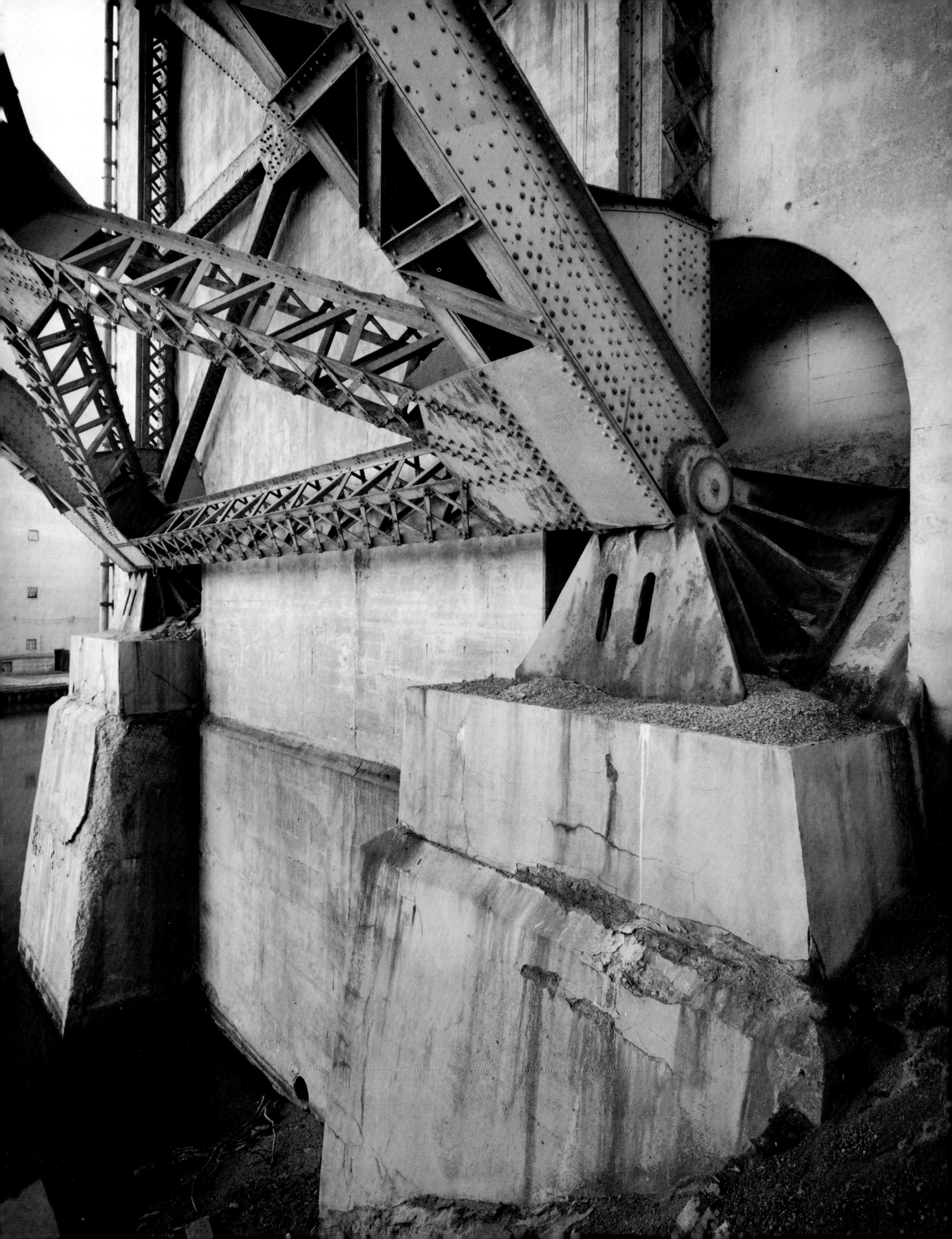

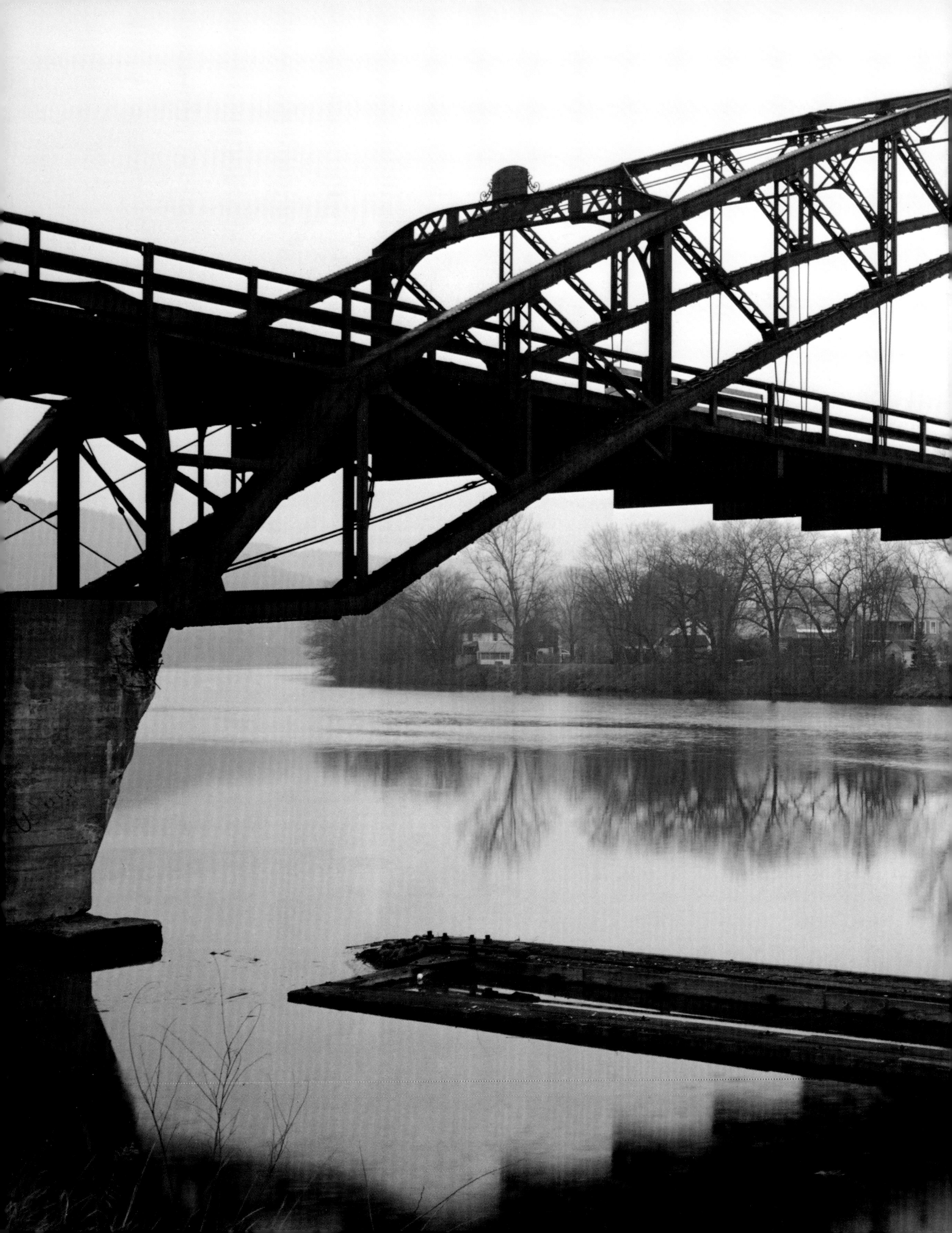

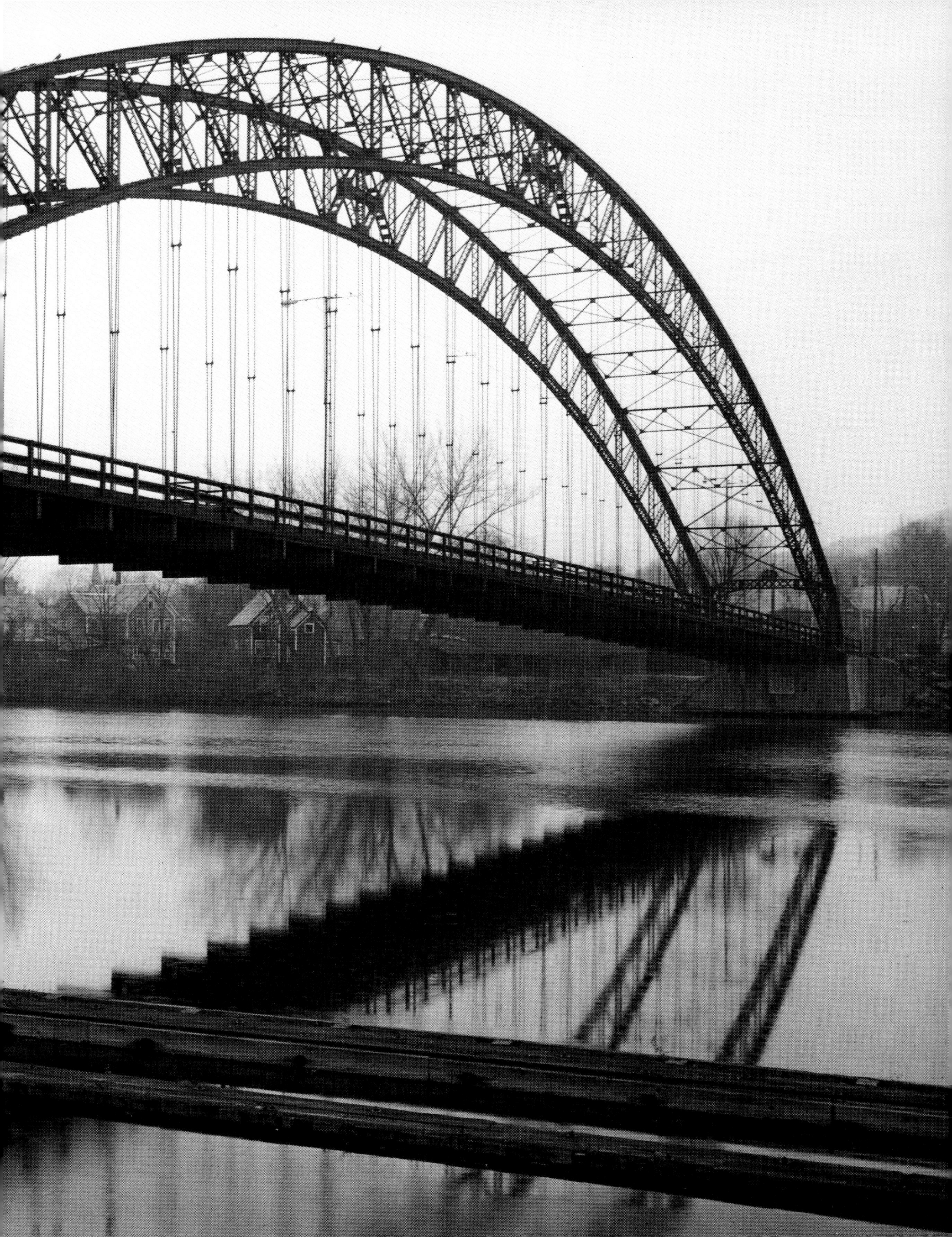

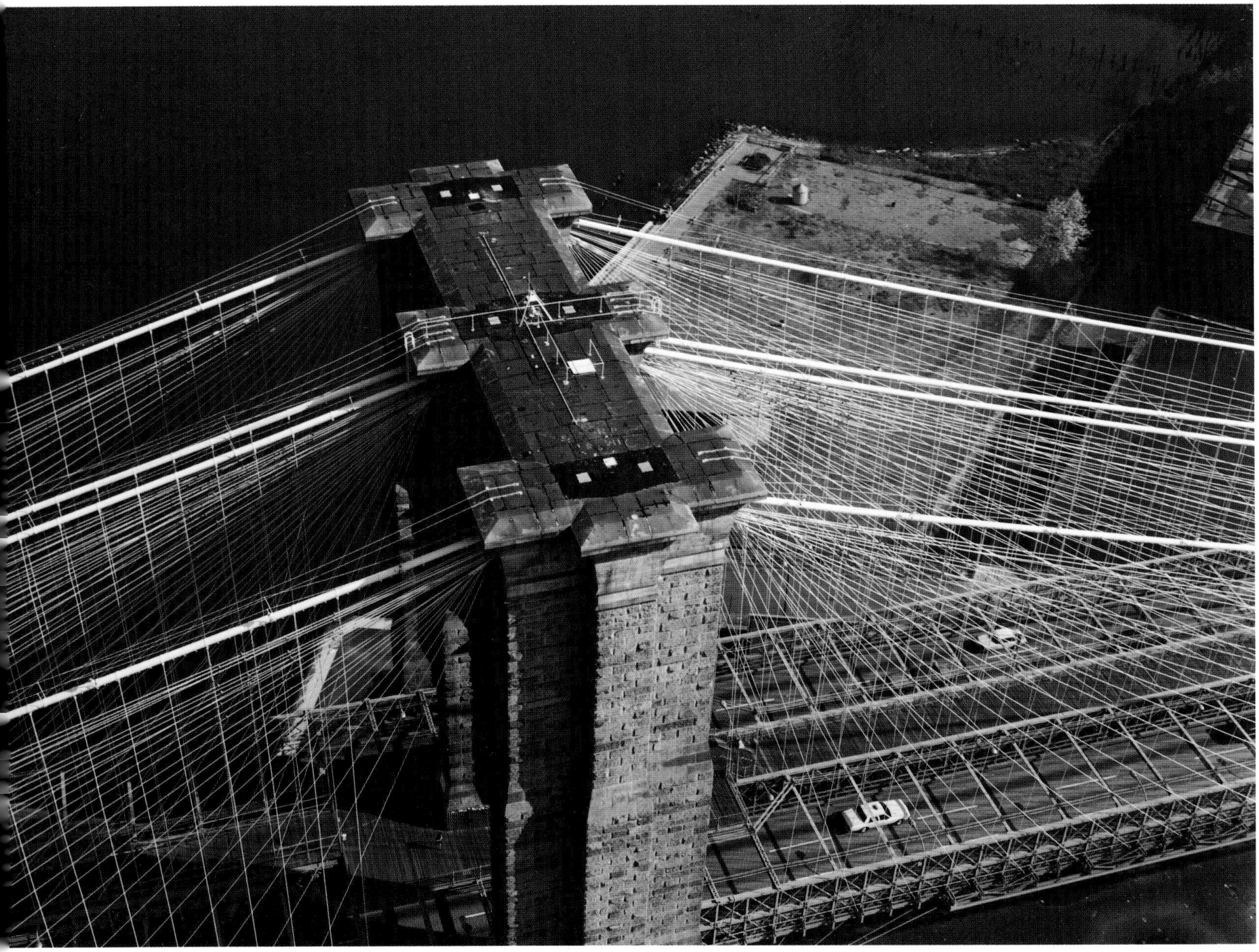

BROOKLYN BRIDGE

Above. *South tower and its main cables, suspenders and spidery diagonal stays, the latter a trademark of John and Washington Roebling that helps prevent the 1883 bridge from moving laterally in the wind.*

Right. *Main cable and stiffening trusses at mid-span.*

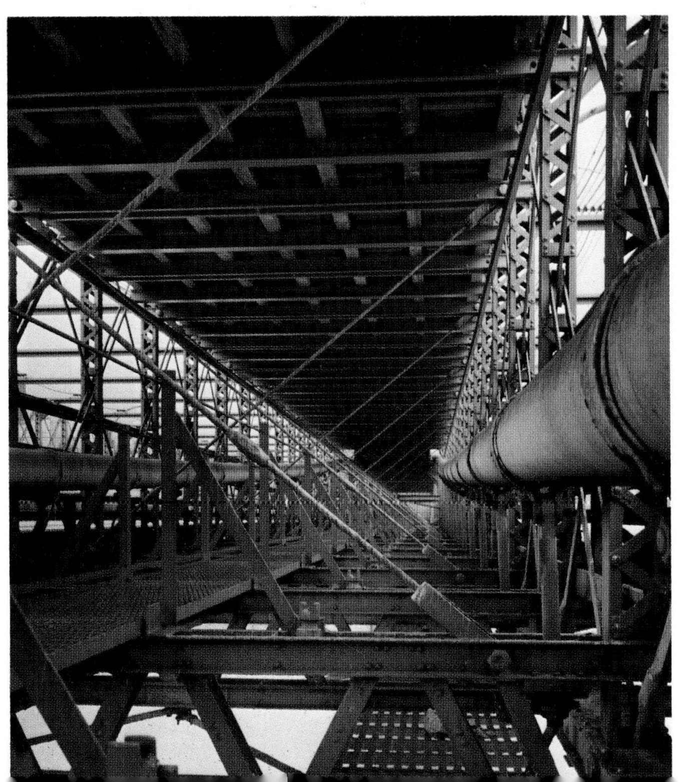

PASCO-KENNEWICK BRIDGES

Below. *1978 and 1921 bridges between Pasco and Kennewick, Wash. The 2,503-foot newer span was the longest cable-stayed bridge in North America when it was constructed. It superseded the multispan truss and cantilever bridge in the background.*

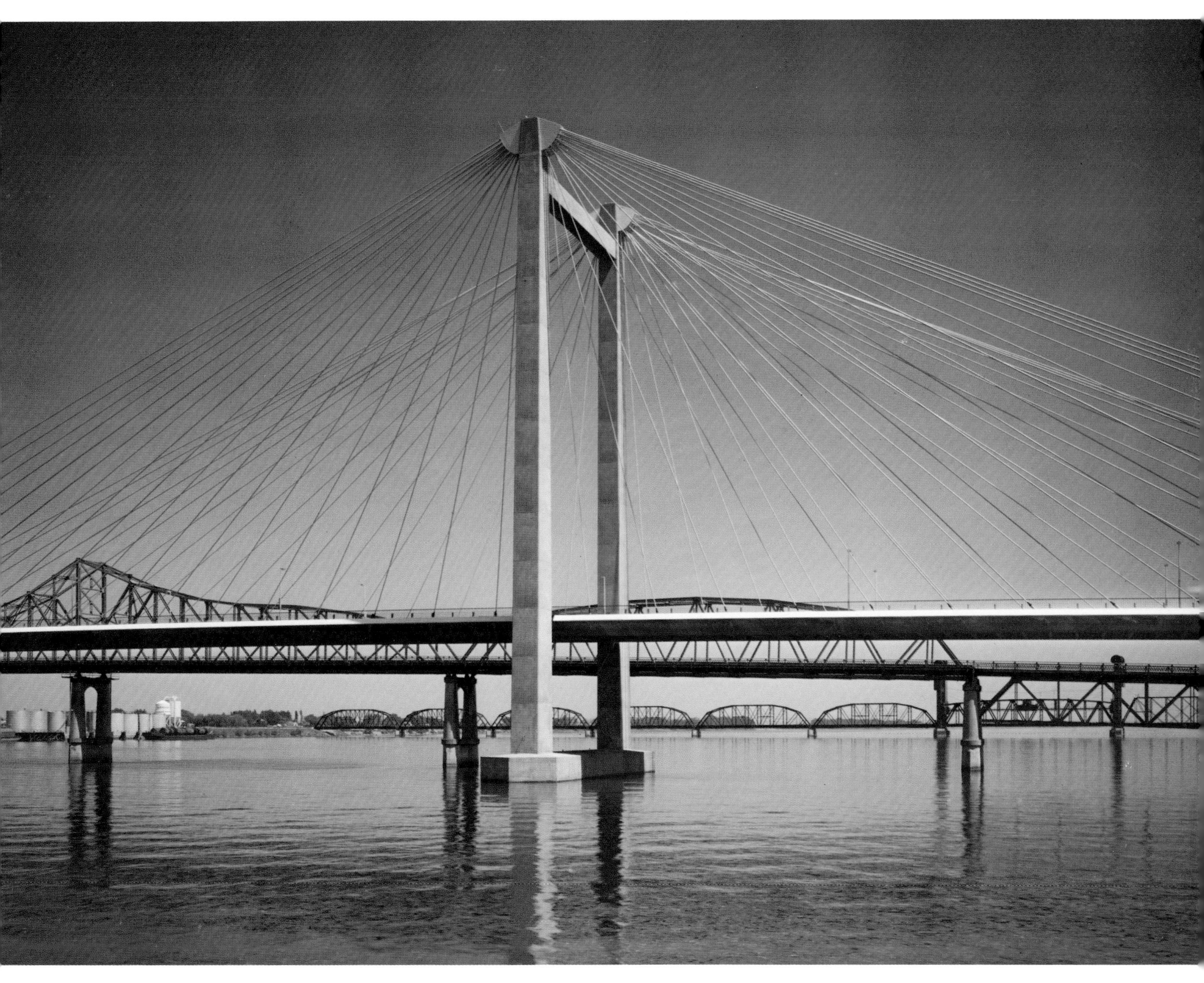

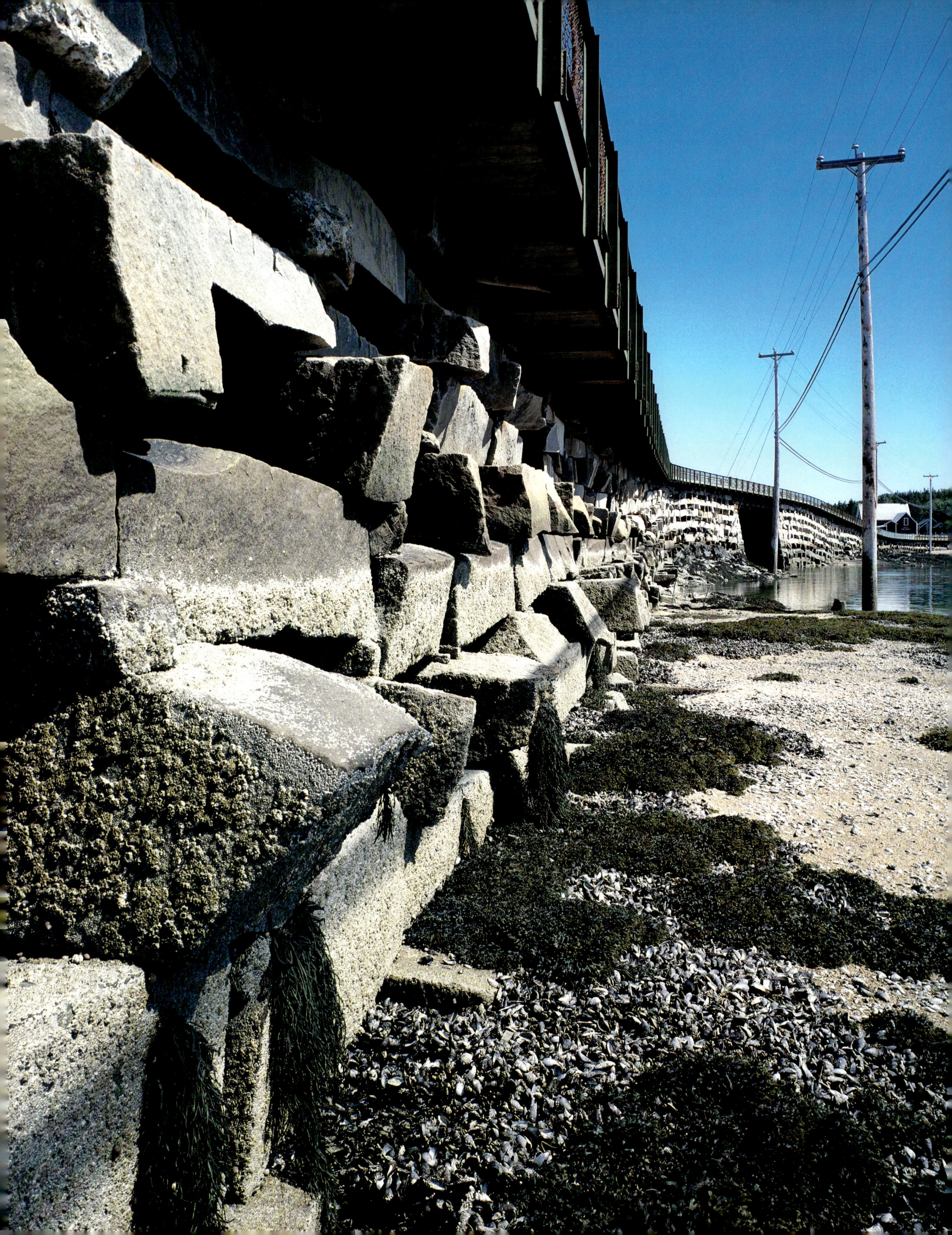

BAILEY ISLAND BRIDGE

Opposite. *Stone slab structural system, Bailey Island, Maine, designed in 1928 by Llewelyn N. Edwards. This choice of material permitted tidal waters to flow through the cribbing while it harmonized with the surrounding seascape.*

MILLION DOLLAR BRIDGE

Below. *Span collapsed during the 1964 Alaskan earthquake. Named for its great expense, this Pennsylvania through-truss bridge, built in 1912 at Cordova, carried the Copper River and Northwestern Railroad on its 196-mile route from the coast to the copper mines of Kennecott.*

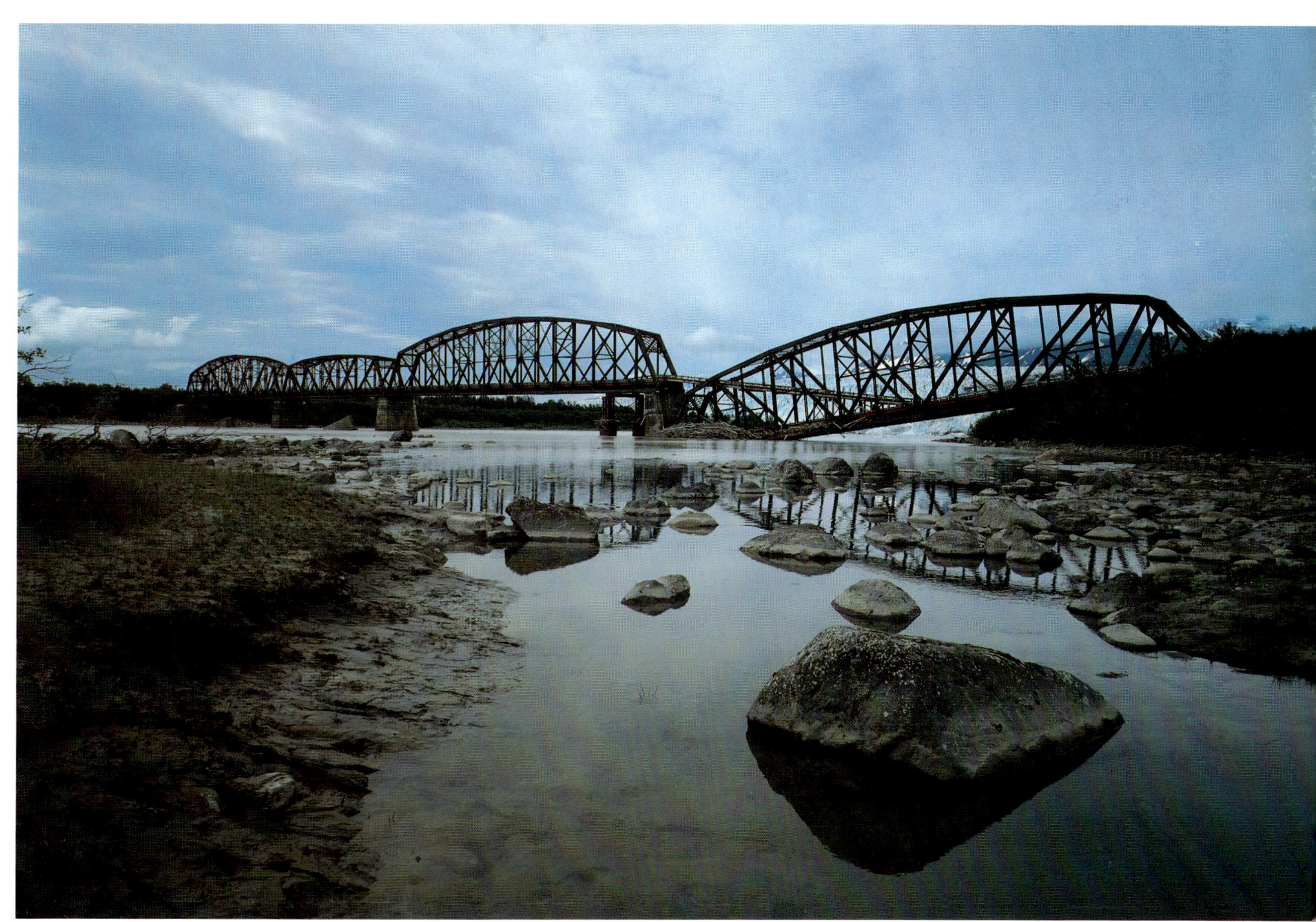

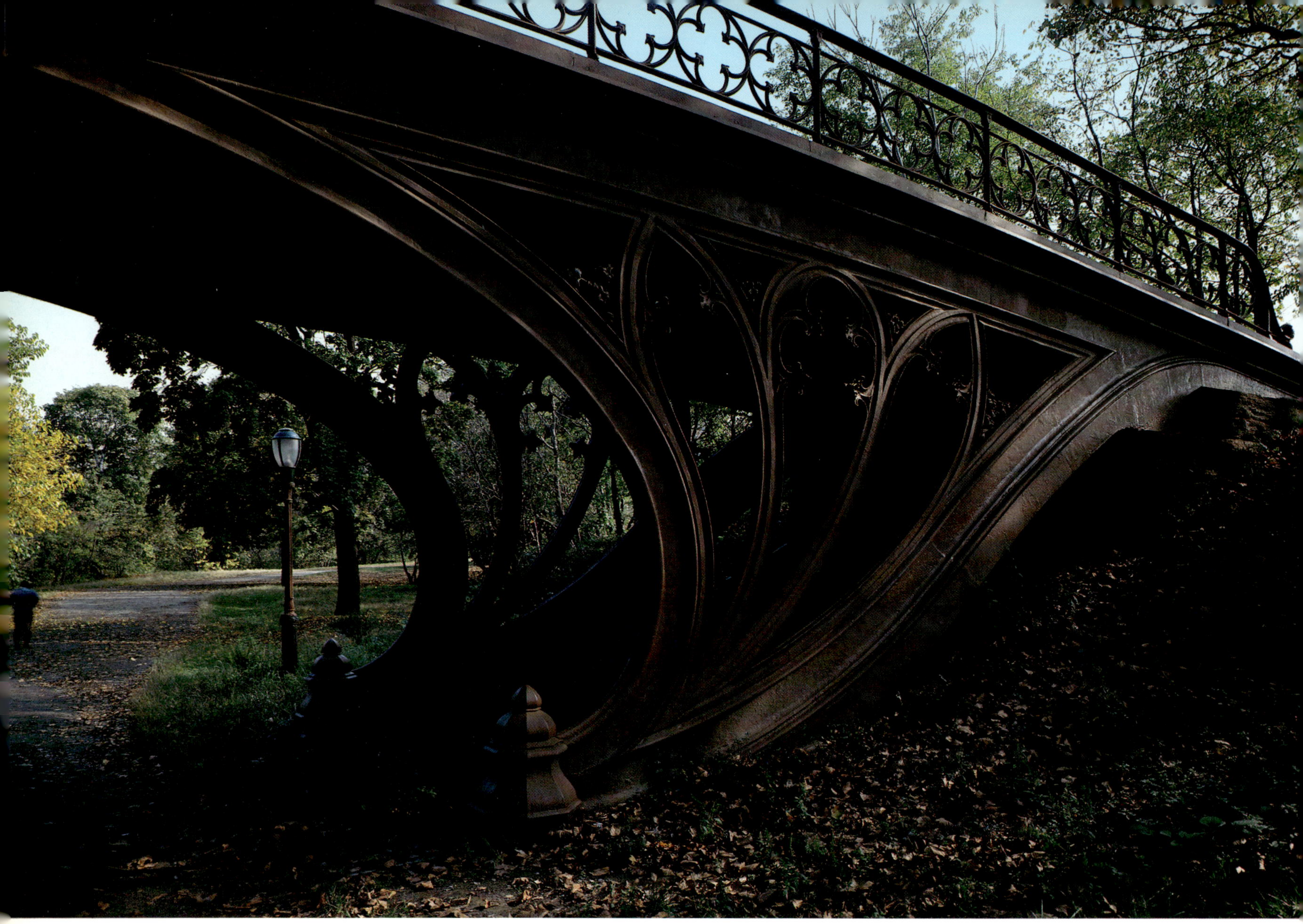

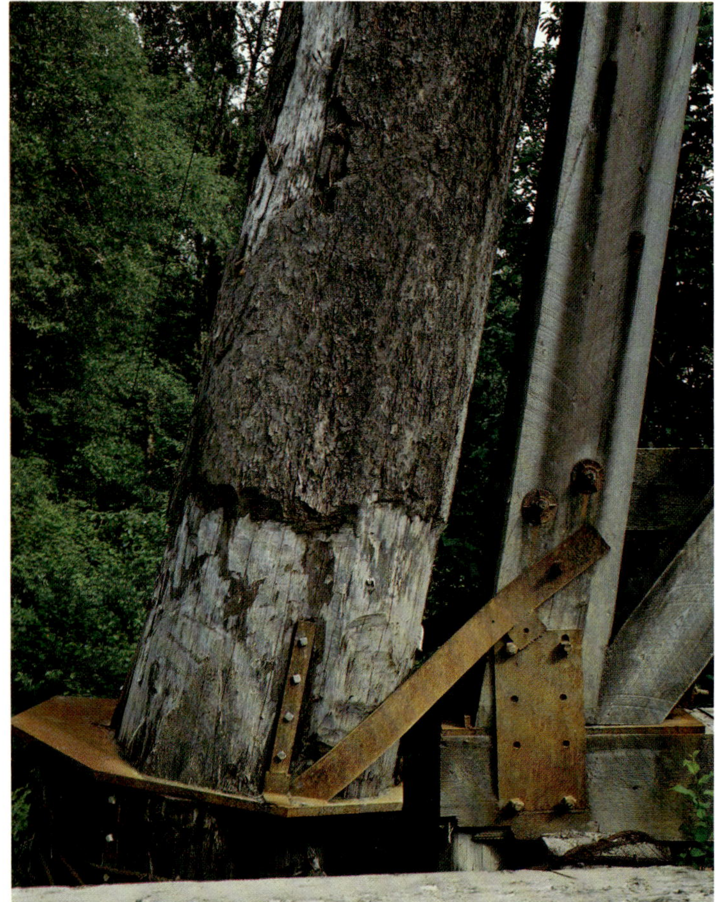

GOTHIC BRIDGE

Above. *Central Park bridle path, New York City, designed by Calvert Vaux and J. Wrey Mould in 1864. Central Park's five cast-iron bridges, built 1859–64, are among the oldest in the country.*

CHOW CHOW BRIDGE

Left. *Crossing the Quinault River near Quinault, Wash. A logging firm superintendent in 1952 designed this cable-stayed bridge, one of the earliest in the Northwest.*

NORTHAMPTON BRIDGE

Opposite. *Lattice truss spans of wrought iron, constructed in 1887 in Northampton, Mass. More costly to build than Pratt truss bridges, the riveted lattice trusses reduced deflection and vibration.*

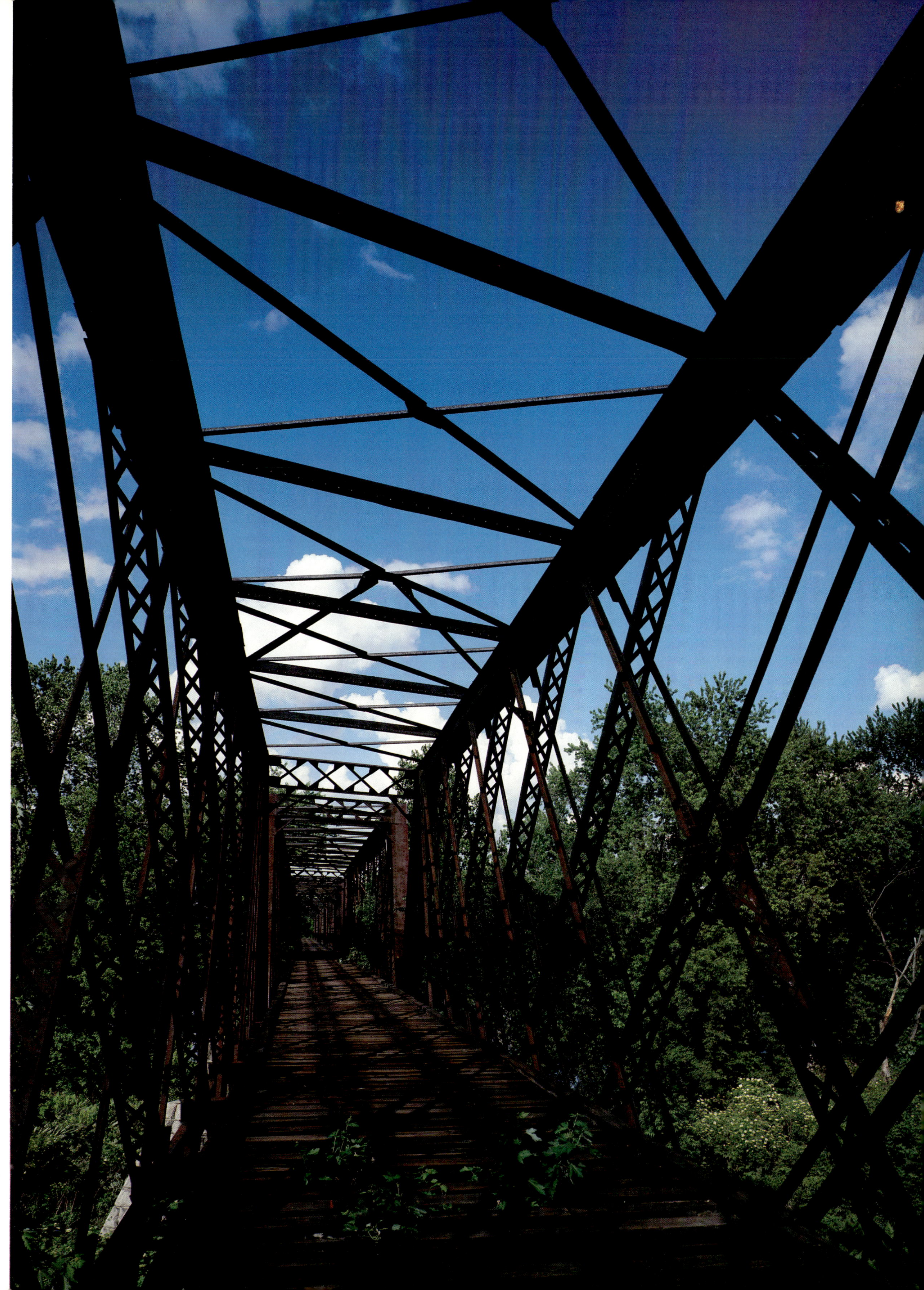

RIVERSIDE AVENUE BRIDGE

Below. *Combination cast- and wrought-iron Whipple through-truss bridge, Greenwich, Conn. Originally part of a railroad bridge in Stratford, Conn., the 1871 span was moved in the 1890s and converted into a highway bridge.*

WIRE BRIDGE

Opposite. *Shingled towers, New Portland, Maine. Partially reconstructed in 1960, the bridge's main cables, anchorages and much of the towers' timber framing date from a century earlier.*

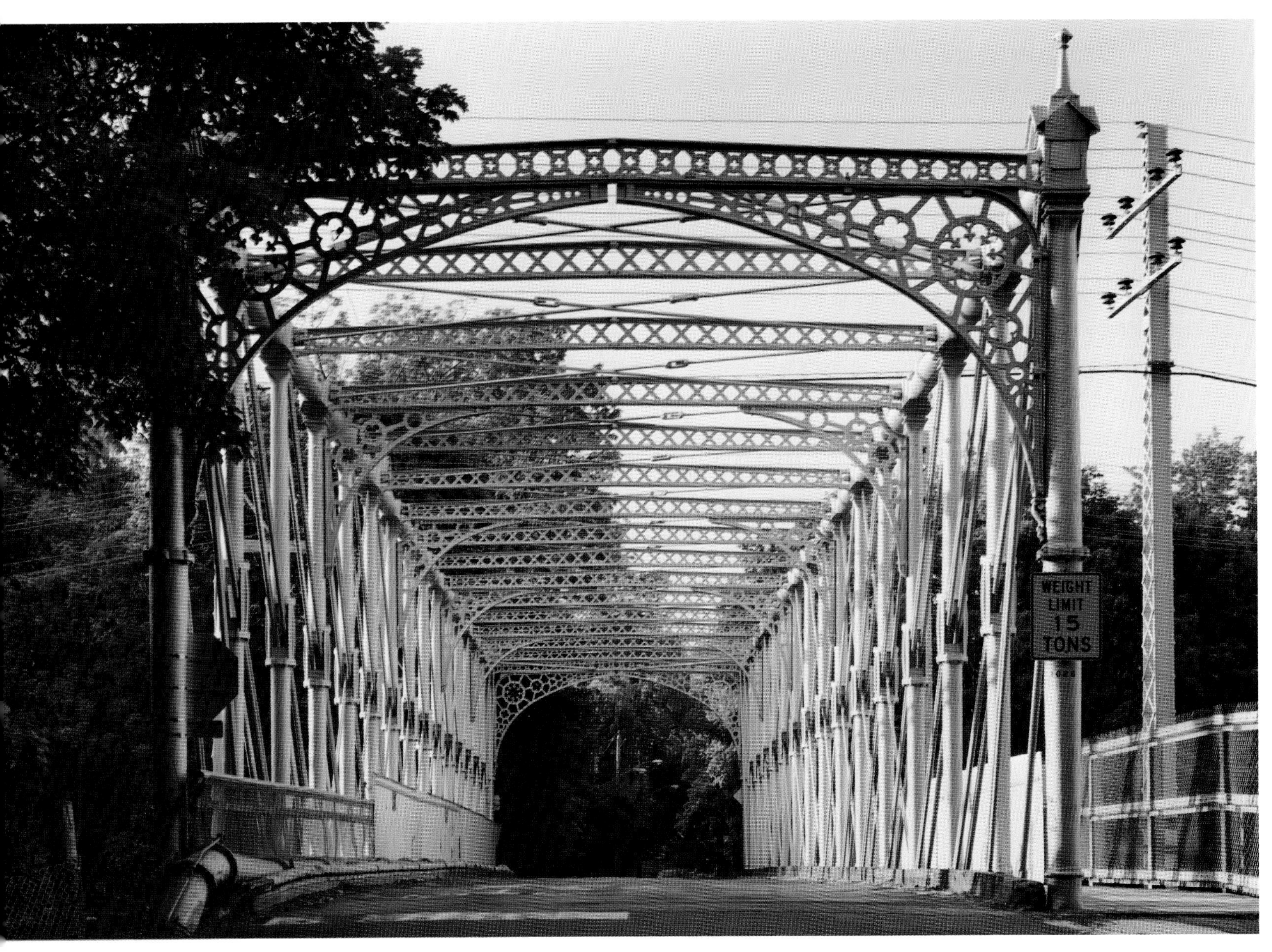

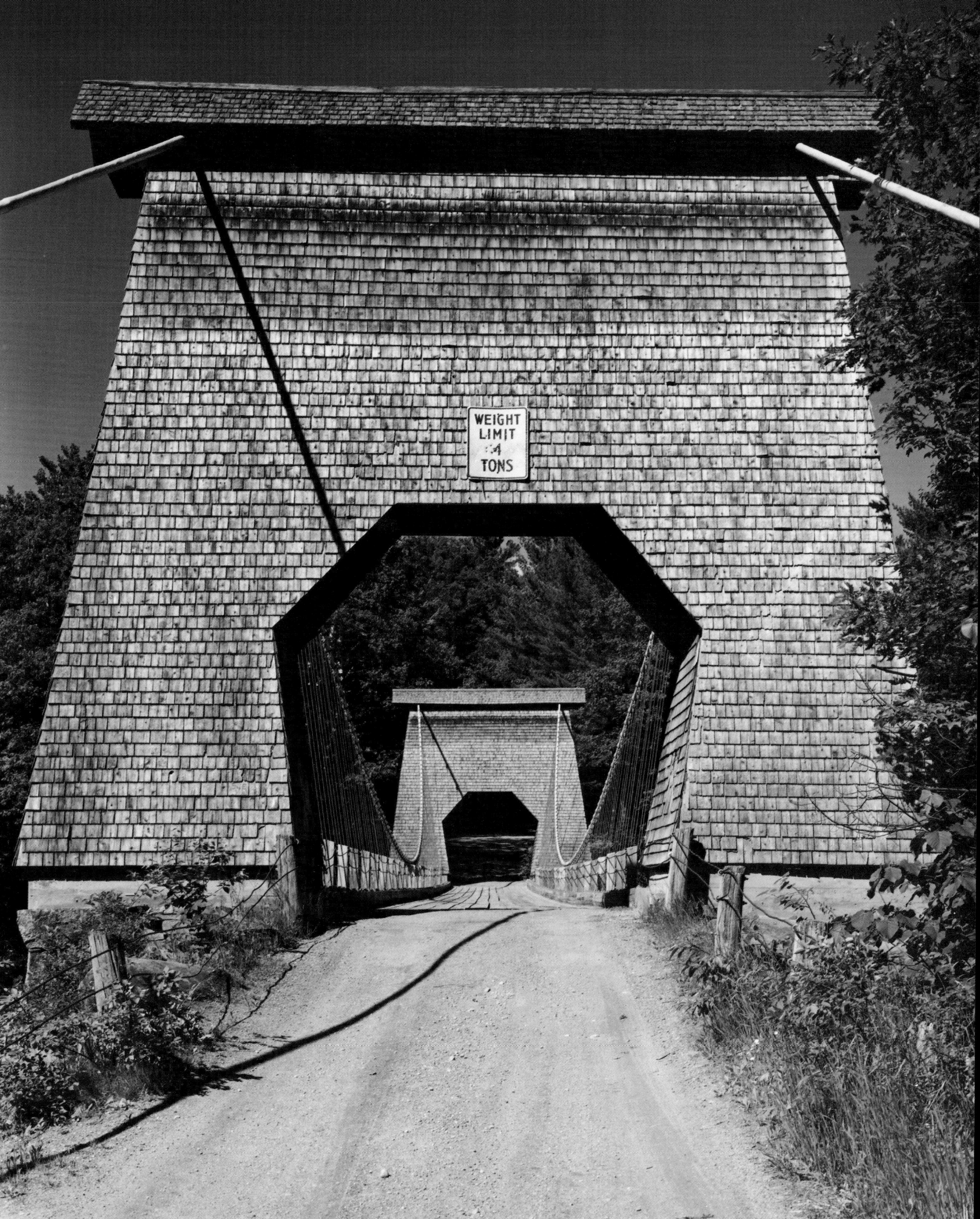
WEIGHT
LIMIT
4
TONS

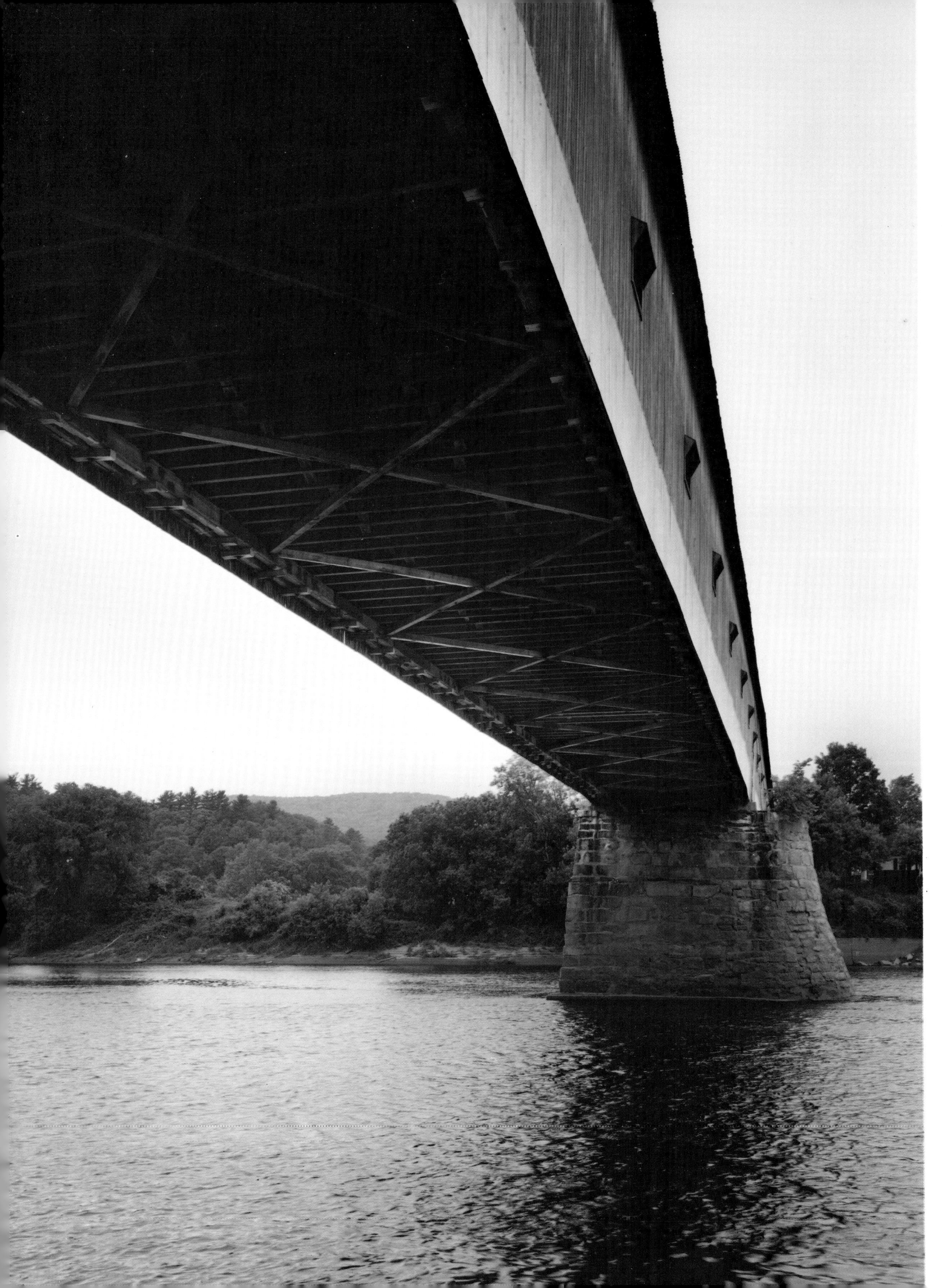

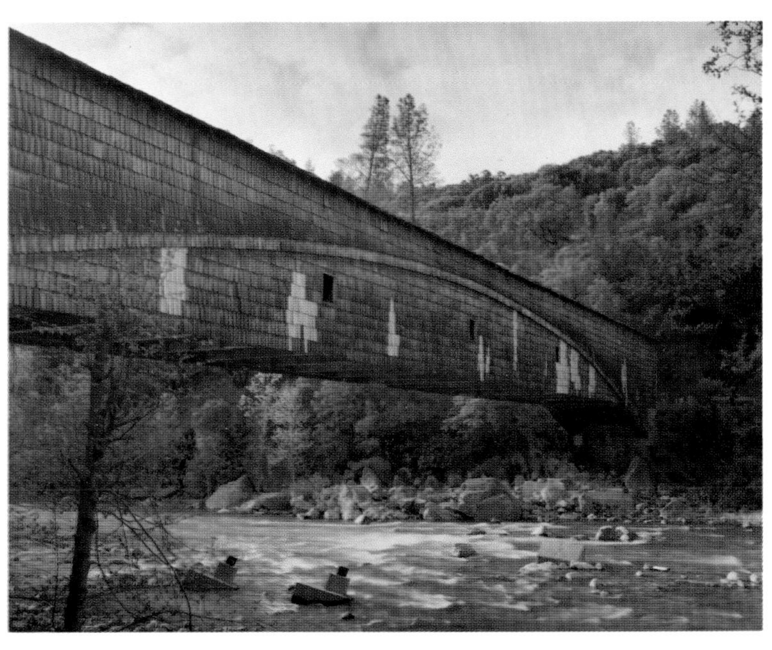

WINDSOR BRIDGE

Opposite. *Covered bridge between Windsor, Vt., and Cornish, N.H., constructed about 1866 with a two-span Town lattice truss.*

BRIDGEPORT BRIDGE

Left. *Howe arch truss covered bridge, Bridgeport, Calif. Completed in 1862, its single span of 233 feet makes this among the longest covered bridges in the world.*

CALIPSO BRIDGE

Below. *Multispan truss railroad bridge over the Yellowstone River, Terry, Mont., built about 1907.*

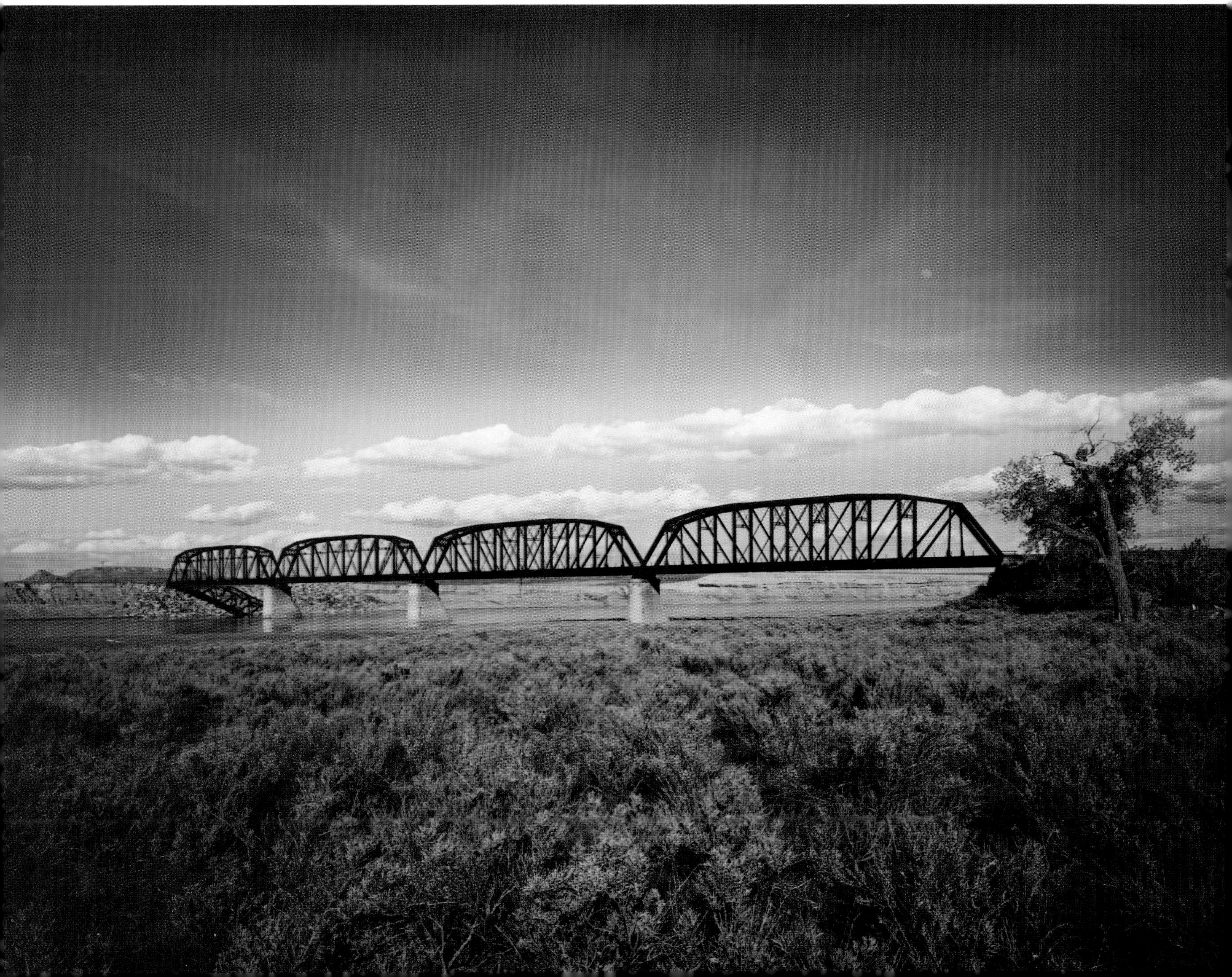

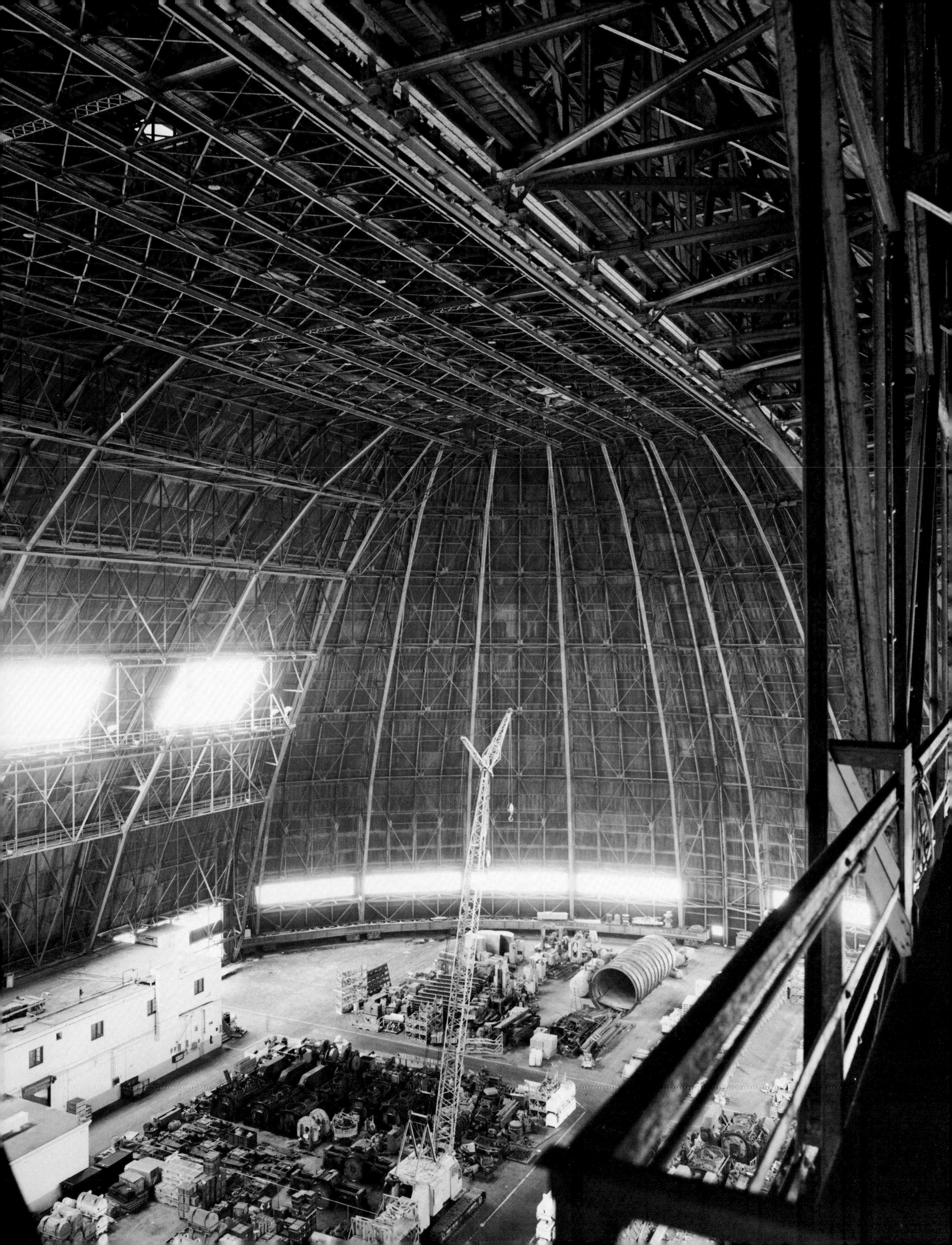

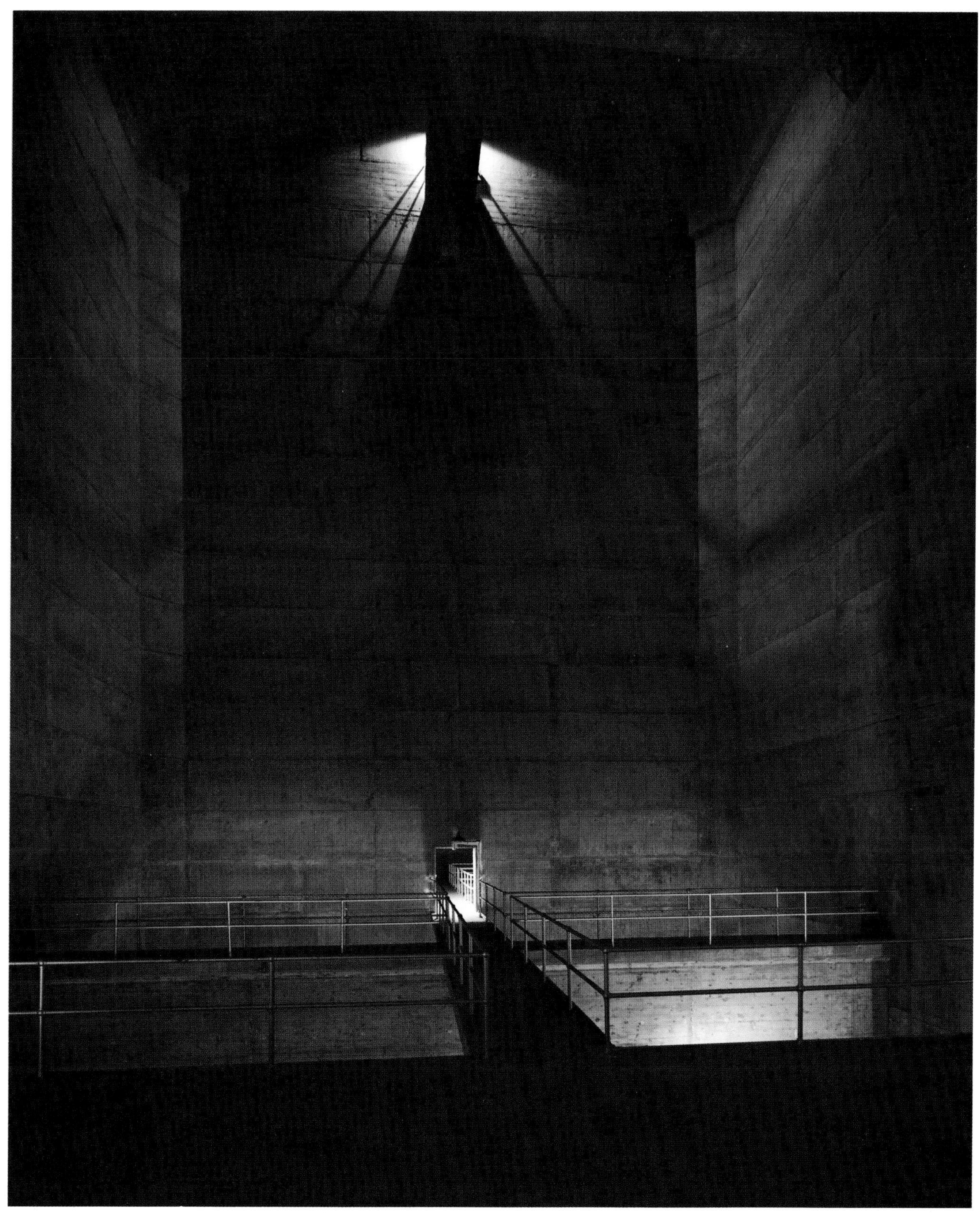

GOODYEAR AIRDOCK

Opposite. *Formerly a factory for constructing and servicing zeppelins. Completed in 1929 near Akron, Ohio, this mammoth, steel-frame structure is 1,175 feet long, 325 feet wide and 211 feet tall.*

SAN FRANCISCO-OAKLAND BAY BRIDGE

Above. *Mid-bay anchorage, a cavernous concrete structure in which the main cables are anchored.*

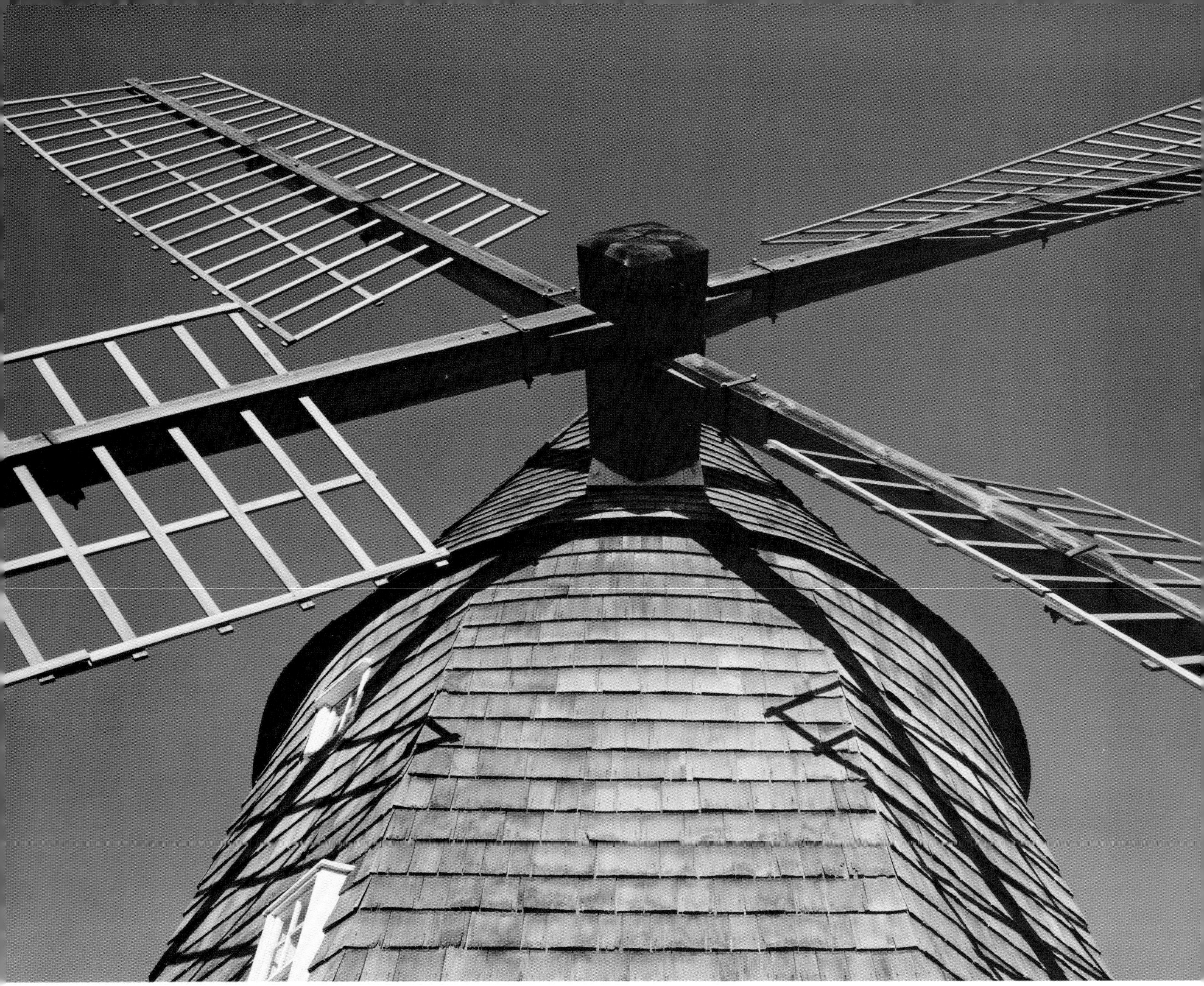

LONG ISLAND WINDMILLS

Above. *Hook Windmill, East Hampton, N.Y., one of 11 remaining windmills on Long Island's South Fork. Constructed in 1806, the windmill was busiest in the late summer and the autumn; commercial flour milling ceased in 1908.*

Right. *Doorway, Pantigo Windmill, East Hampton, N.Y. The 1804 structure survives with the aid of periodic reshingling.*

Opposite. *Worn treads of the Pantigo Windmill's wooden stairway.*

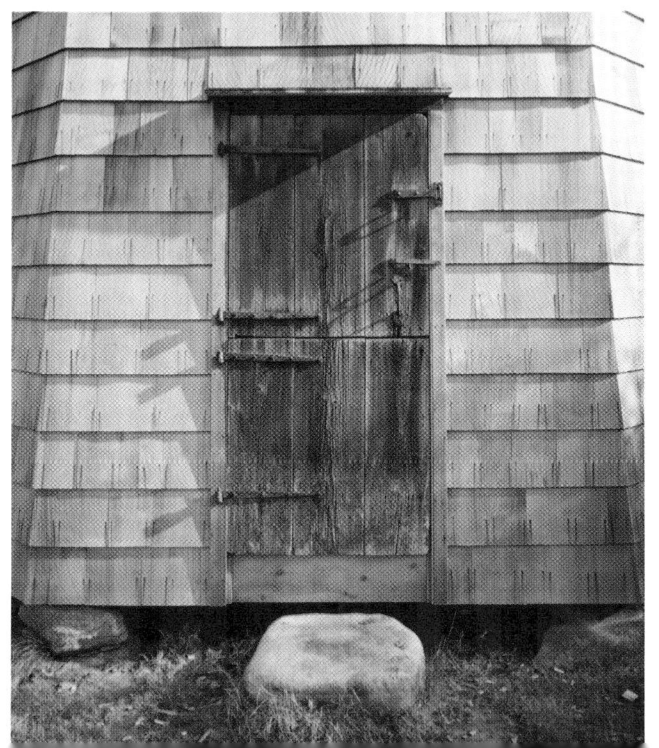

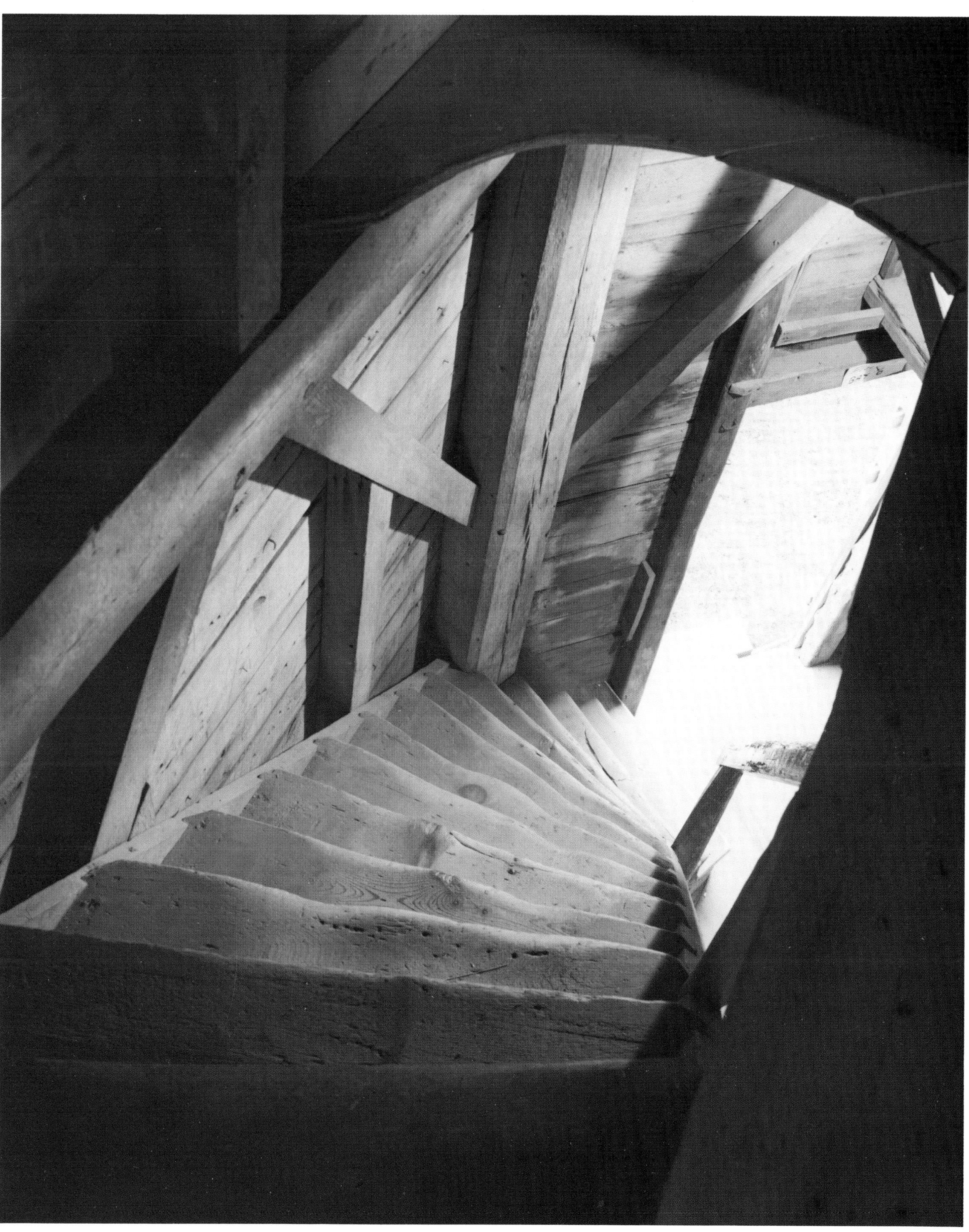

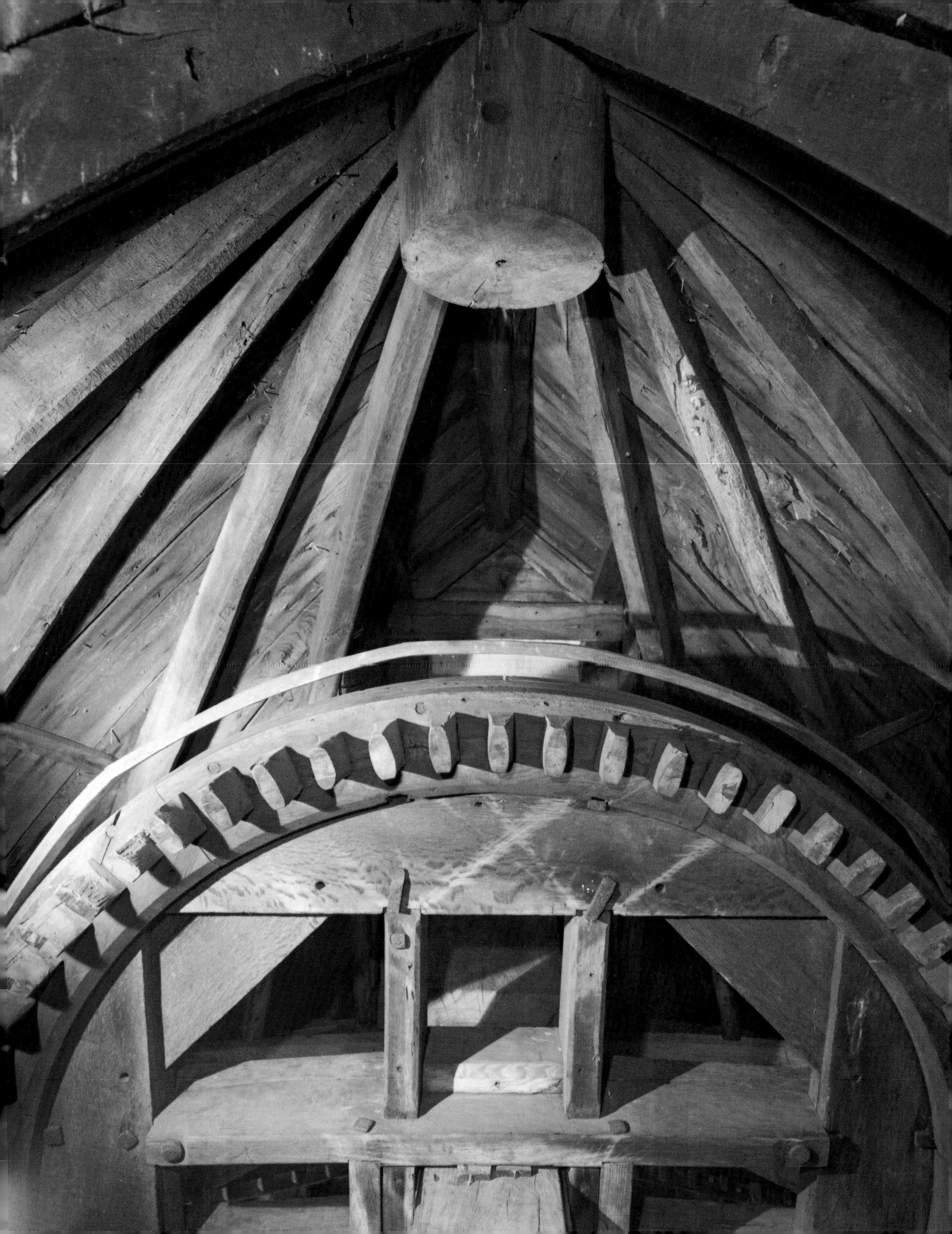

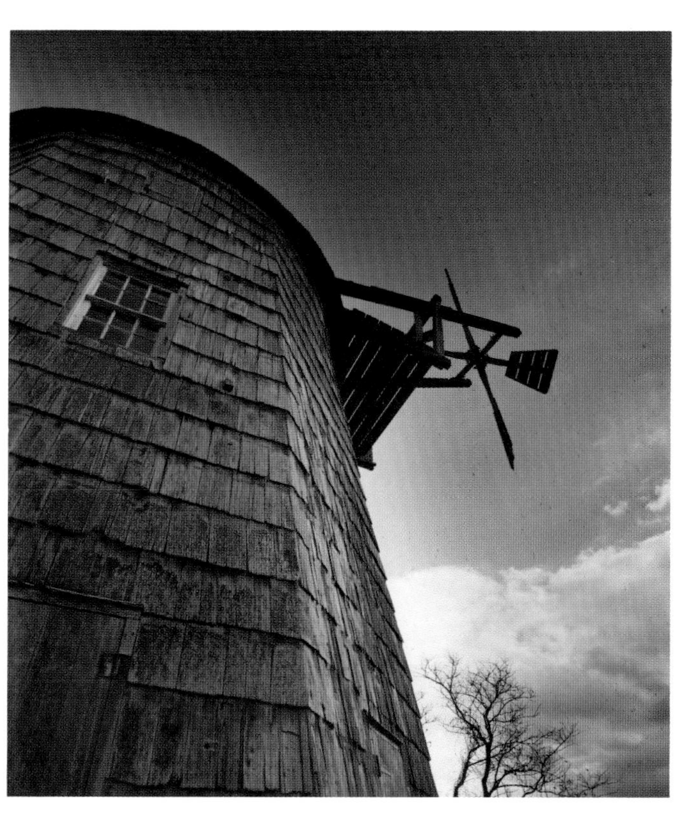

PANTIGO WINDMILL

Opposite. *Bowed rafters of the conical cap, with a clasp-arm brake wheel that is not original.*

WAINSCOTT WINDMILL

Left. *Fanstage designed to keep the windmill's sails turned into the wind. Located originally in Southampton, the 1813 windmill was moved to Wainscott, N.Y., in the 1850s, where it was operated until the early 1900s.*

HAYGROUND WINDMILL

Below. *Mill sails and the tintering gear for the burr stones, used to regulate the grinding fineness. Inscribed "built 1809," this windmill also was moved, from Bridgehampton to East Hampton, in 1950.*

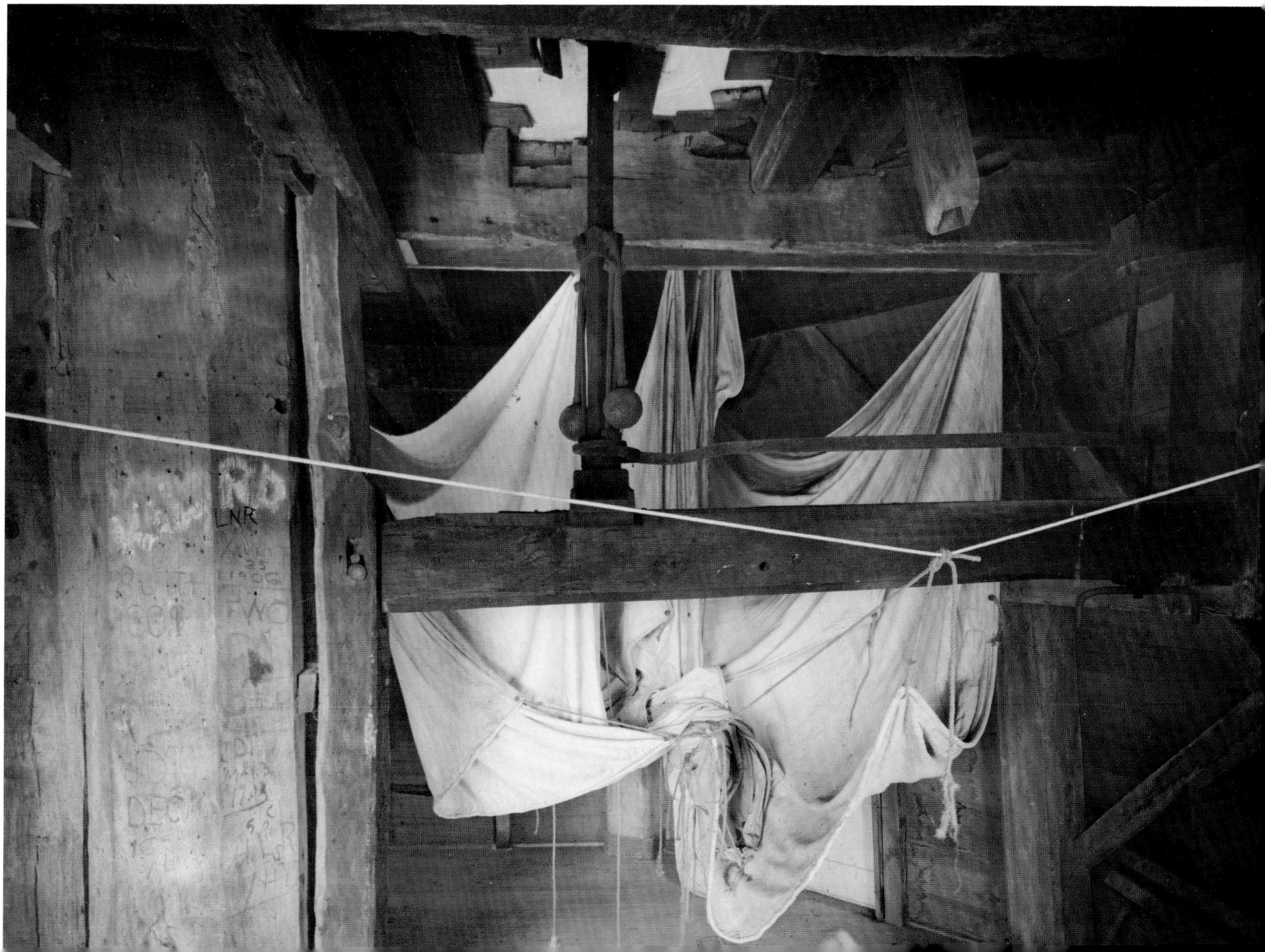

FIRE

O! for a Muse of fire,
that would ascend
The brightest heaven
of invention!

WILLIAM SHAKESPEARE
King Henry V

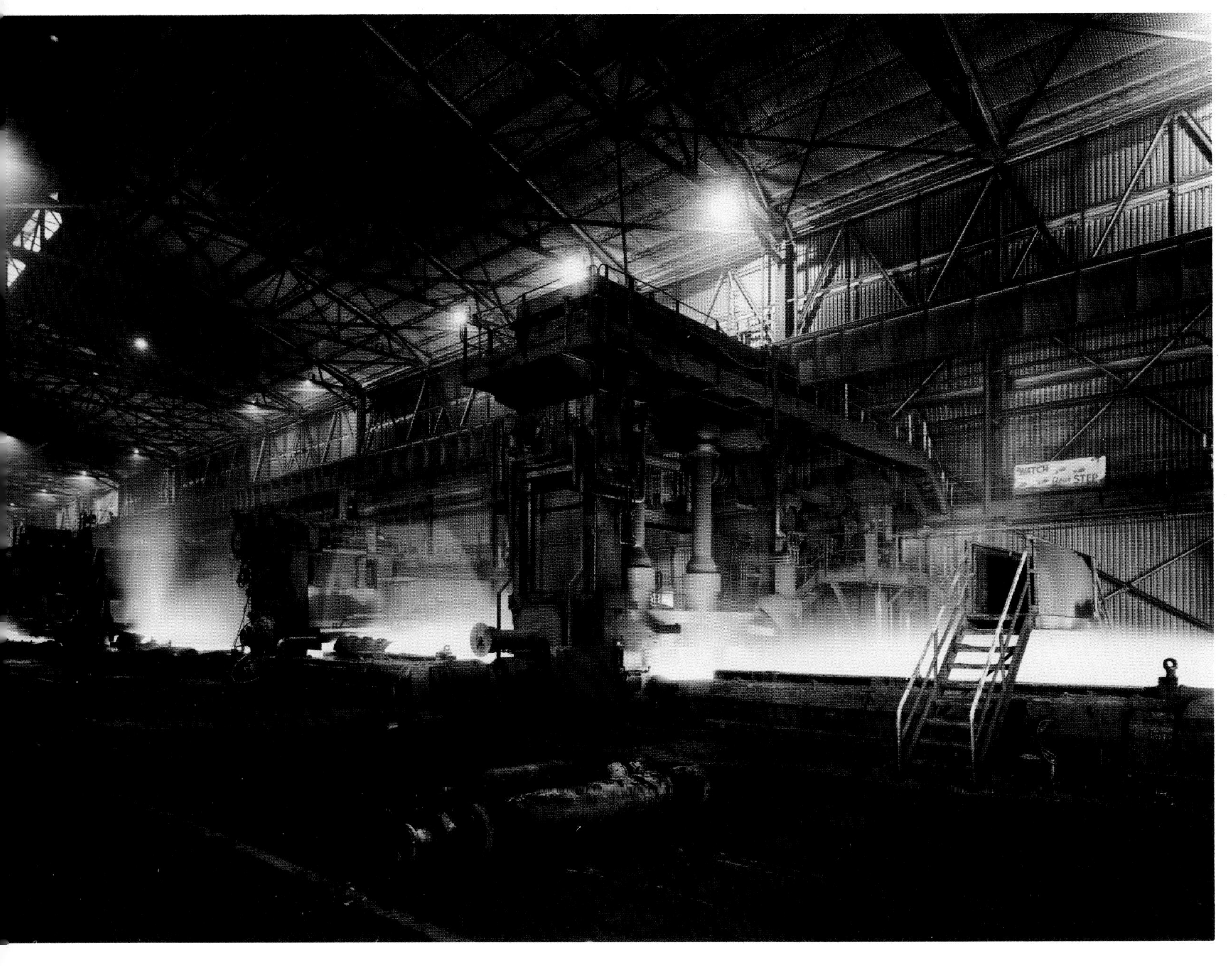

REPUBLIC STEEL COMPANY

Above. *Roughing stands for the 10-inch bar mill, Cleveland. The machinery is used to remove extraneous materials from steel slabs processed in the bar mill.*

WYMAN-GORDON COMPANY

Opposite. *Forging press, North Grafton, Mass. This and the adjacent 50,000-ton press, one of the largest fabrication tools in the world, are used to die-cut aluminum alloy components for air and space needs.*

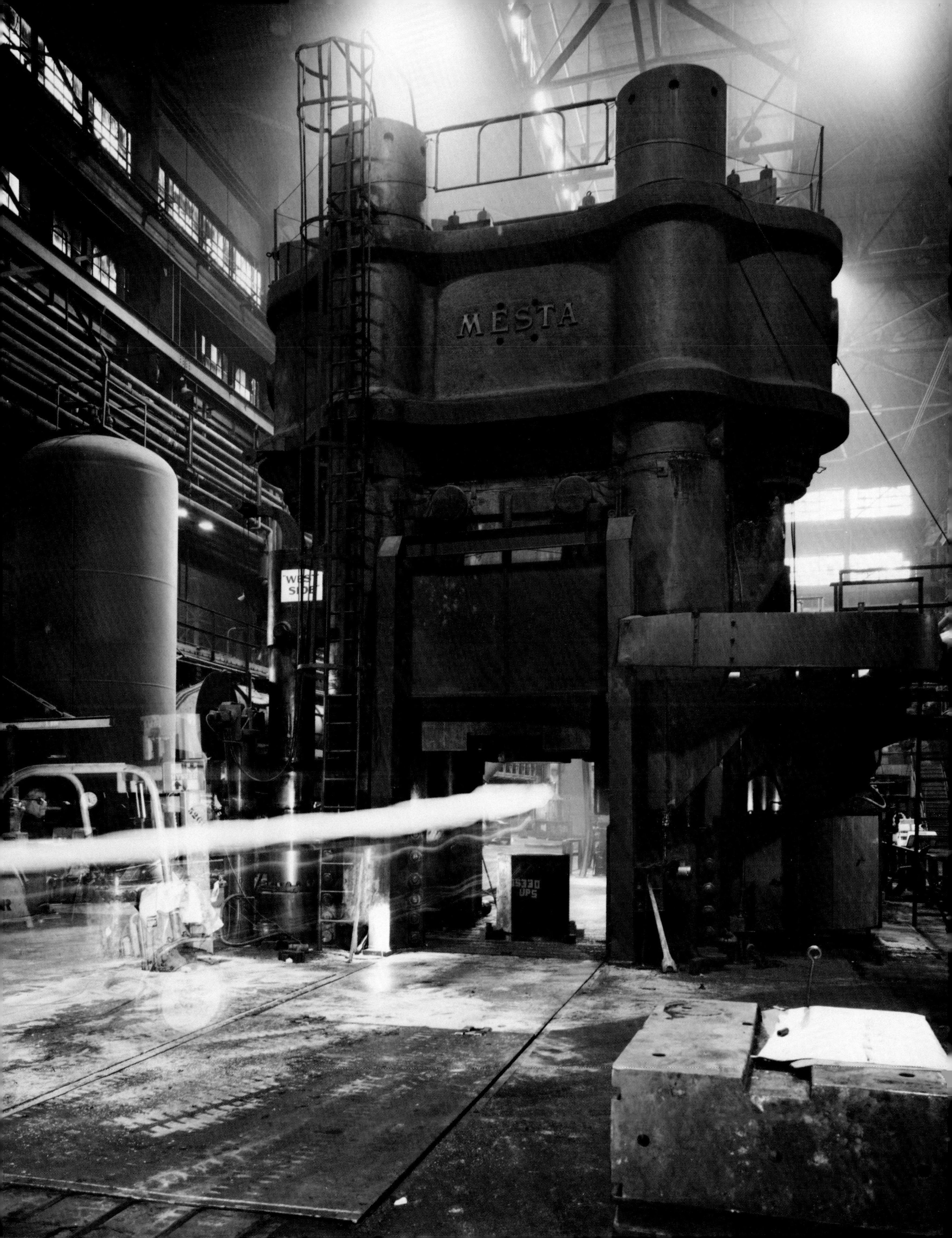
MESTA
WEST SIDE

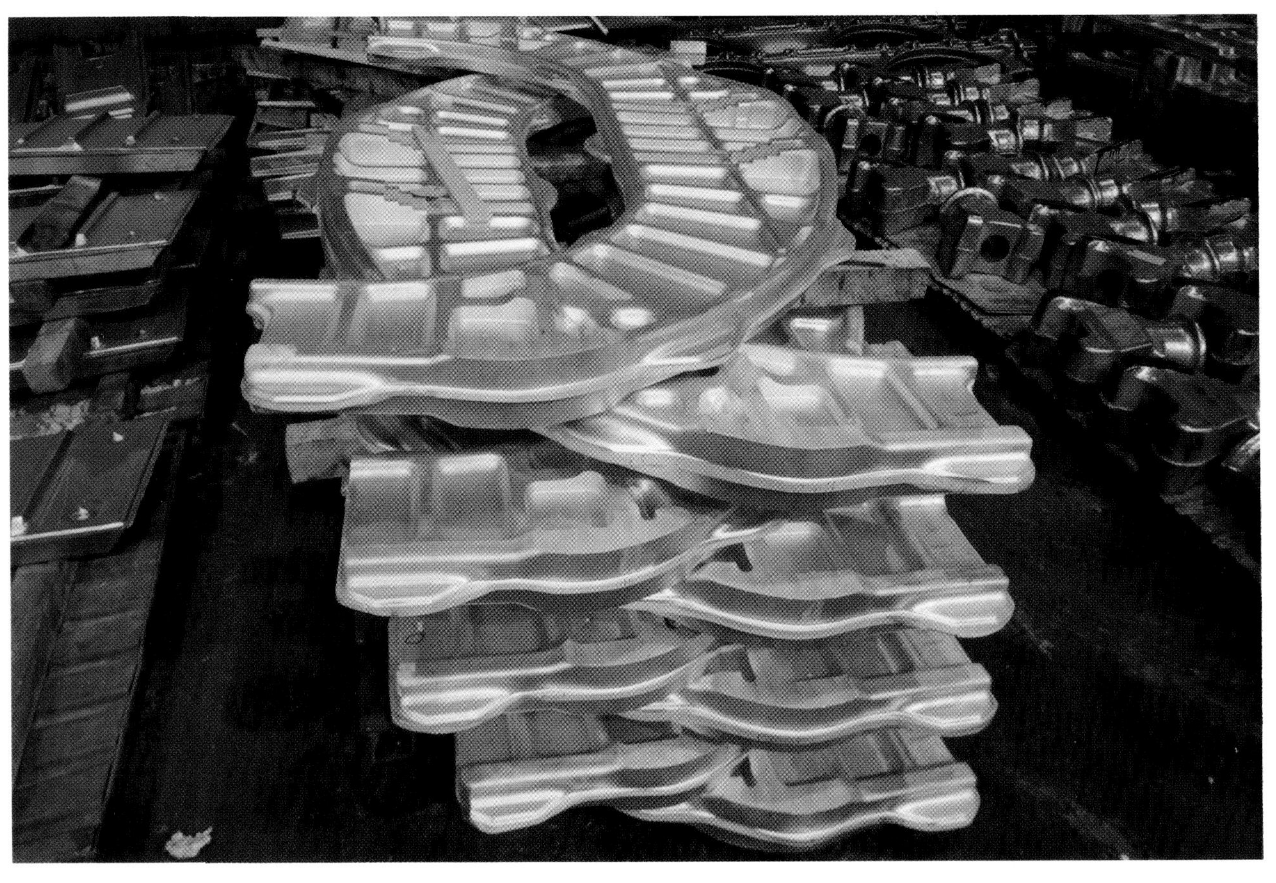

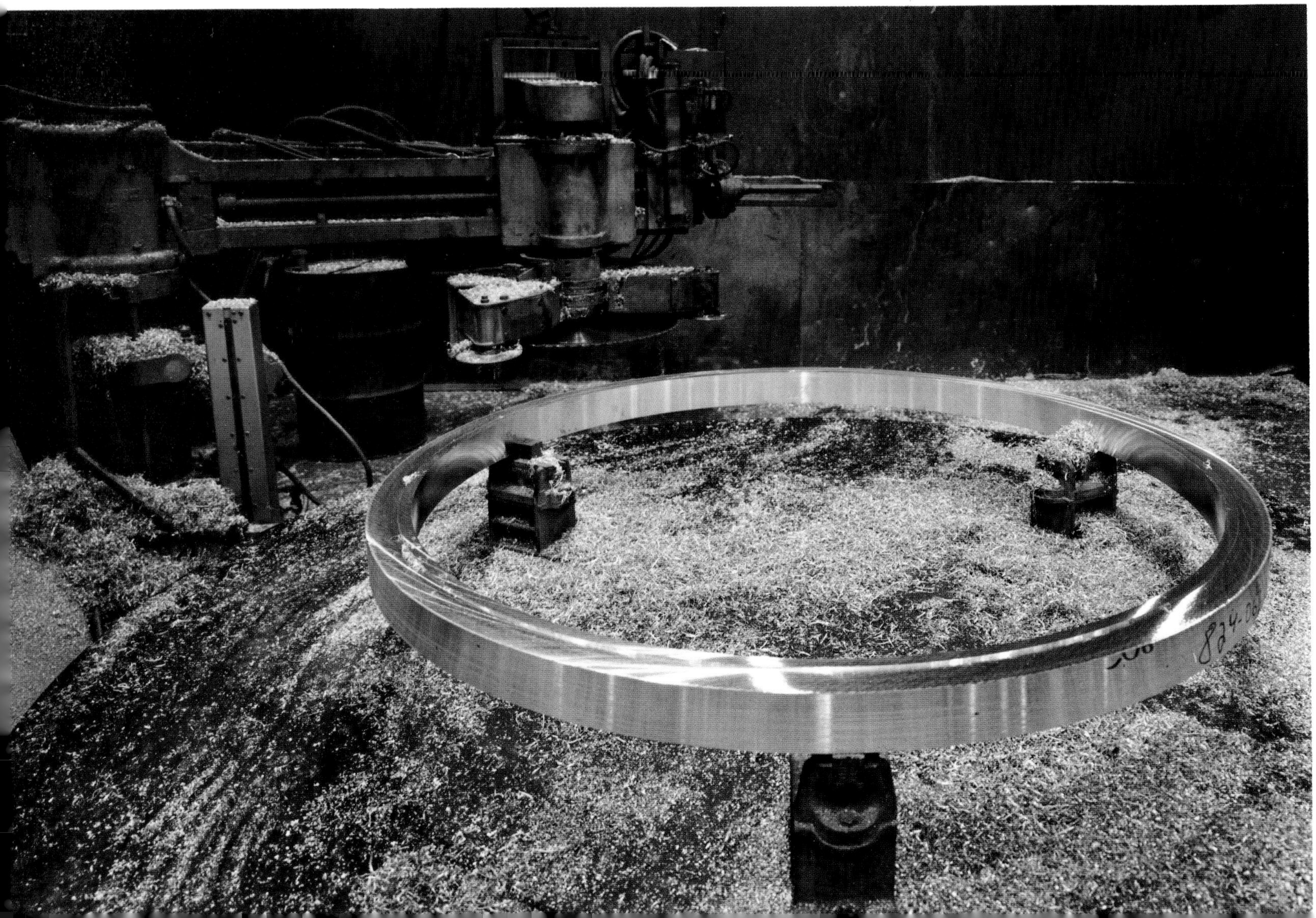

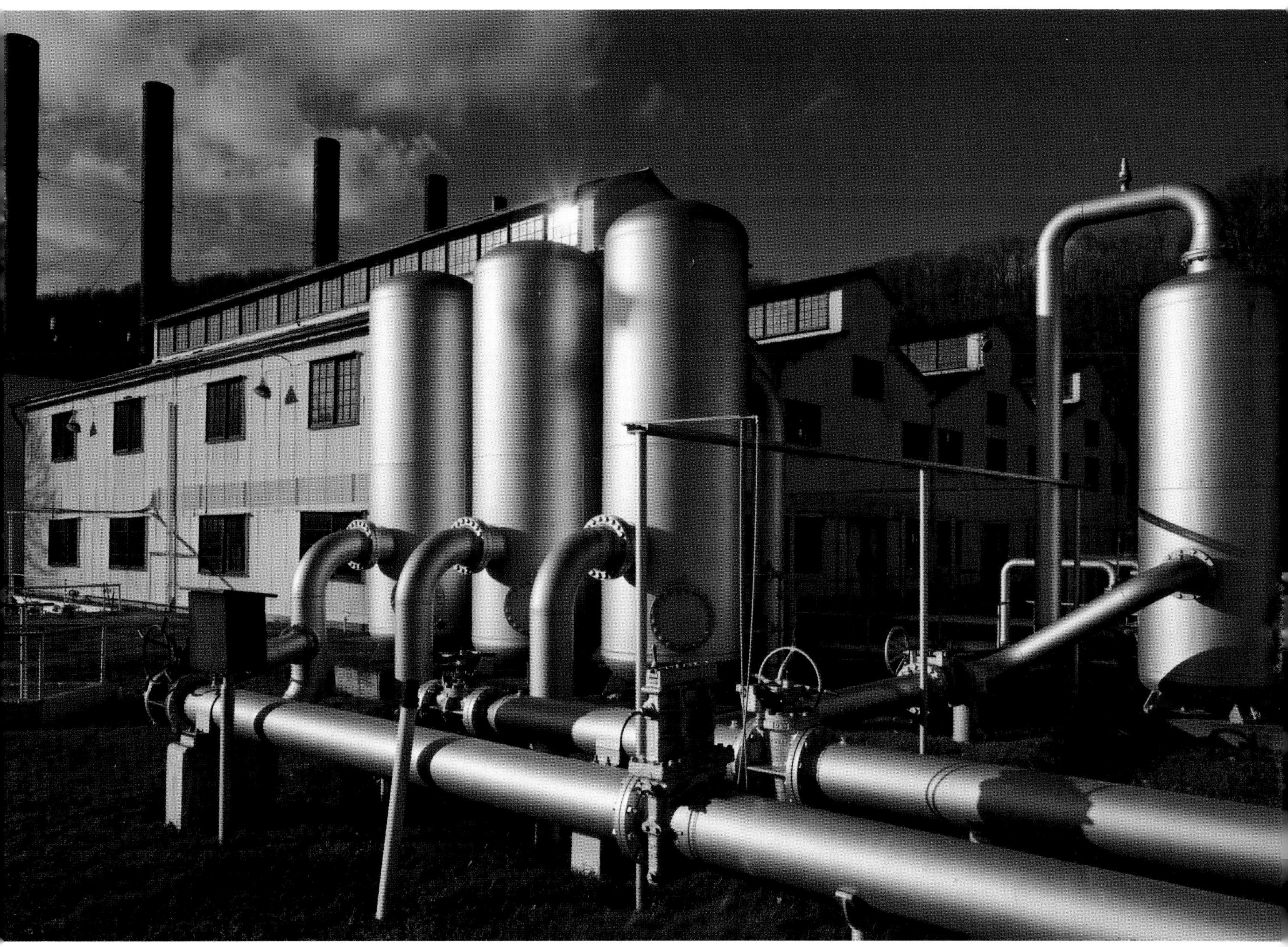

W Y M A N - G O R D O N   C O M P A N Y

Opposite above. *Cast-aluminum alloy aircraft parts in the North Grafton, Mass., factory before being finished.*

A L U M I N U M   C O M P A N Y   O F   A M E R I C A

Opposite below. *Aluminum ring lathe at Alcoa, Cleveland, used primarily in the manufacture of airplane components.*

B U R N S V I L L E   N A T U R A L   G A S

Above. *West Virginia's last known operating steam-powered natural gas pumping station, constructed at Burnsville in 1917 with additions 1936–43.*

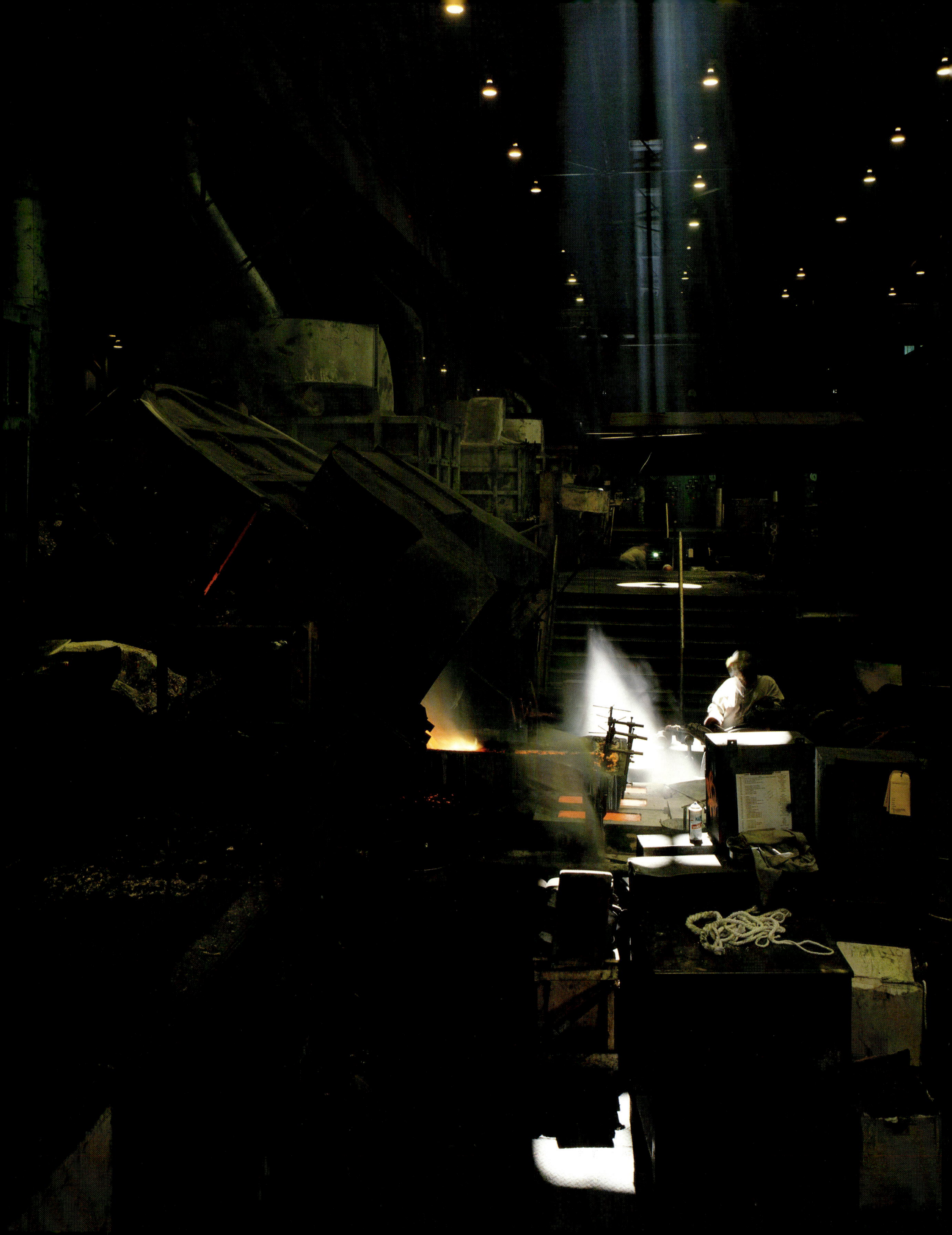

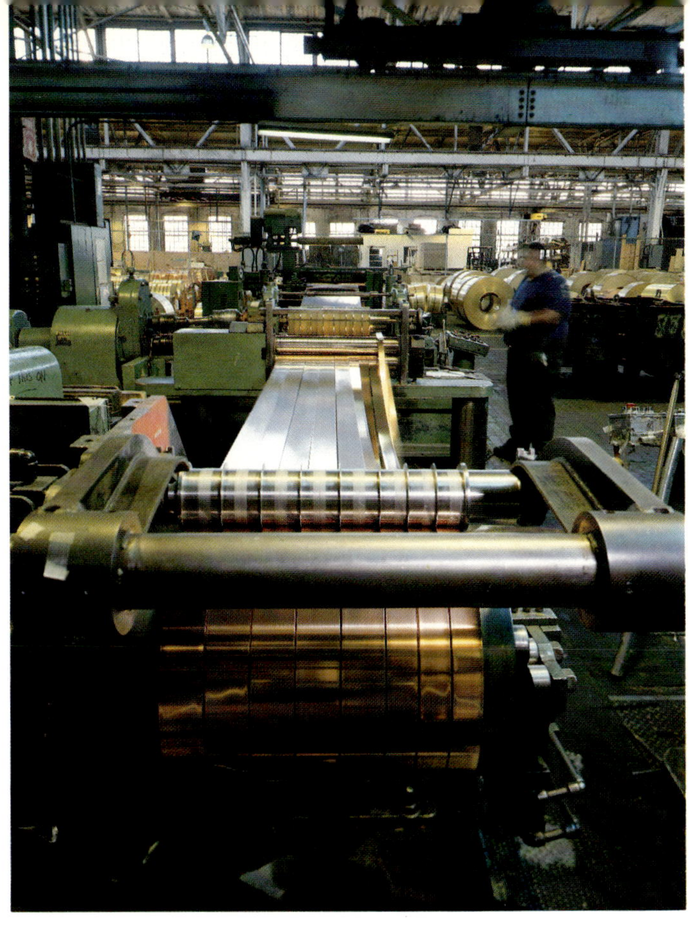

AMERICAN BRASS COMPANY

Opposite. *Holding furnace for molten copper and tin, after which the resulting brass is poured into molds that produce slabs 20 or 30 feet long and 5 inches thick. The Connecticut-based company established this brassworks in Buffalo, N.Y., about 1907.*

Left. *Slitting machine, used to cut rolled sheets of brass that are made from the molded slabs.*

Below. *Rolled sheets of brass, ready to be finished on site or shipped out.*

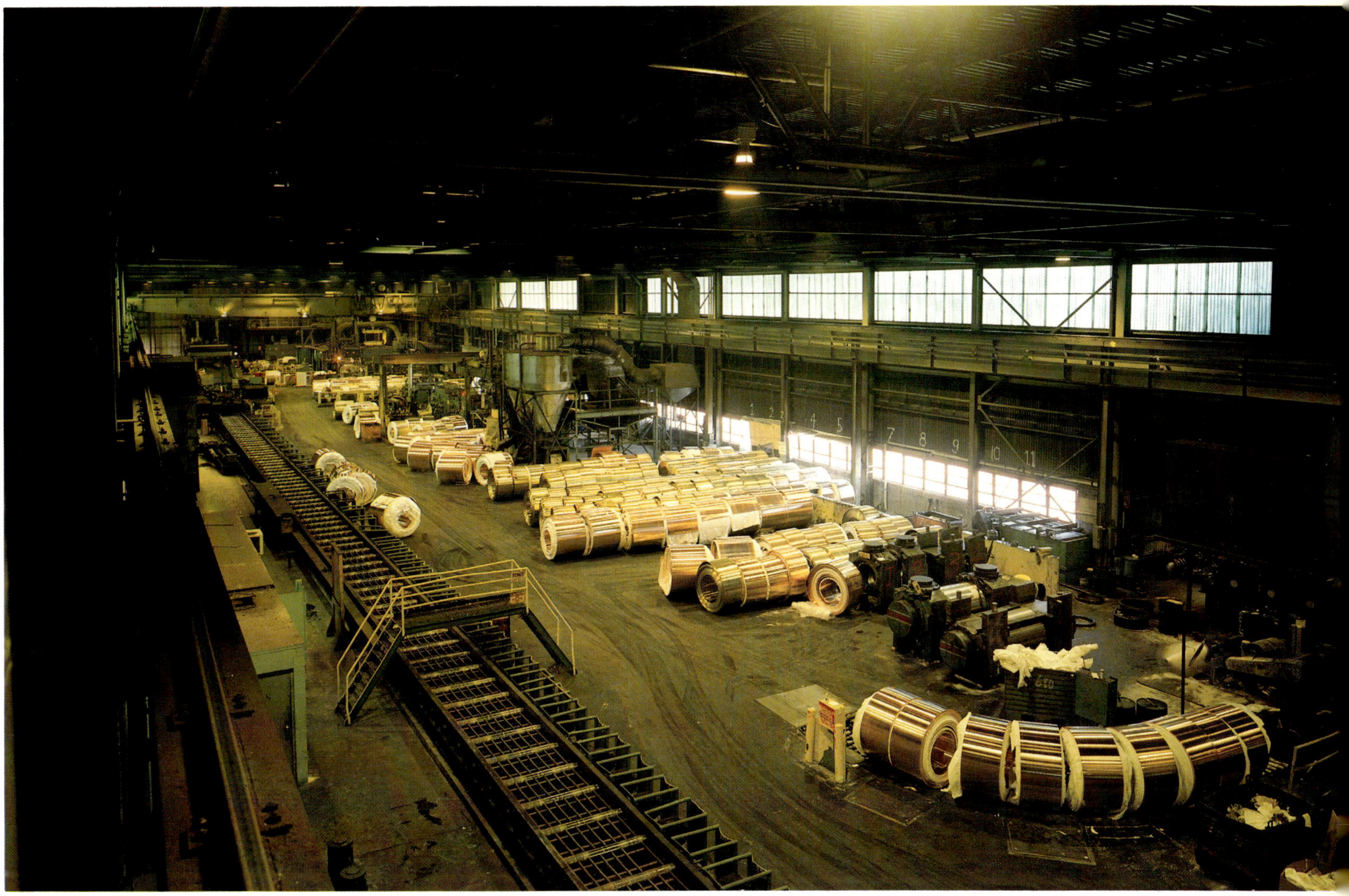

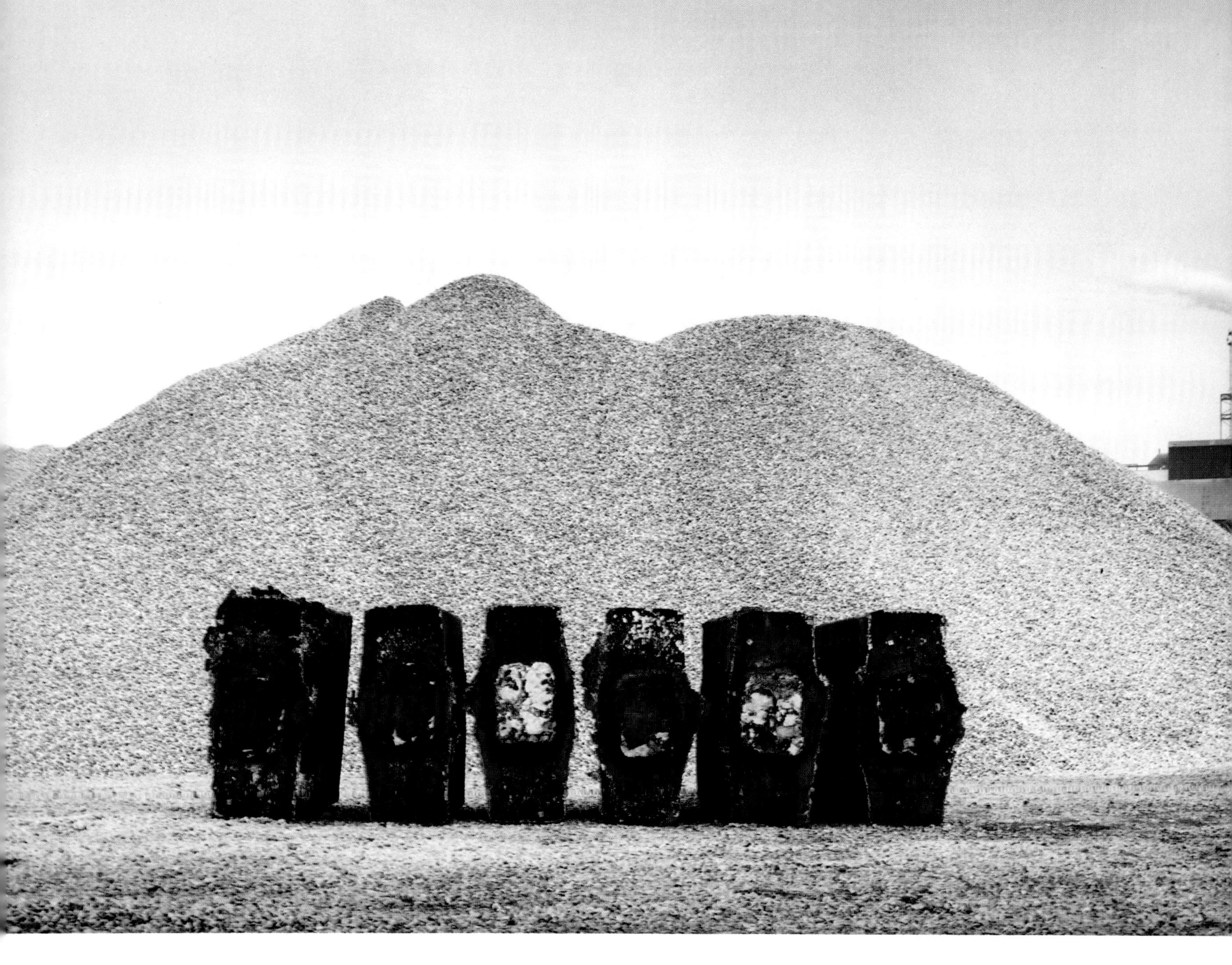

CORRIGAN, MCKINNEY STEELWORKS

Above. *Steel ingots in front of a gravel pile on the site of the former Cleveland company. Corrigan, McKinney erected a steel mill along the Cuyahoga River in the early 1900s and soon became one of the city's largest producers. It was acquired by Republic Steel in 1935.*

WATKINS MILL

Opposite. *Work bench in the woolen mill, Lawson, Mo. Waltus Watkins built this steam-powered mill in 1861.*

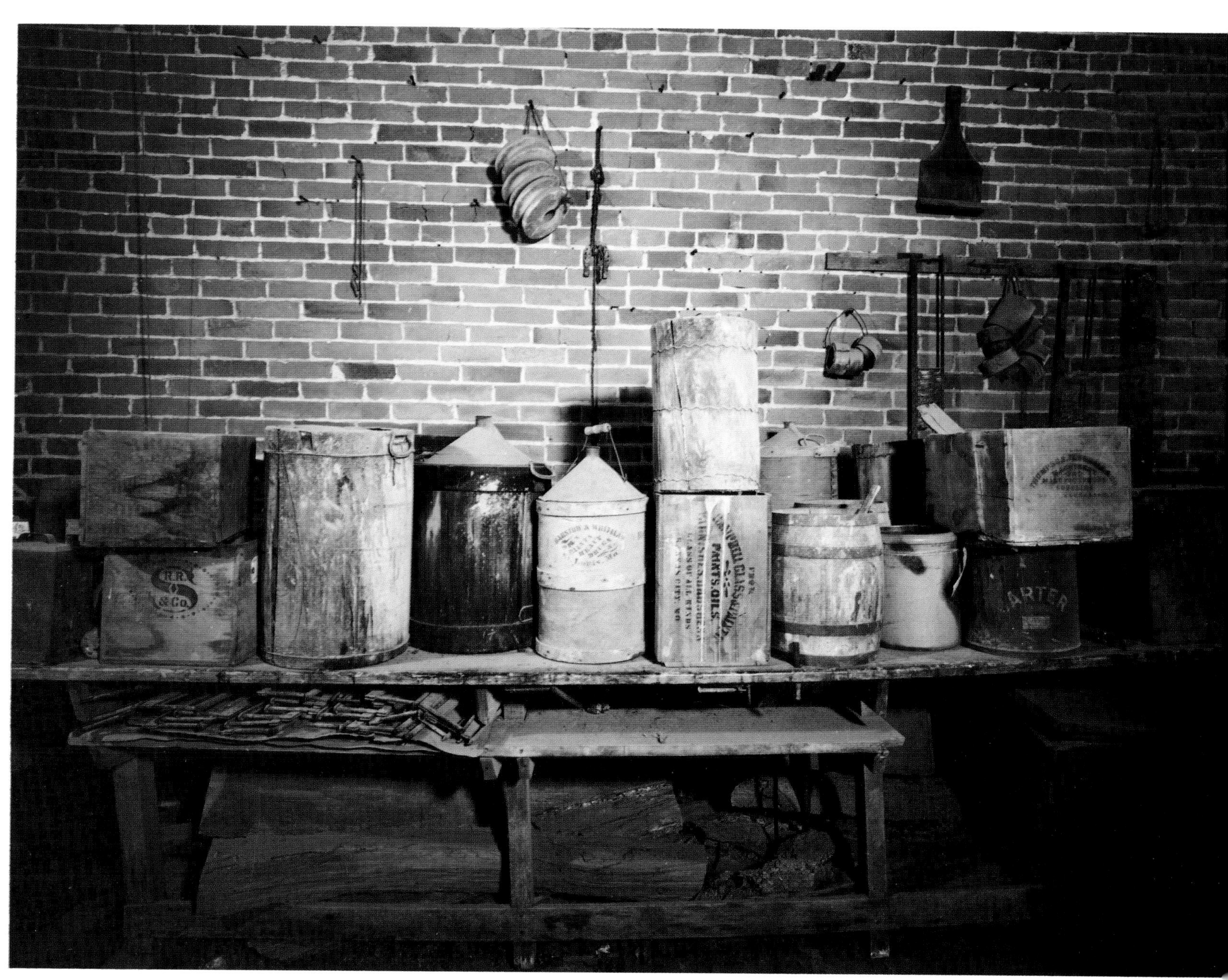
R.R.
S
&Co.
PAINTS.OILS.
ARTER

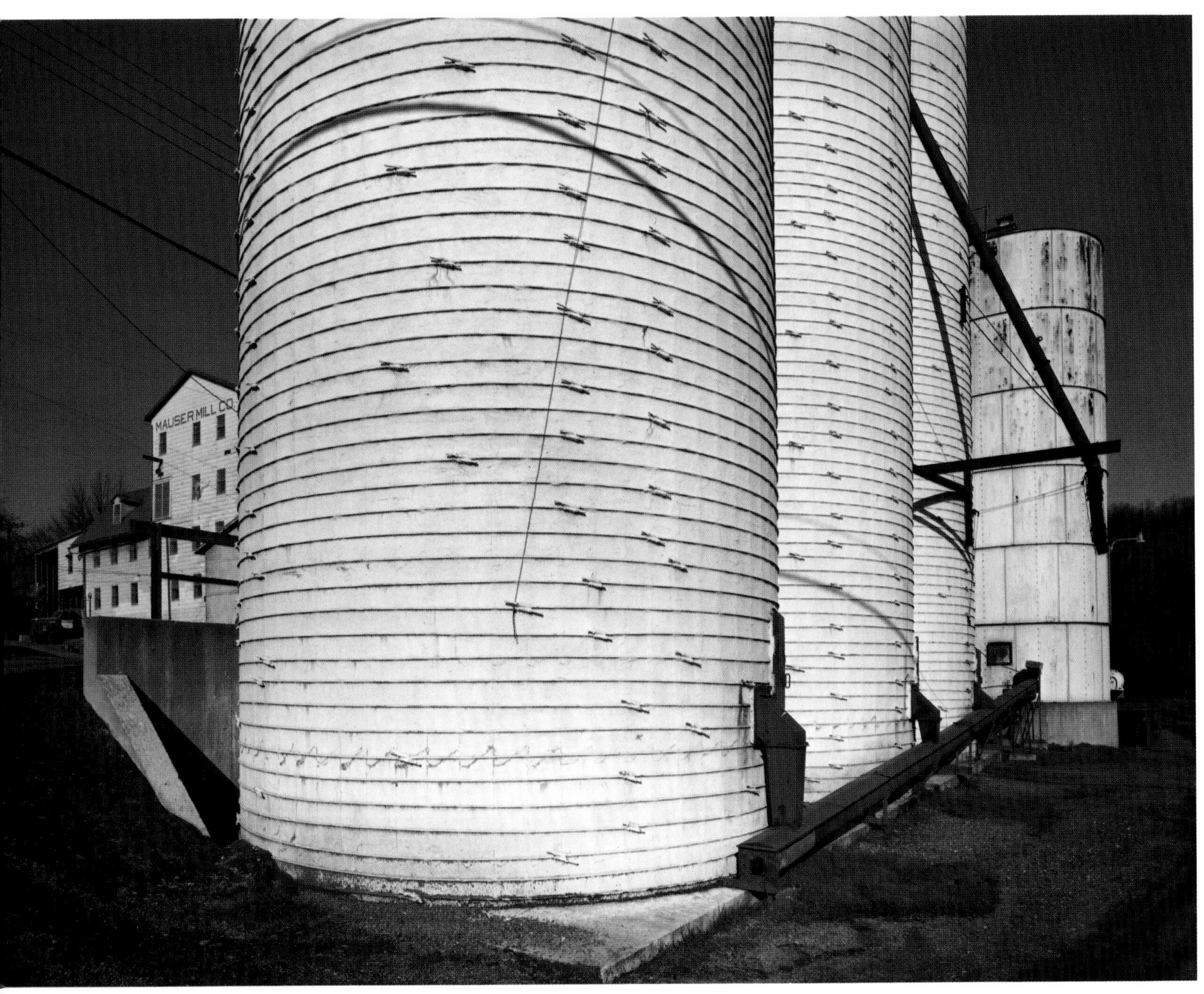

MAUSER MILL COMPANY

Above. *Grain elevator and storage bins, Lehigh, Pa., dating from the early 1900s. This grain-handling complex along the Lehigh Canal also includes a late 19th-century flour mill.*

AMERICAN WIRE AND STEEL

Opposite. *Iron stairway ascending the blast furnaces, Cleveland. For many years a subsidiary of U.S. Steel, American Wire began making wire in the early 1900s.*

WHITE MOTOR COMPANY

Overleaf. *Ventilation stacks on a factory roof, Cleveland, opened about 1908. The company is one of the few survivors of Cleveland's early automobile industry.*

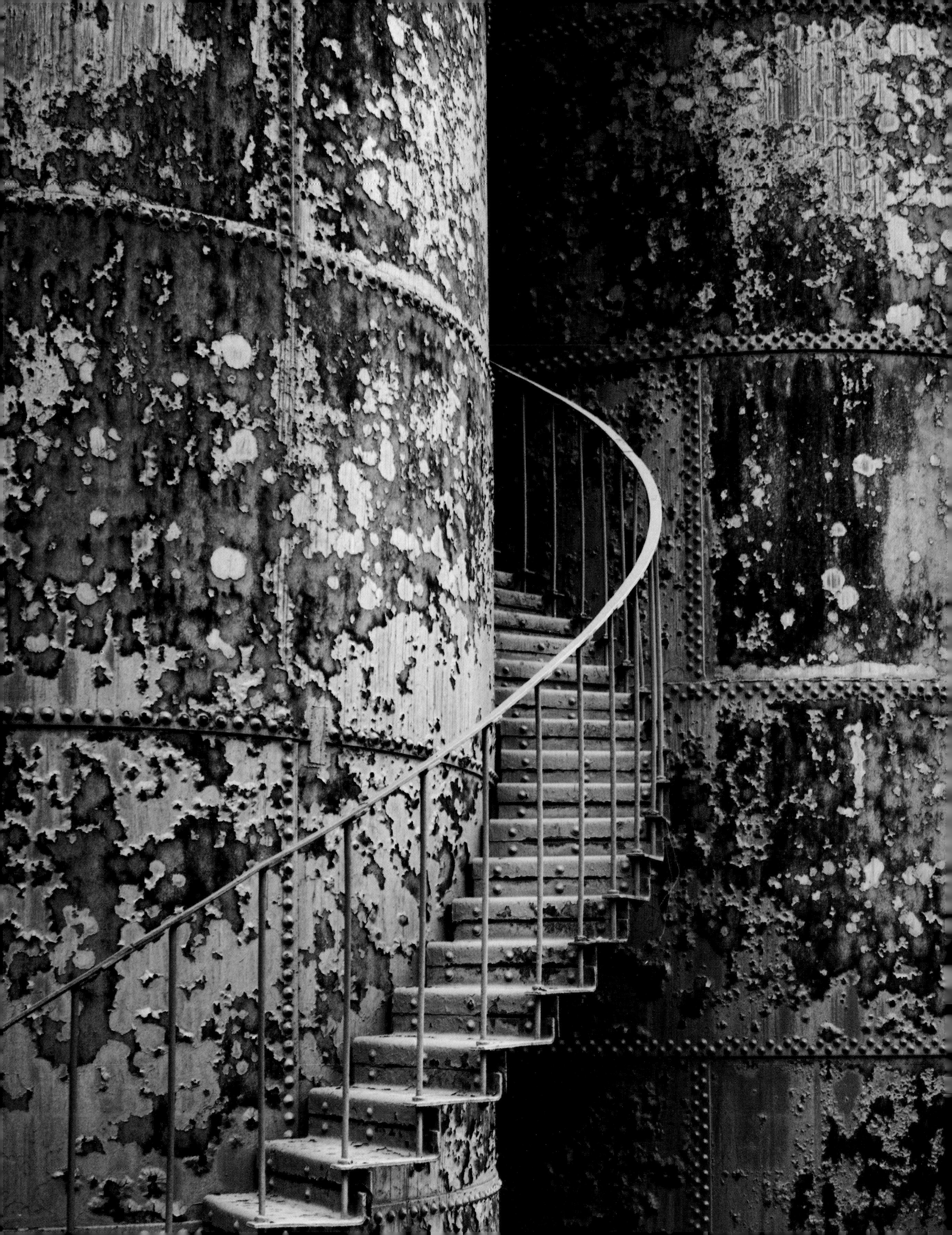

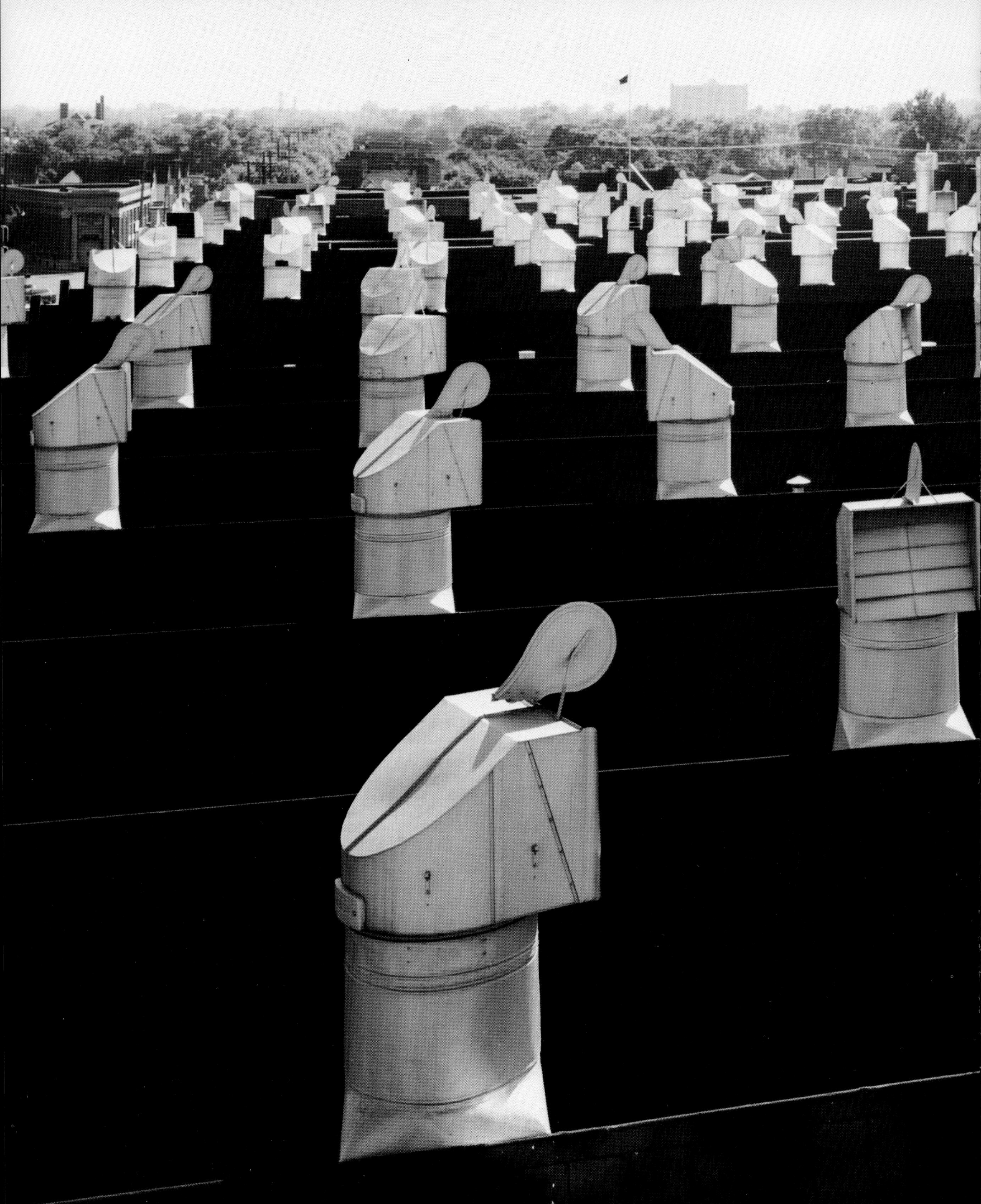

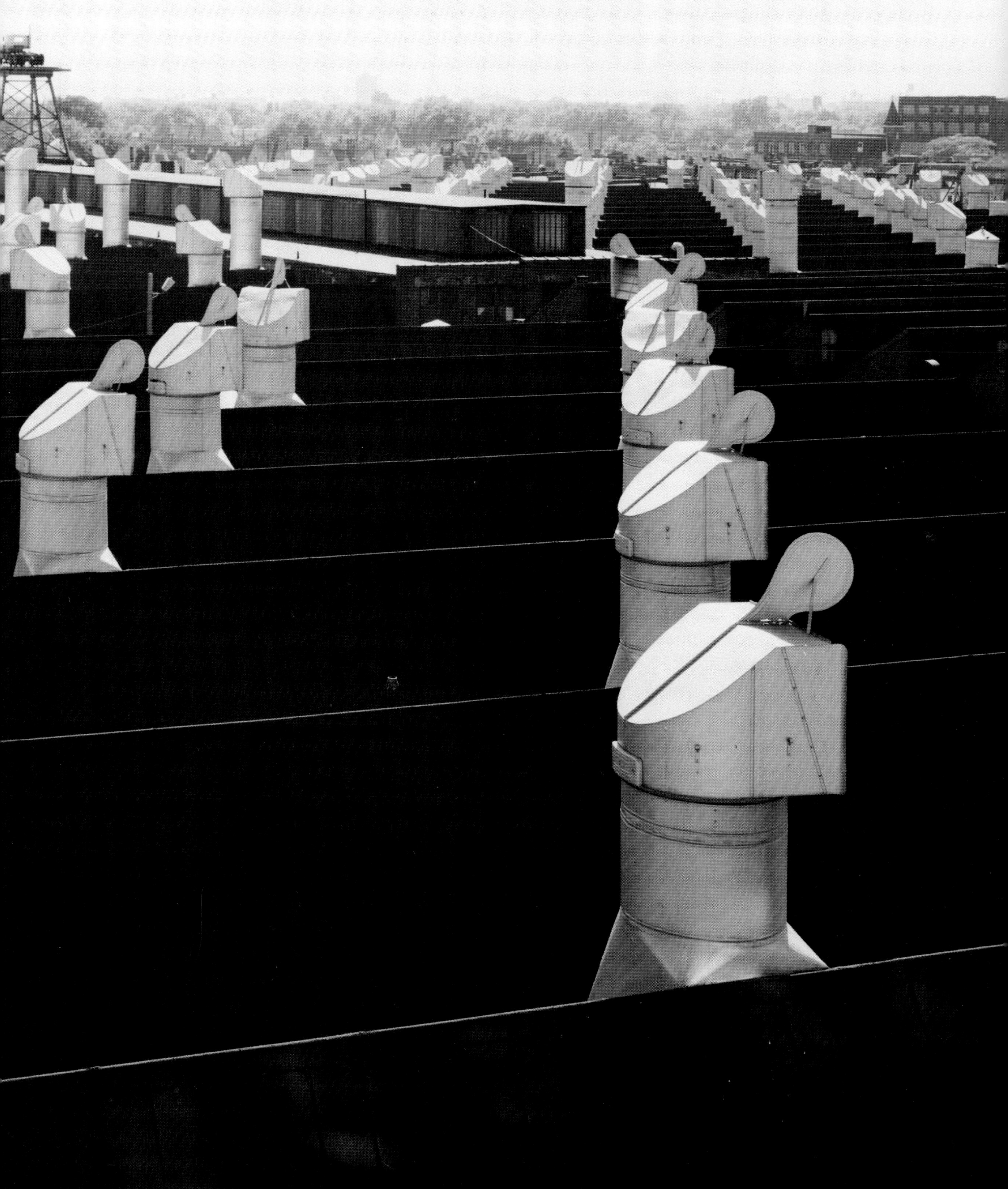

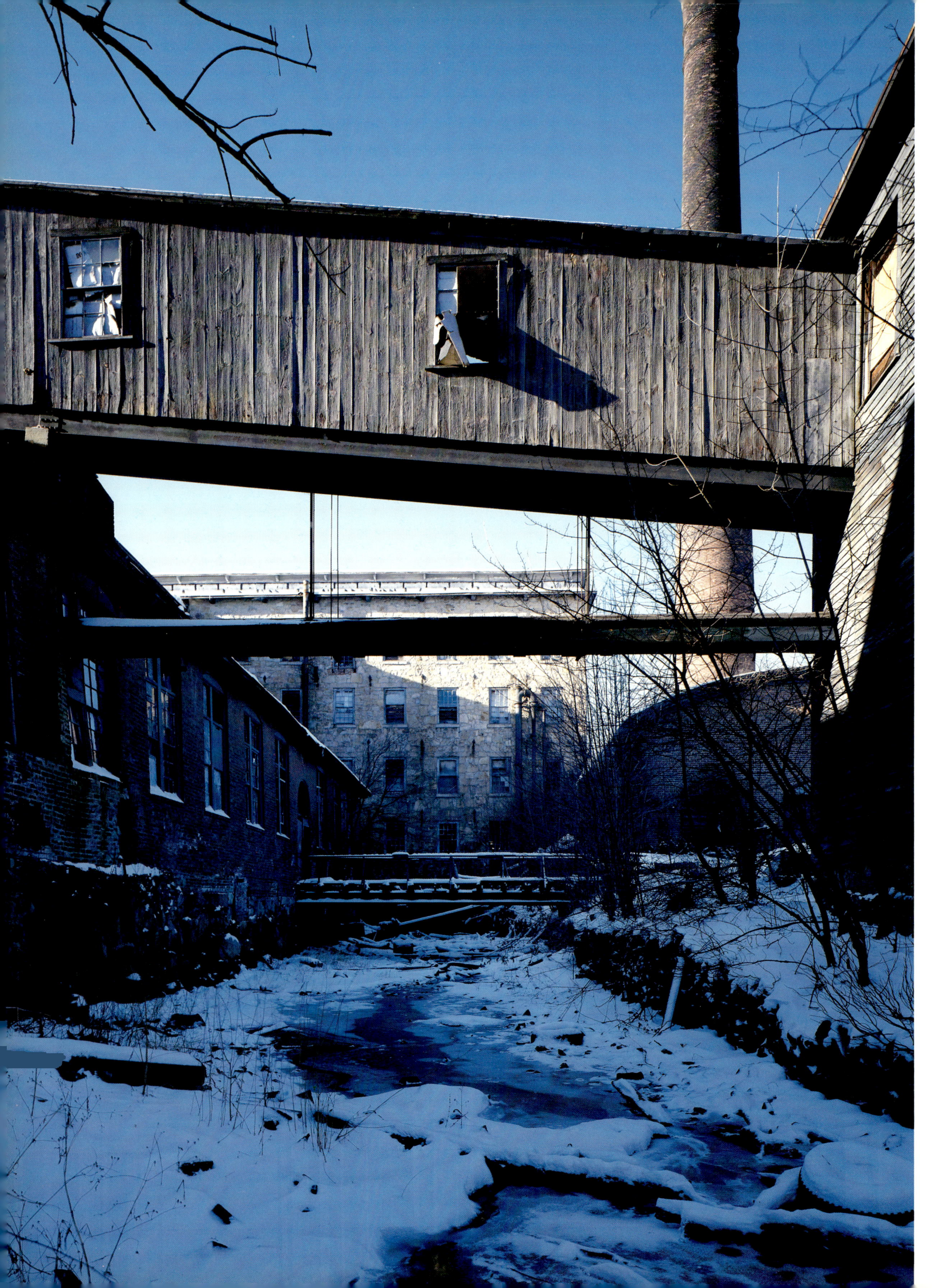

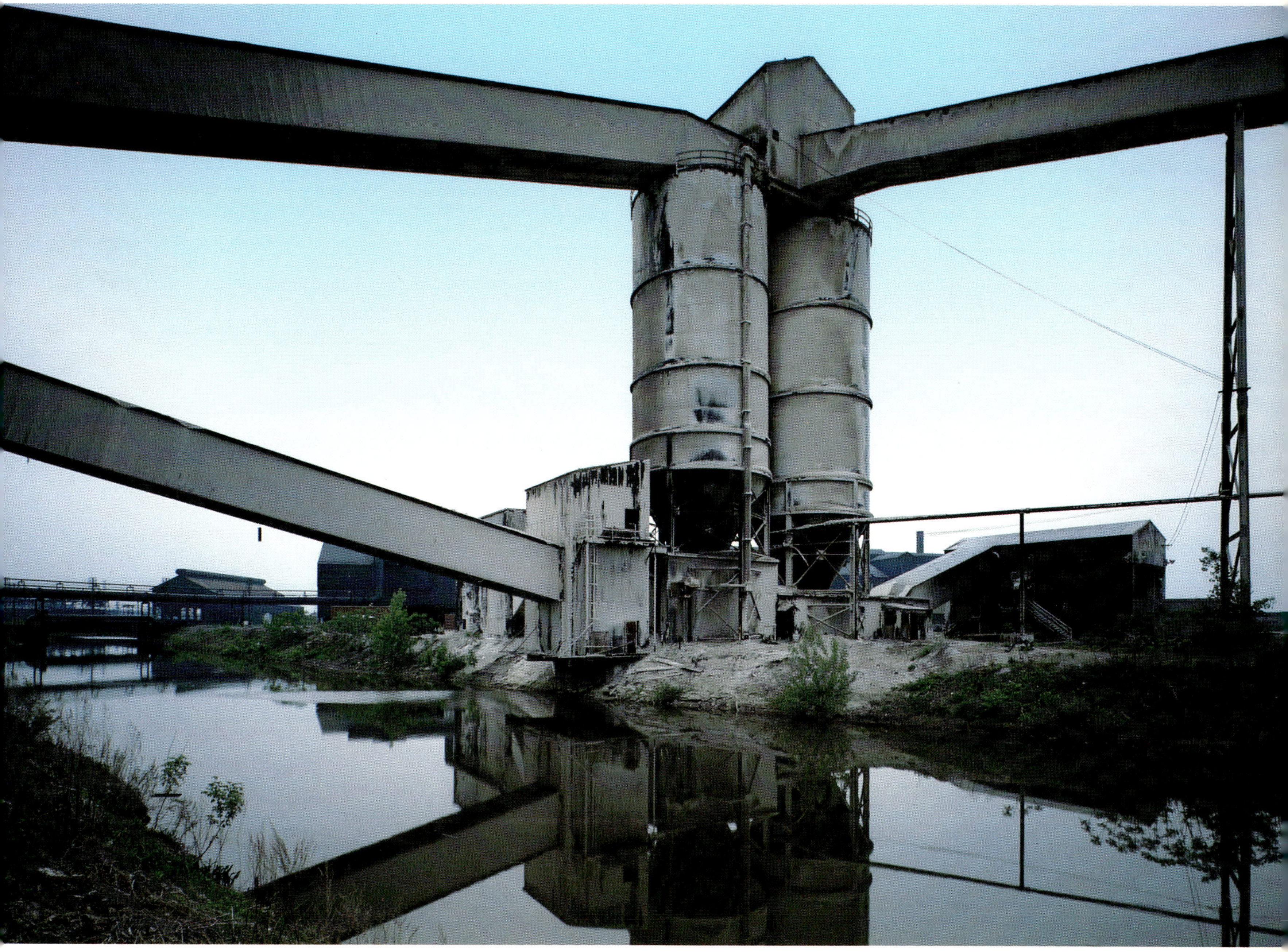

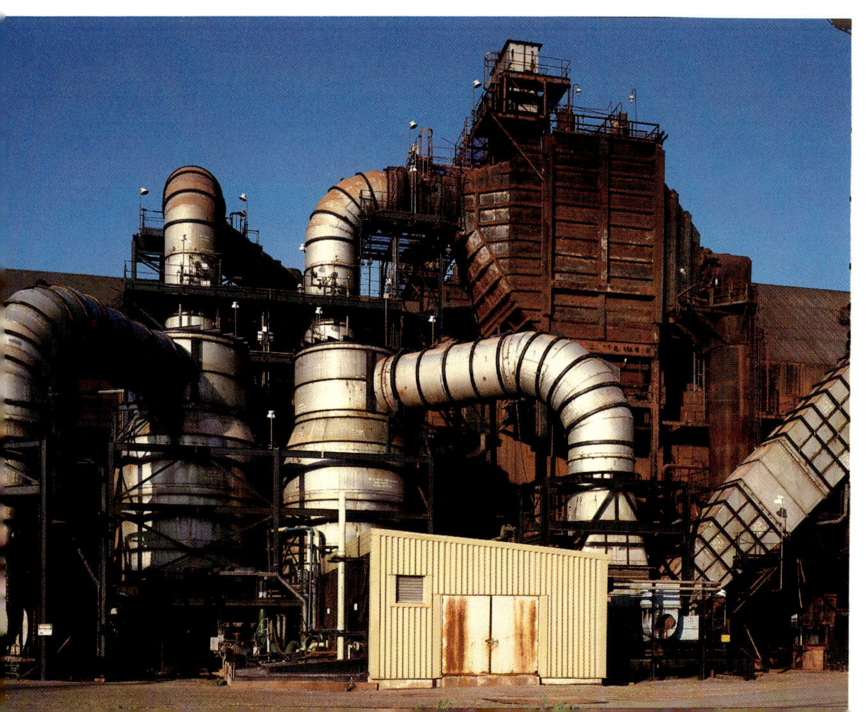

UNITED WASTE COMPANY

Opposite. *Shoddy mill, Dedham, Mass., a converted cotton mill used to recycle waste material for packing and insulation.*

BETHLEHEM STEEL

Above. *Elevators that carried limestone, coke and iron ore to the blast furnaces of Bethlehem Steel's Erie Lackawanna plant, Buffalo, N.Y.*

Left. *Sintering plant from the 1950s, which collected dust and particulate from the blast furnaces and recycled them back into the furnaces.*

GUYNS MILL

Right. *Steam engine flywheel. The Lexington, Ky., grist mill was built about 1880.*

WATKINS MILL

Below. *Carding machine in the 1861 woolen mill, Lawson, Mo. The company was in business until the early 1900s.*

FISHER-FALLGATTER MILL

Opposite. *Dust remover used to take particulate out of the grain-cleaning machines in the 1884 flour mill, Waupaca, Wis.*

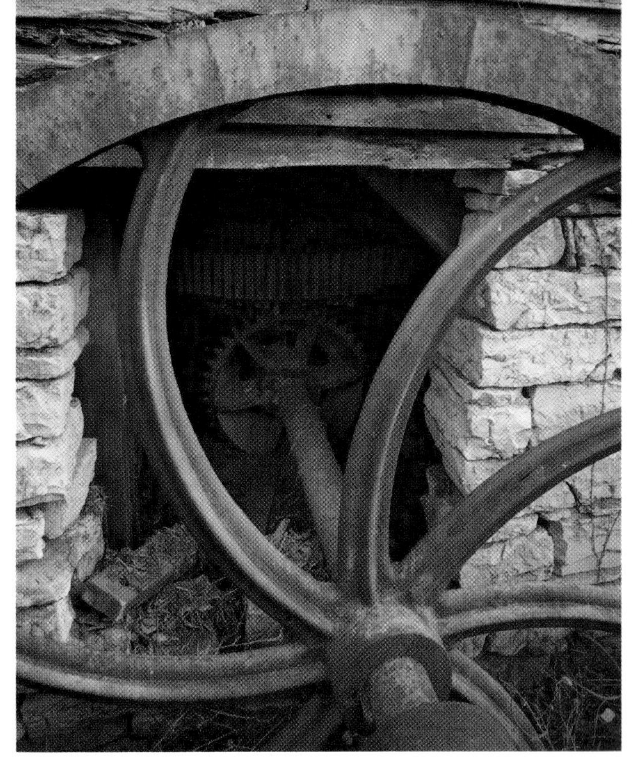

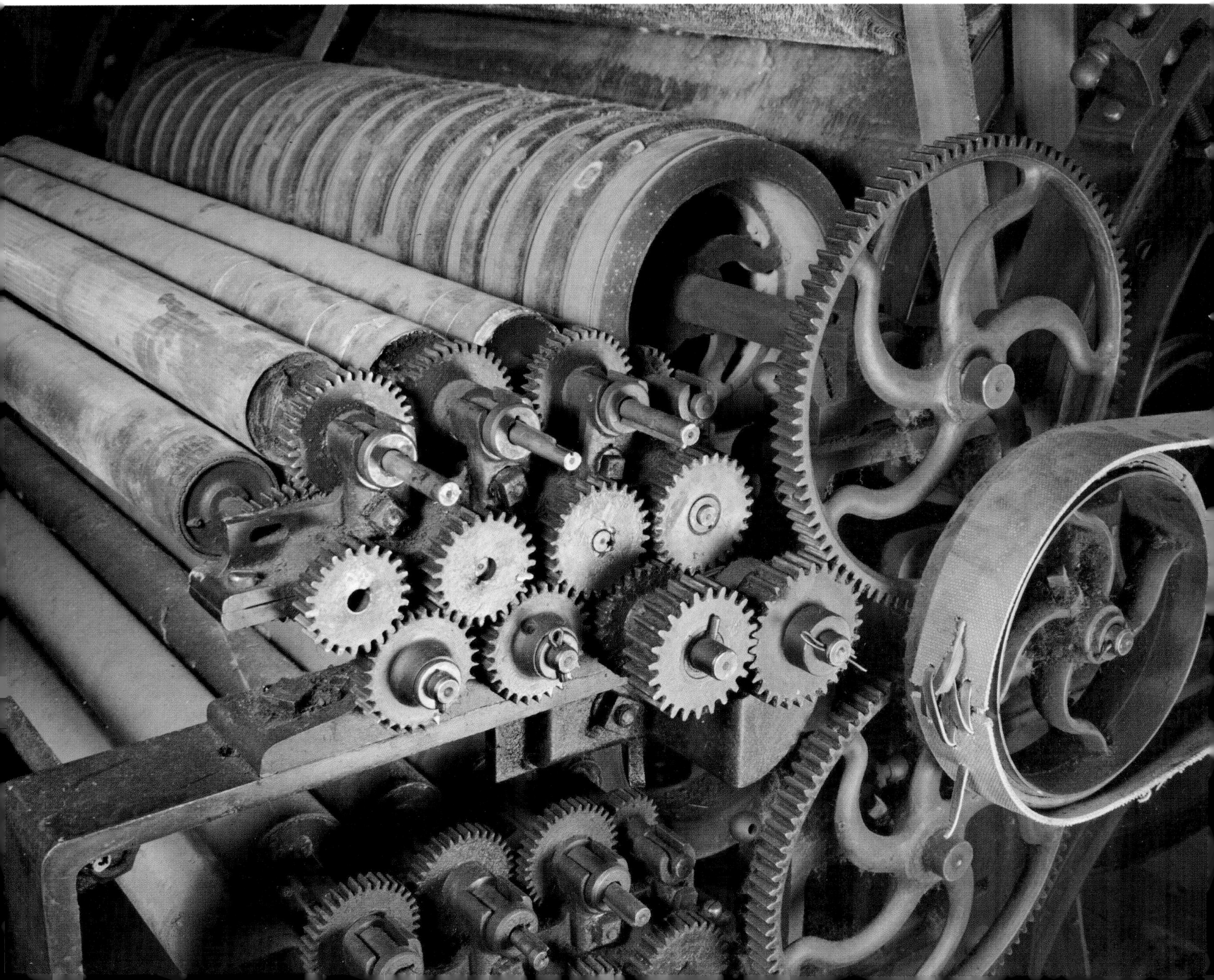

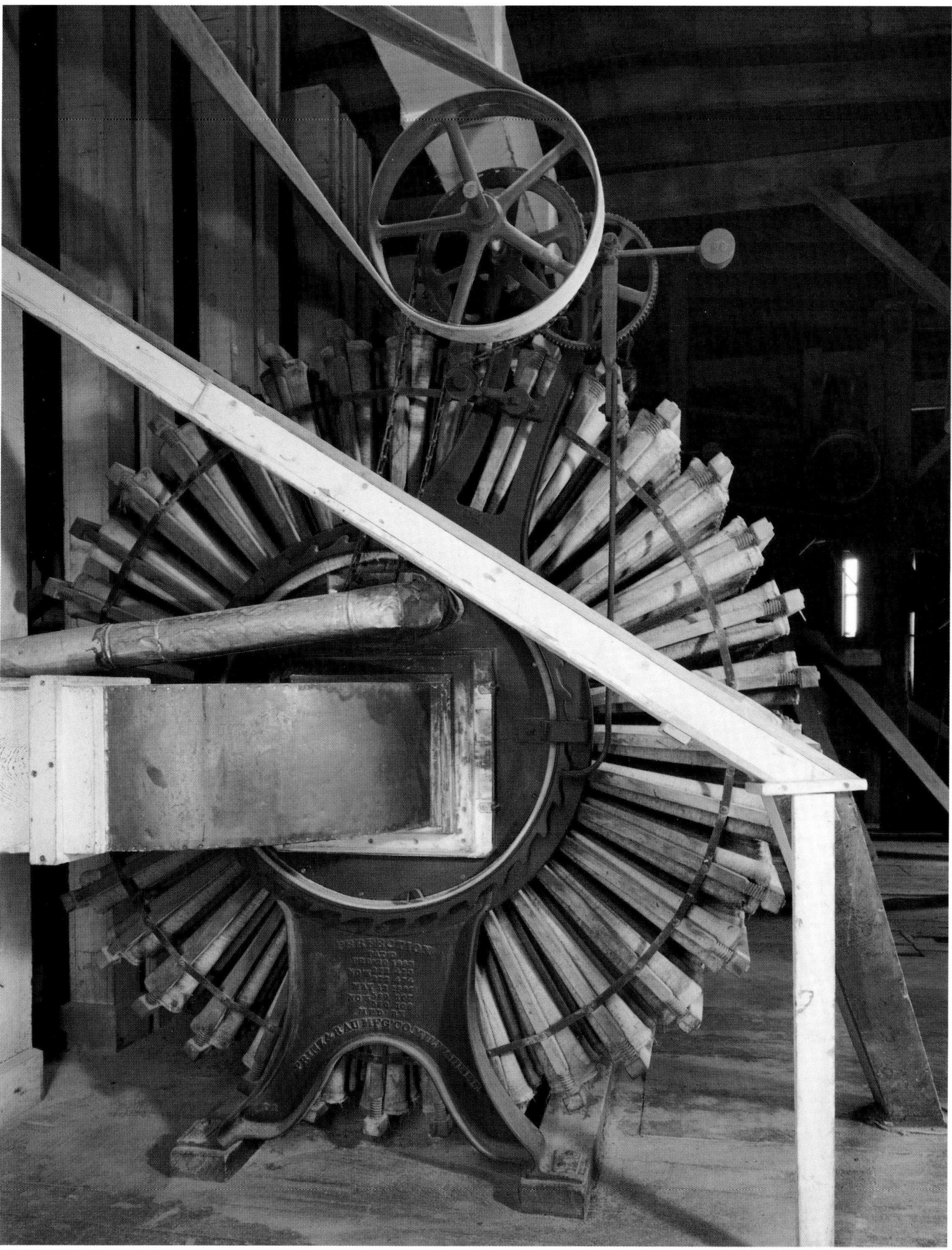
PERFECTION

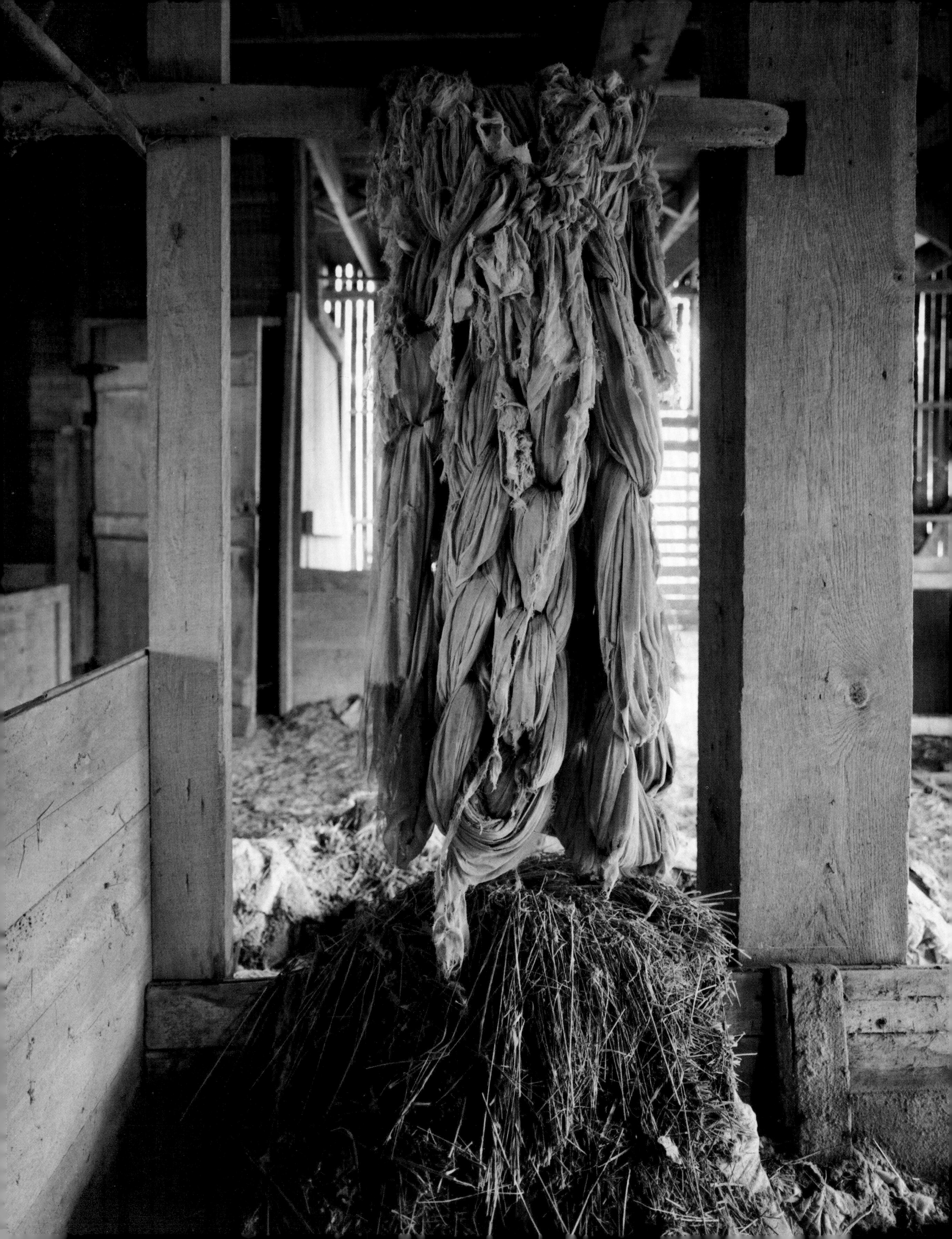

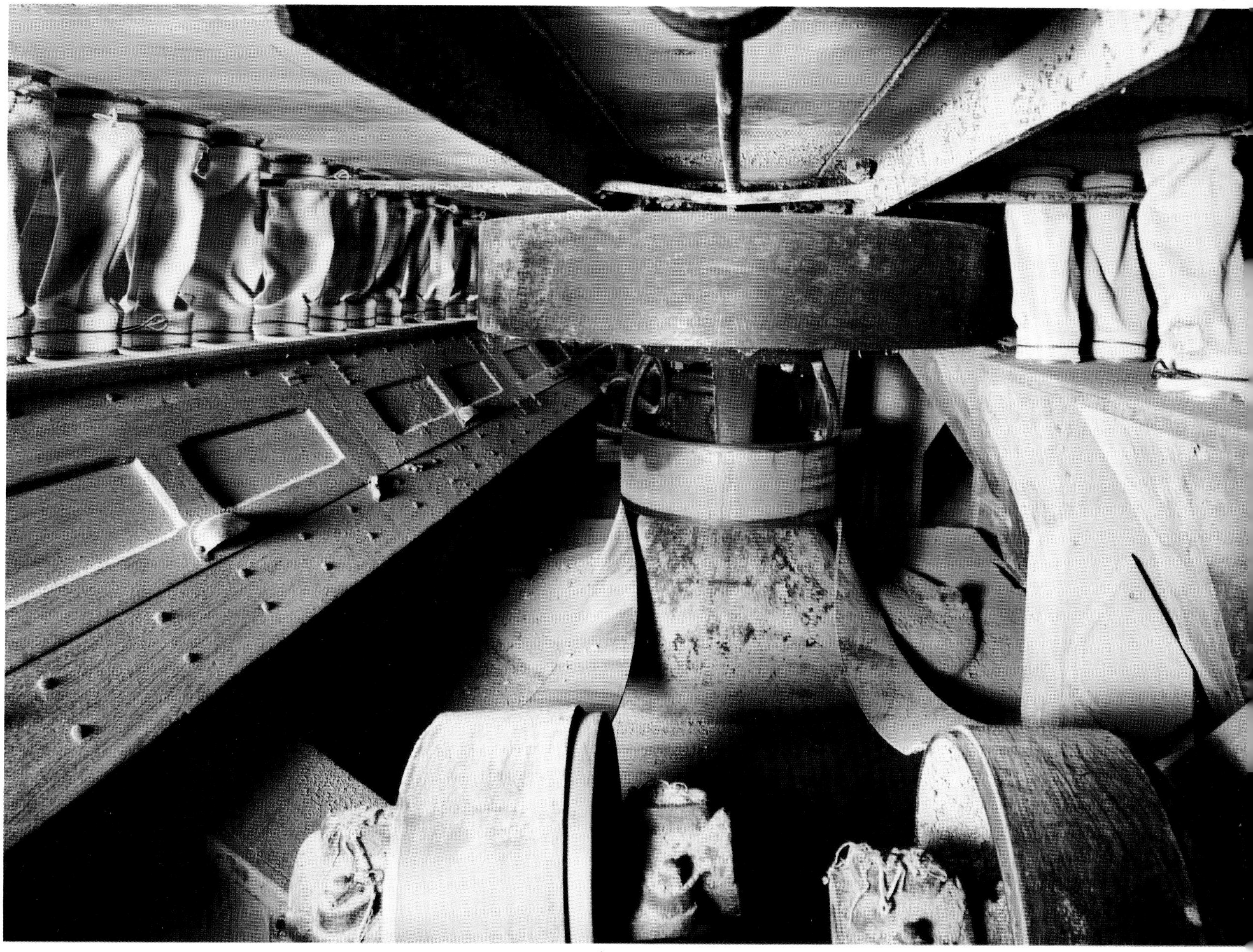

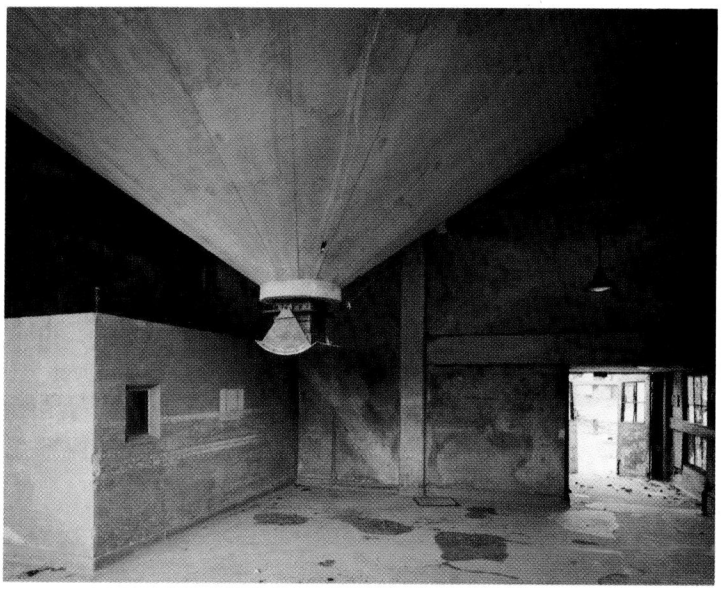

GUYNS MILL

Opposite. *Heavy timber posts and tobacco plant bedcloth inside the abandoned mill, Lexington, Ky.*

FISHER-FALLGATTER MILL

Above. *Drive mechanism beneath the plain sifter. Before it closed in 1969, the mill specialized in rye flour.*

PICATINNY ARSENAL

Left. *Powder house, Dover, N.J., constructed in the 1920s. A reinforced-concrete control room bunker is to the left of the cannon powder blender.*

WATKINS MILL

Right. *Painted arm of the broadloom, manufactured by Alfred Jenks and Son of Bridesburg, Pa., about 1870. All of the machinery at the steam-powered mill was belt driven.*

Below. *Spinning jack employed to spin-twist wool to strengthen it for weaving.*

Opposite. *Fulling machine used to break down wool fibers before spinning.*

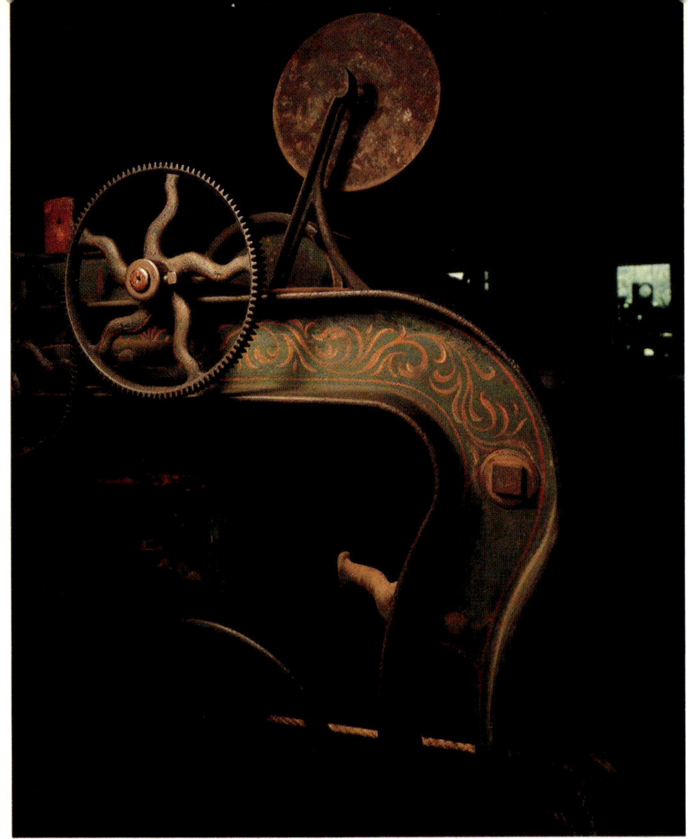

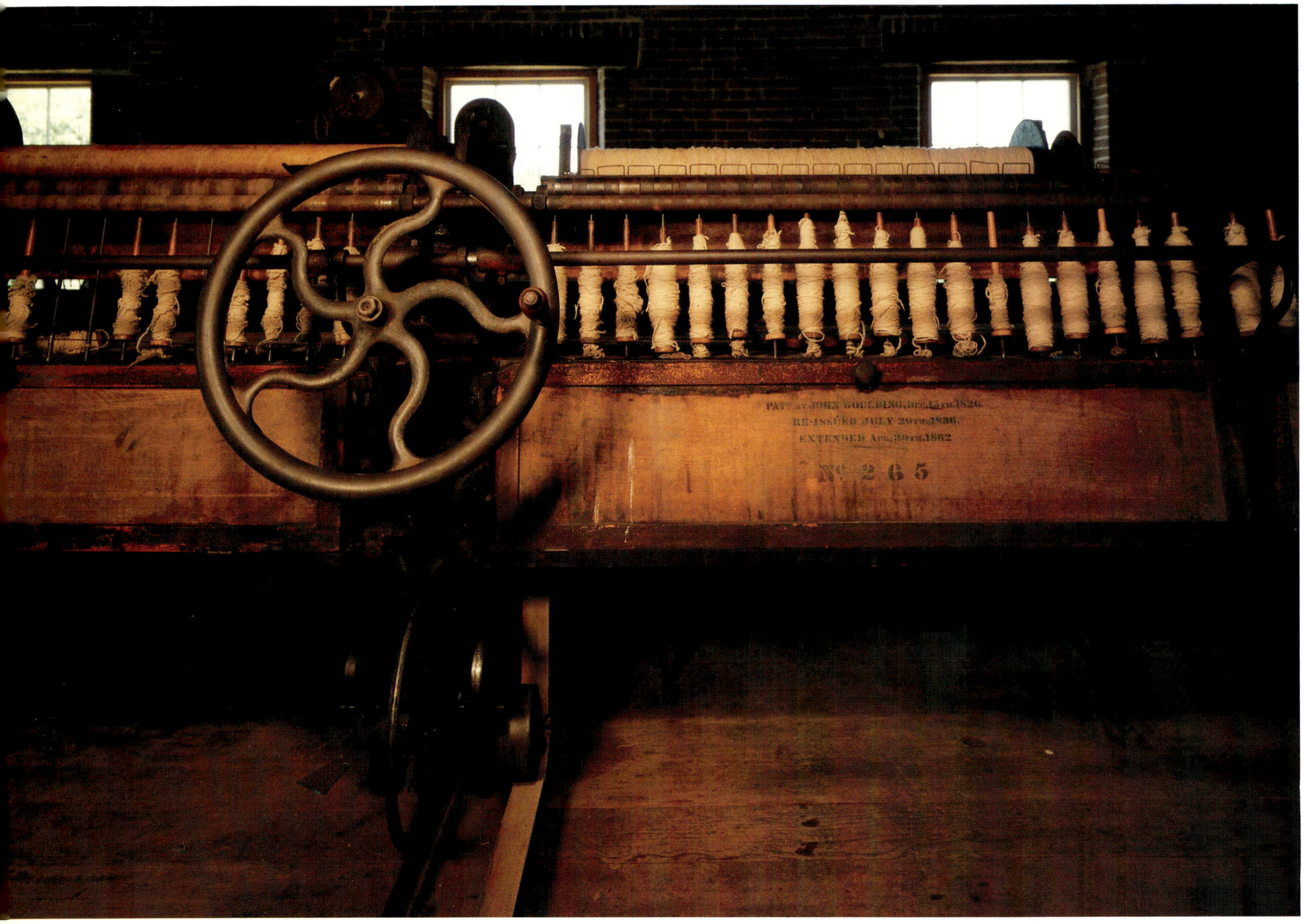

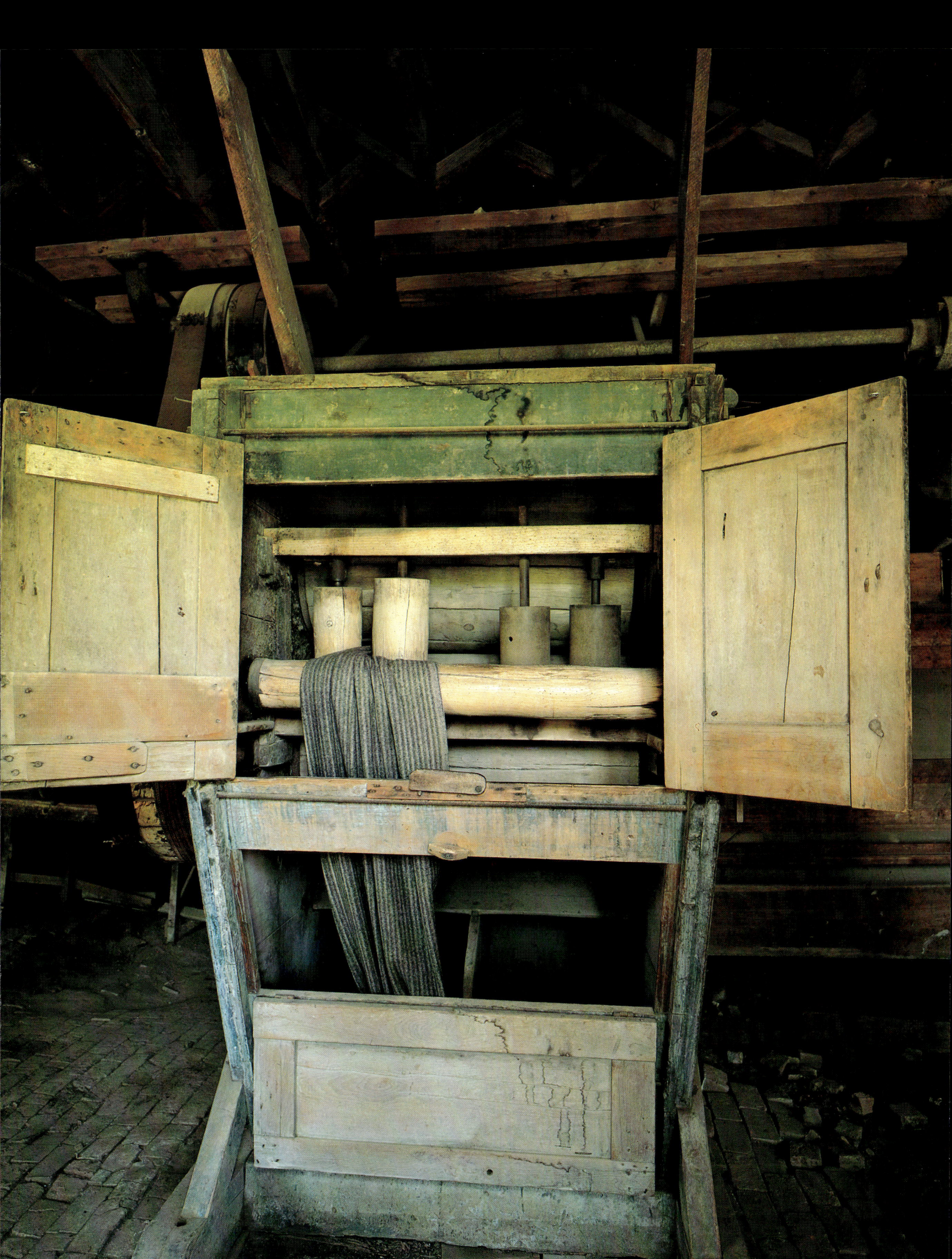

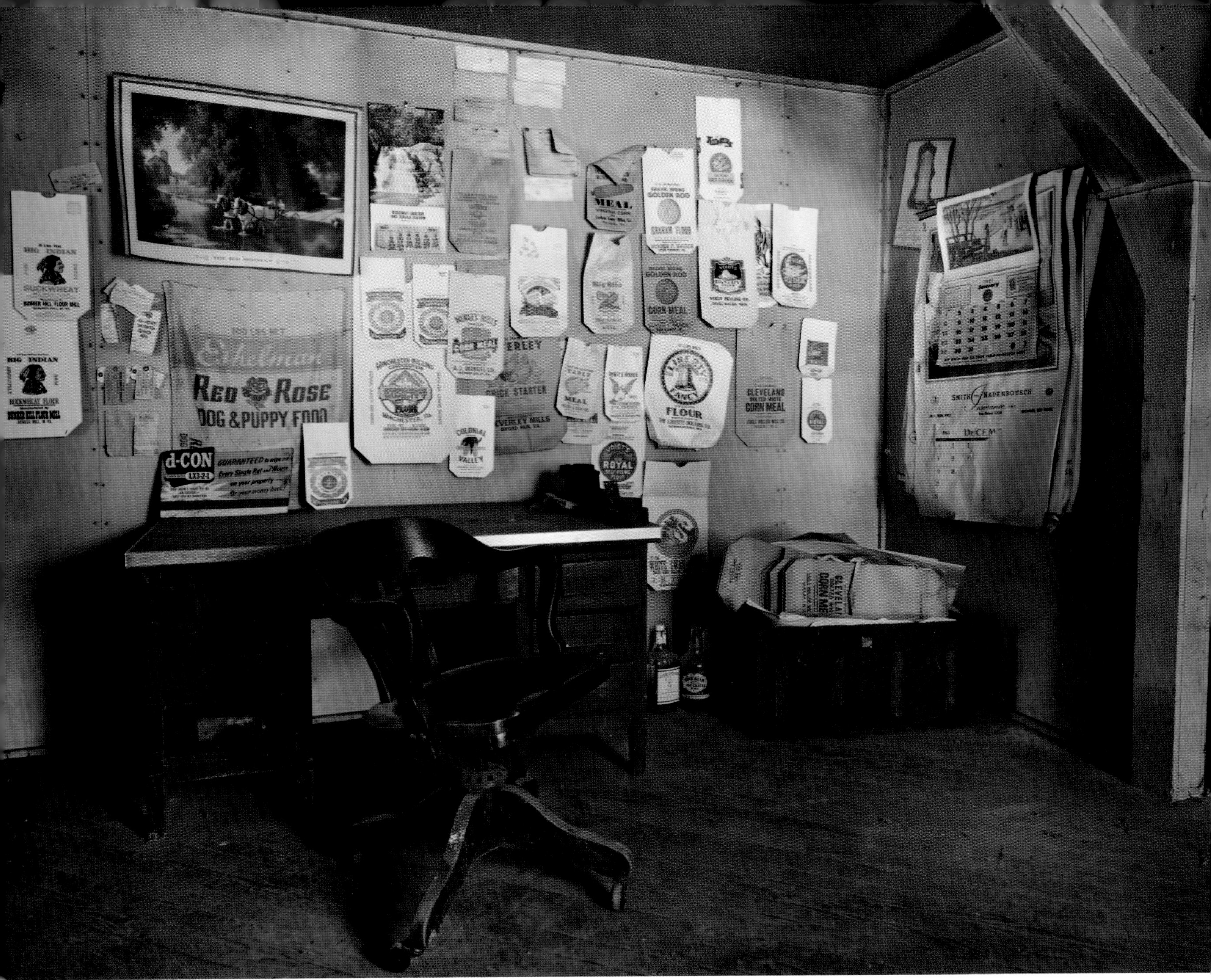

BUNKER HILL MILL

Above. *Office in the mill building, Bunker Hill, W. Va. This water-powered flour mill dates from the 17th century. Reconstructed after an 1887 fire, it closed in 1964.*

SAN JOSE GRIST MILL

Opposite. *Interior of the mill at the San Jose Mission National Historic Site, San Antonio, Tex. Built 1789–94, this may be the earliest surviving grist mill in the country. It was restored by the WPA in the 1930s.*

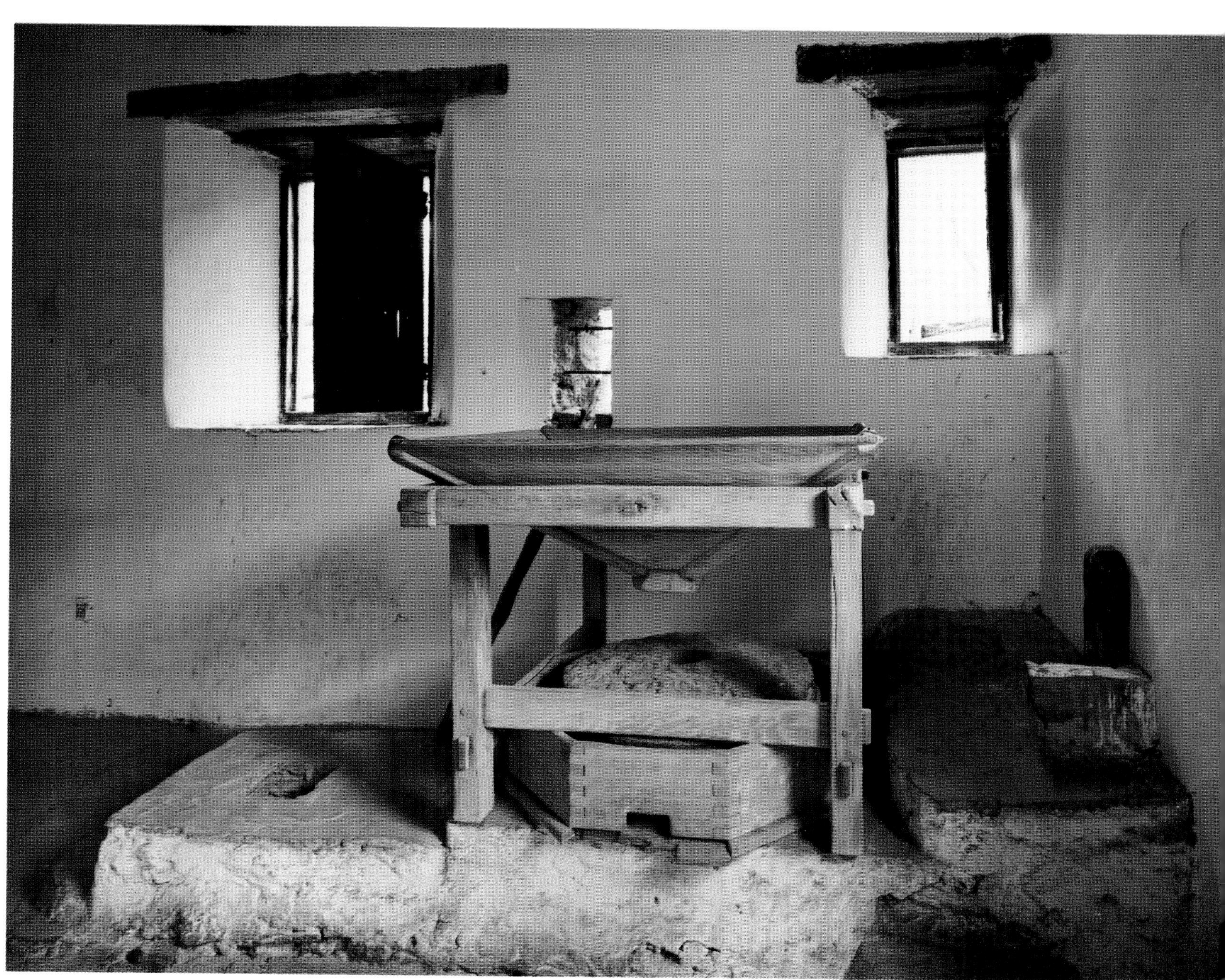

WATER

"D'ye think,"
said Mr. Dooley,
"'tis th' mill that makes
th' wather run?"

FINLEY PETER DUNNE
On Wall Street

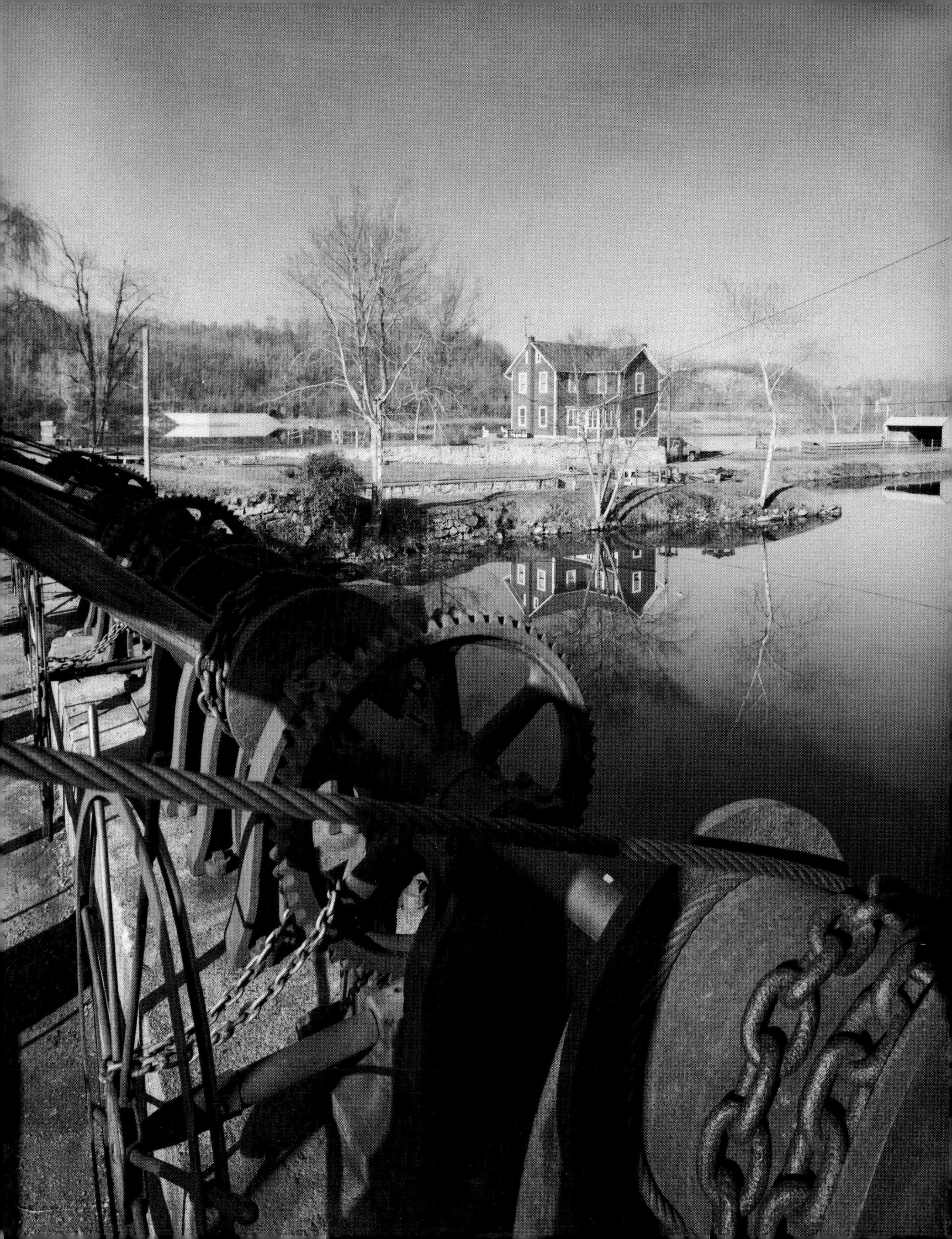

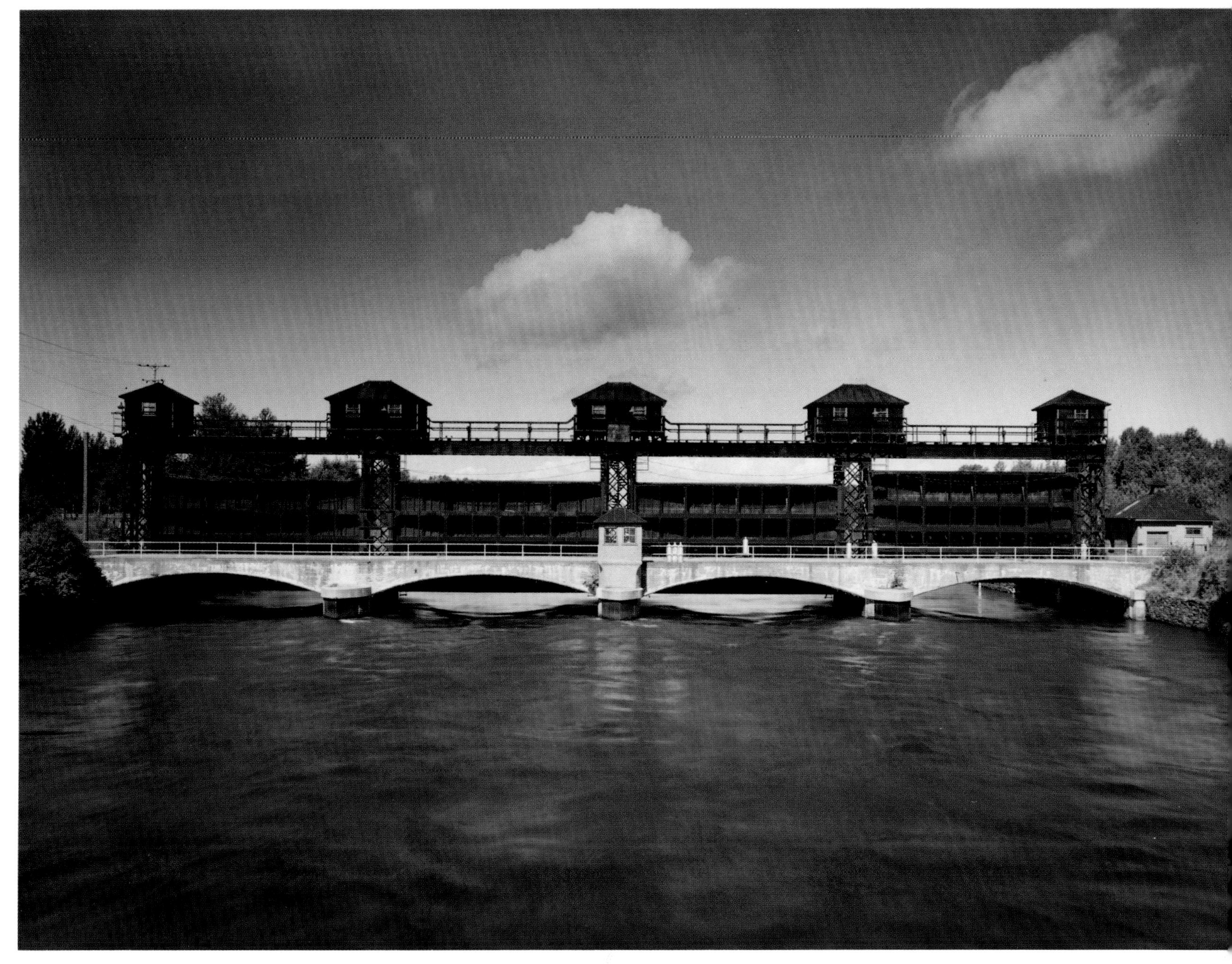

LEHIGH CANAL

Opposite. *Guard Lock No. 8 and the lock tender's house, Glendon, Pa. Completed in 1829, this canal paralleling the Lehigh River allowed barges to haul coal from the mines surrounding Mauch Chunk (Jim Thorpe) for more than a century.*

MICHIGAN LAKE SUPERIOR POWER

Above. *Headgates (movable dam) of the canal feeding into the company's hydroelectric plant at Sault Ste. Marie, Mich. When built in 1902, this system used a larger volume of water than any other in the world.*

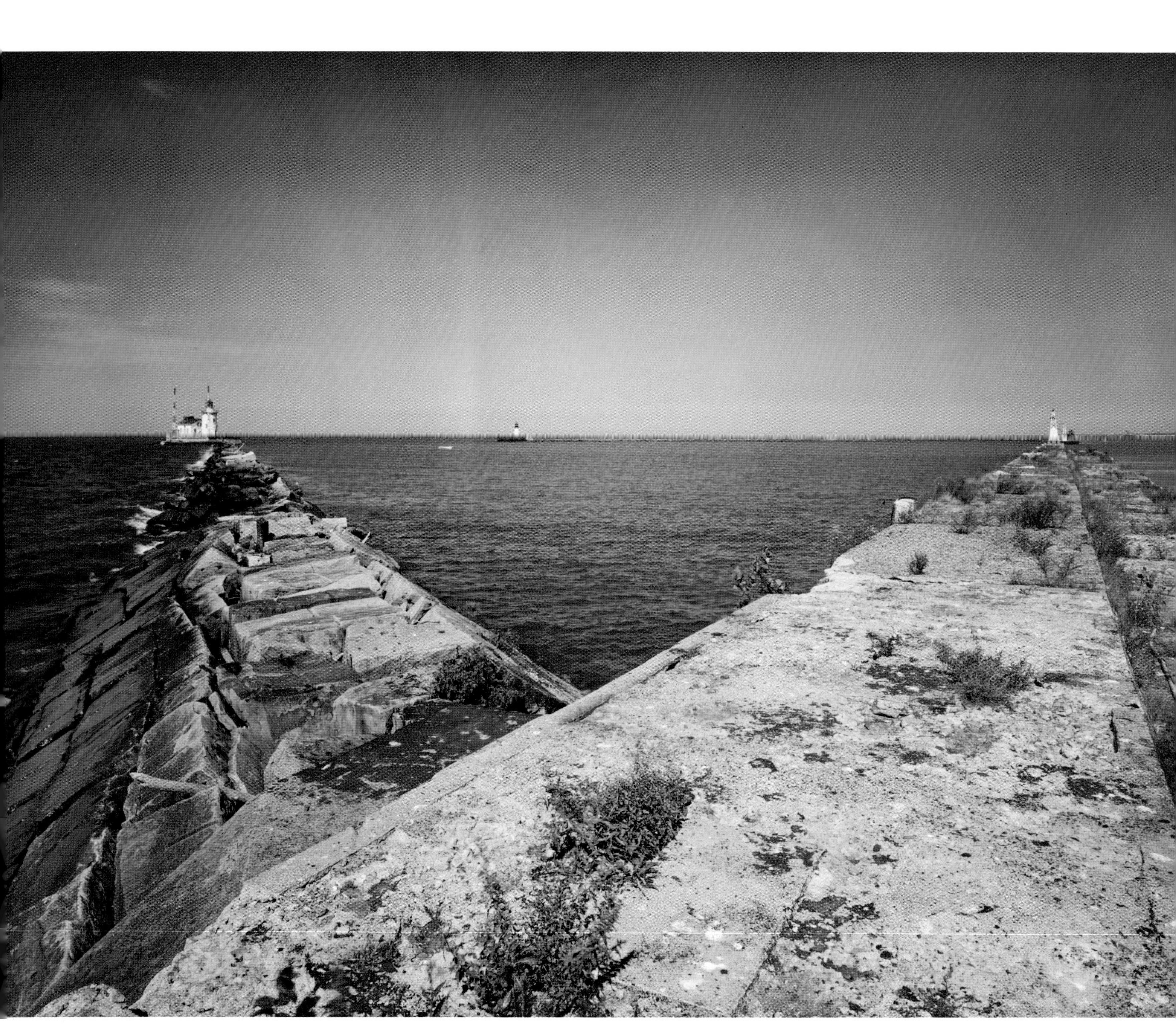

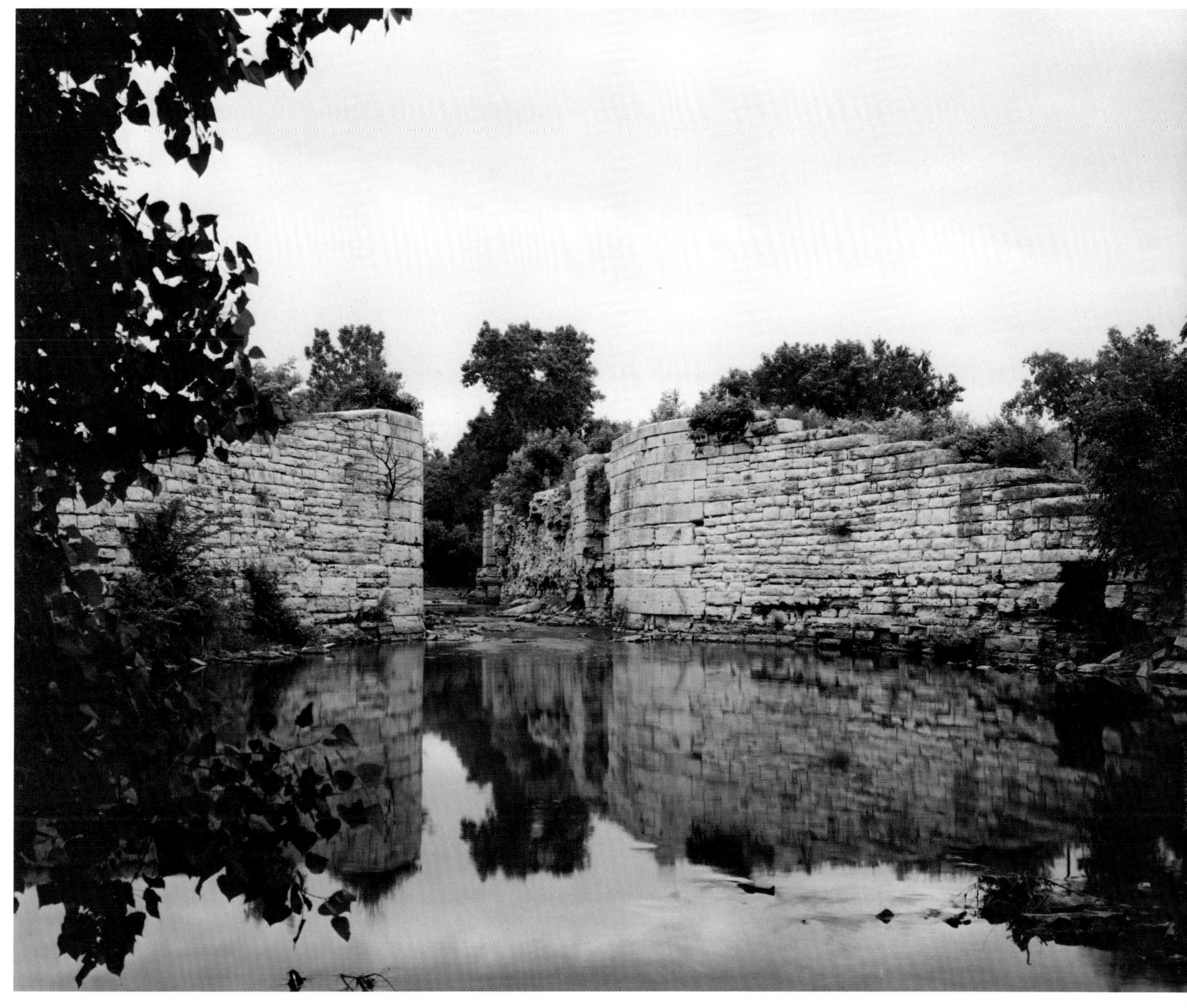

CLEVELAND BREAKWATER

Opposite. *Lake Erie waterfront, Cleveland. Constructed 1875–1915, the breakwater forms an integral part of the city's harbor, receiving the flow of the serpentine Cuyahoga River after it travels through Cleveland.*

ILLINOIS AND MICHIGAN CANAL

Above. *Lock No. 1, Lockport, Ill. With the completion of the canal in 1848, the Great Lakes and the Gulf of Mexico were at last linked with a navigable waterway via the Mississippi and Illinois rivers.*

WAWONA

Overleaf. *Under restoration by Northwest Seaport, Inc., in Seattle. Launched at Fairhaven, Calif., in 1897, this schooner was used to ship lumber from the Pacific Northwest and later served as a fishing vessel and, during World War II, as a barge, stripped of rigging and masts.*

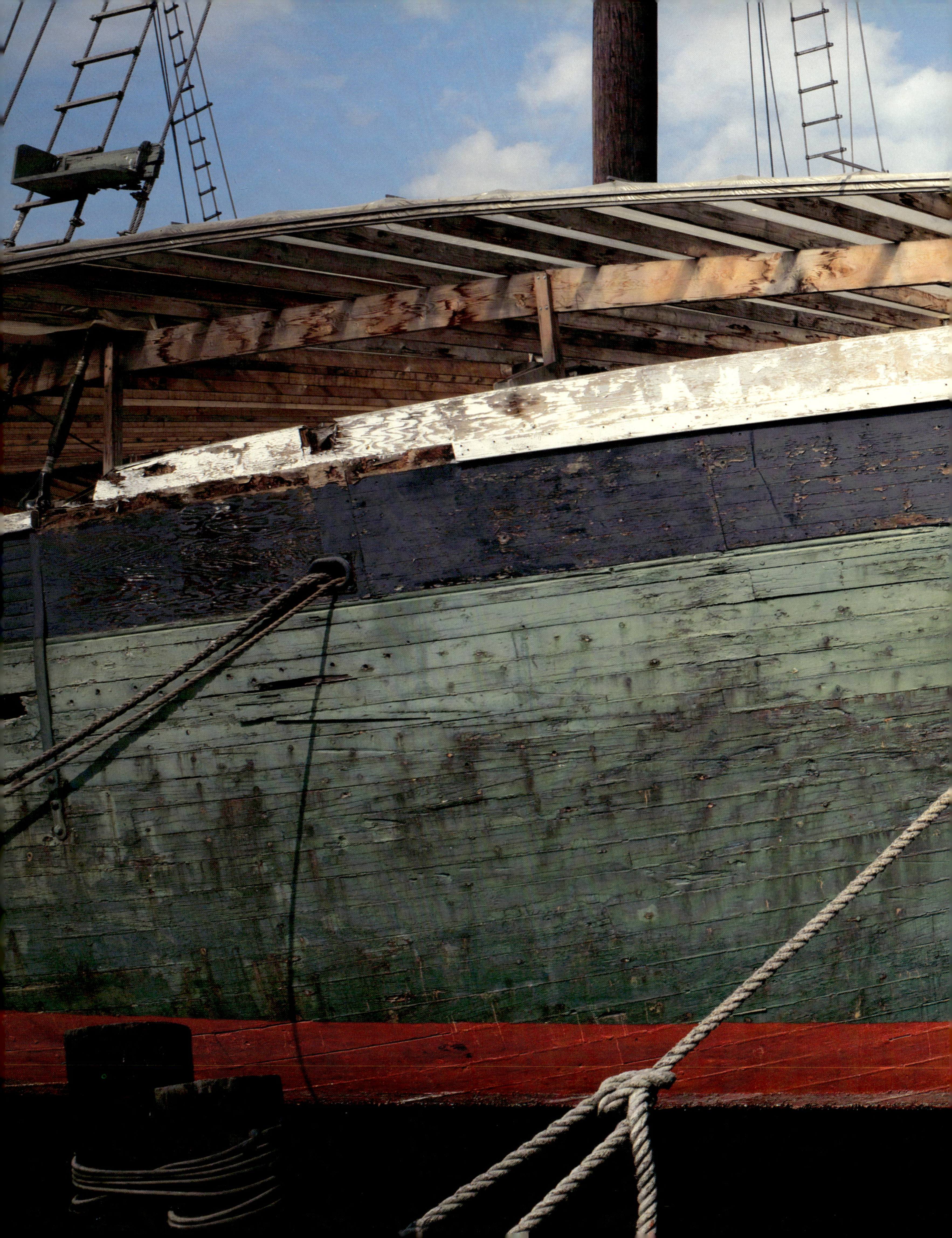

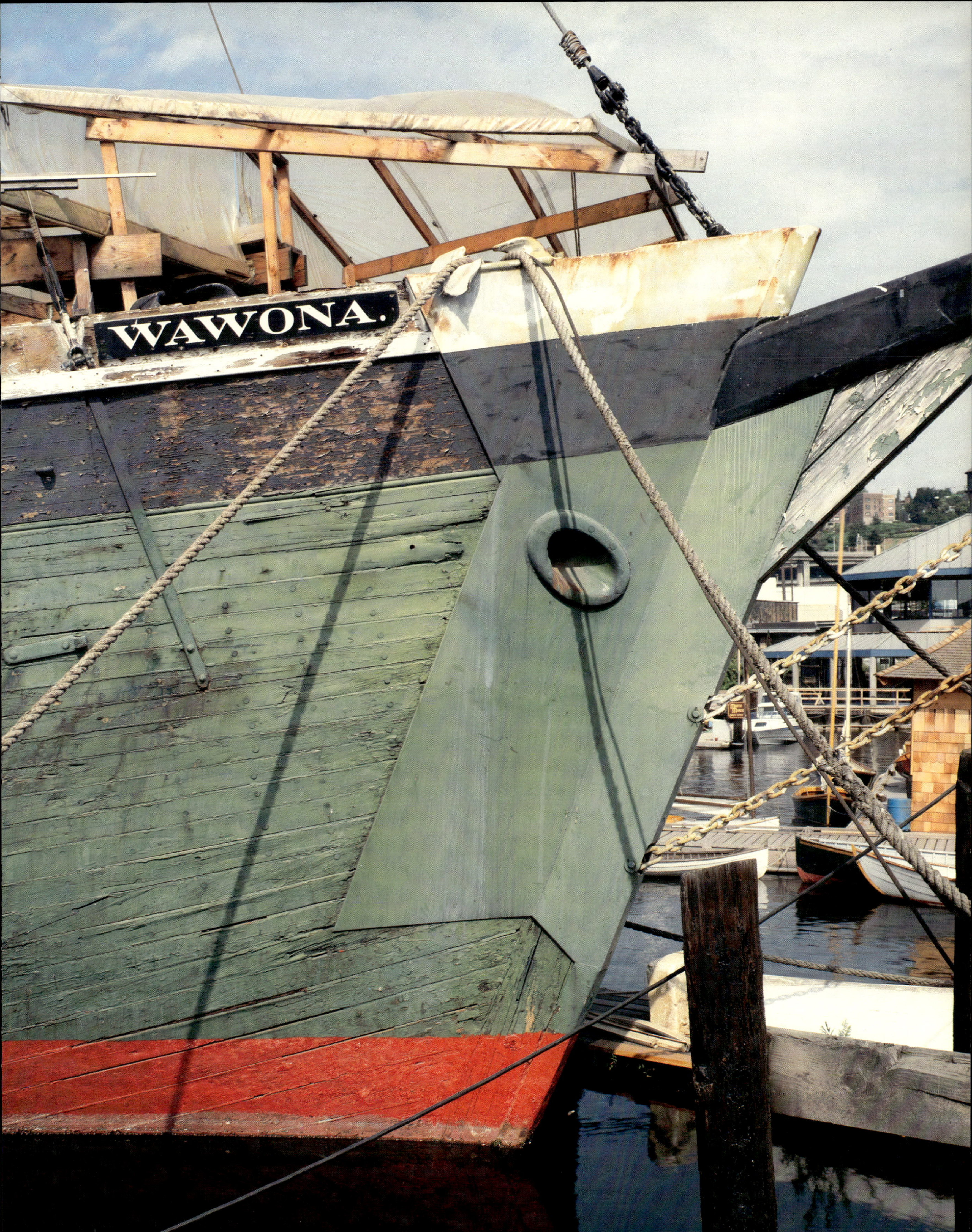
WAWONA.

EMERSON SAWMILL

Right. *On the Scroon River, Warrensburg, N.Y. This water-powered mill was part of a small industrial hamlet.*

Opposite. *Timber framing and diamond-shaped windows. The mill, built in 1900, was washed away in 1980.*

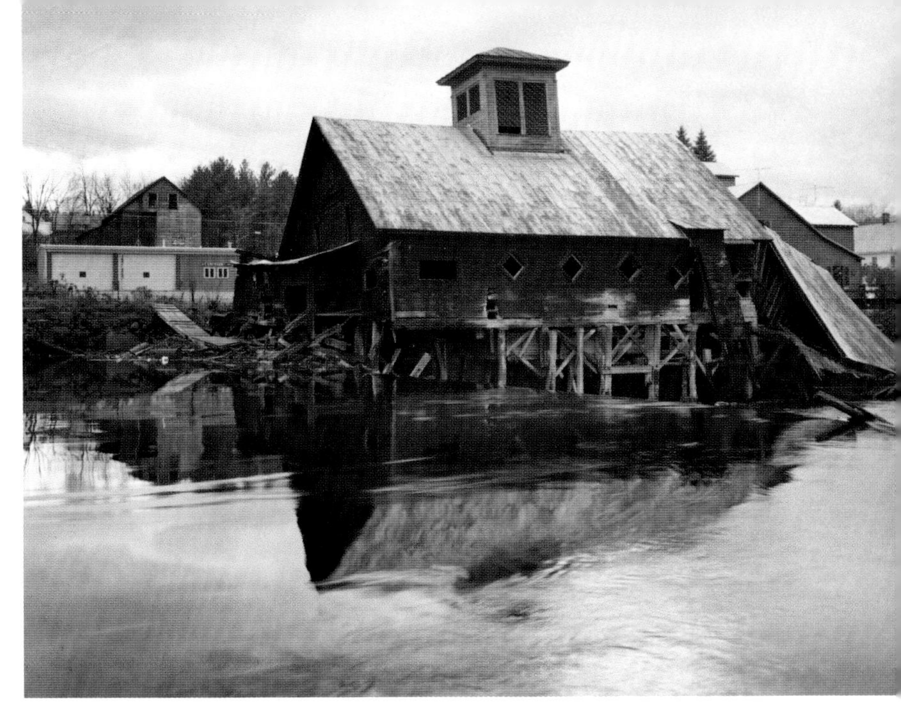

CHATTAHOOCHEE RIVER INDUSTRIES

Below. *Abandoned 19th-century textile mills, Columbus, Ga., some reminiscent of New England designs.*

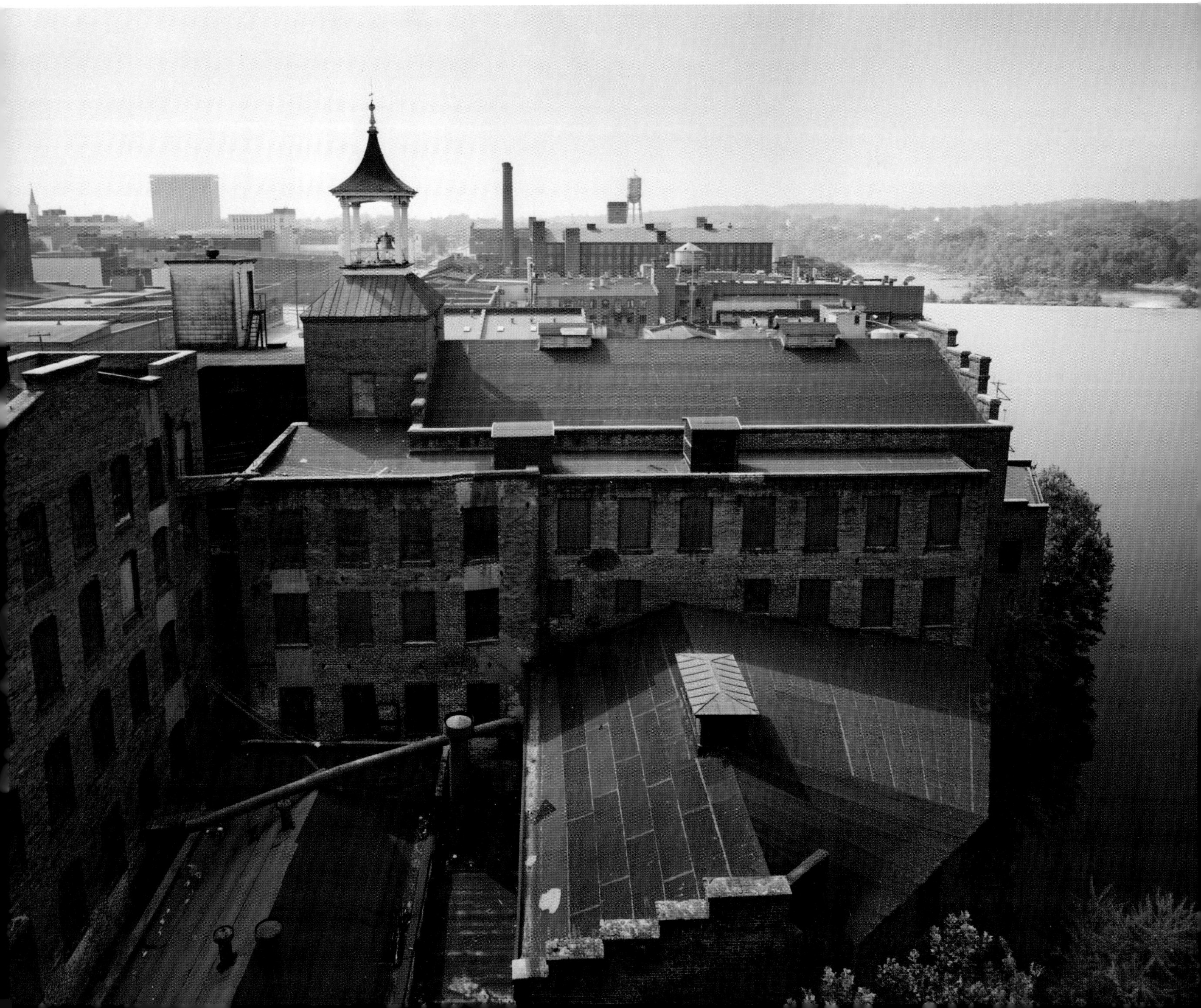

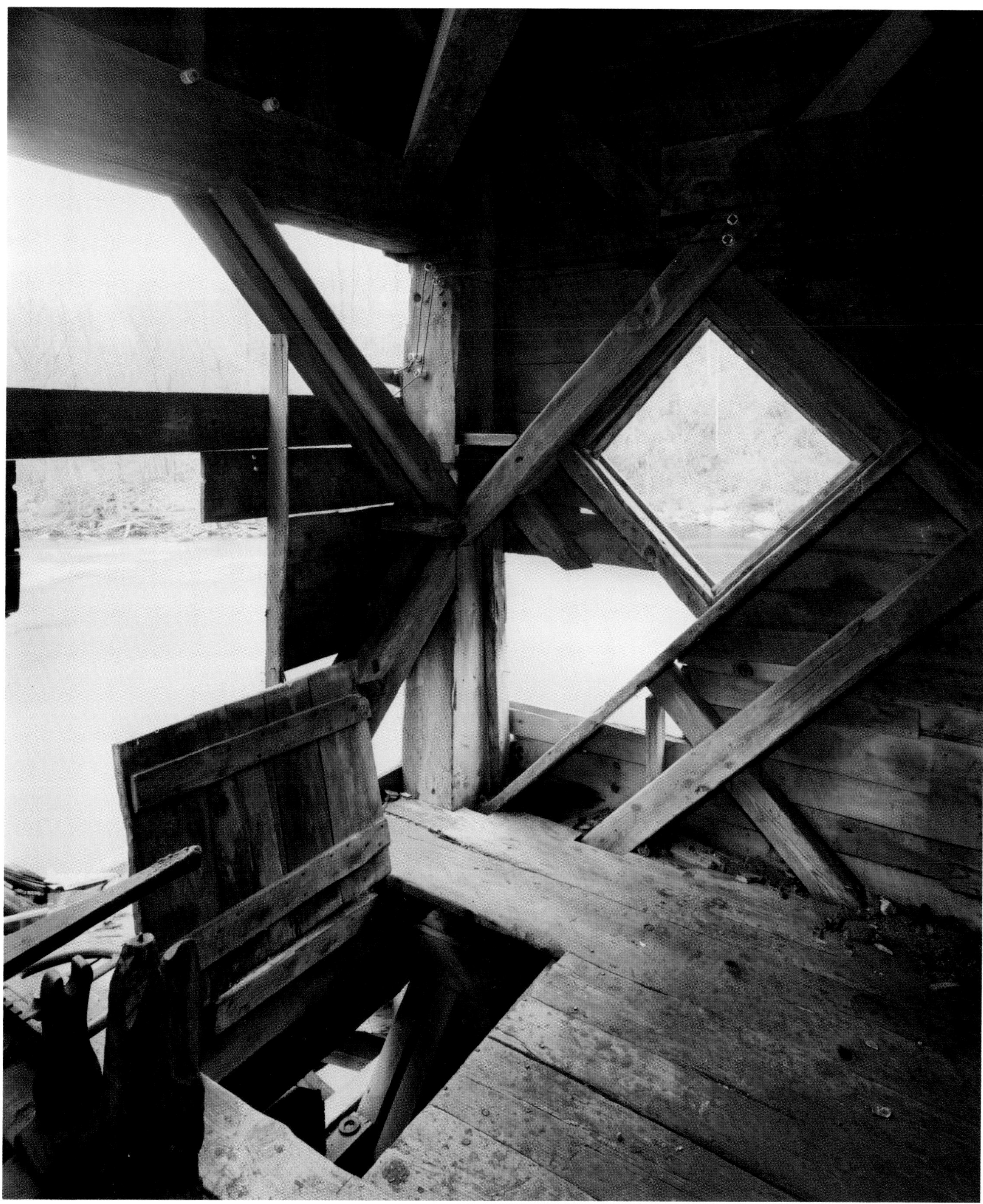

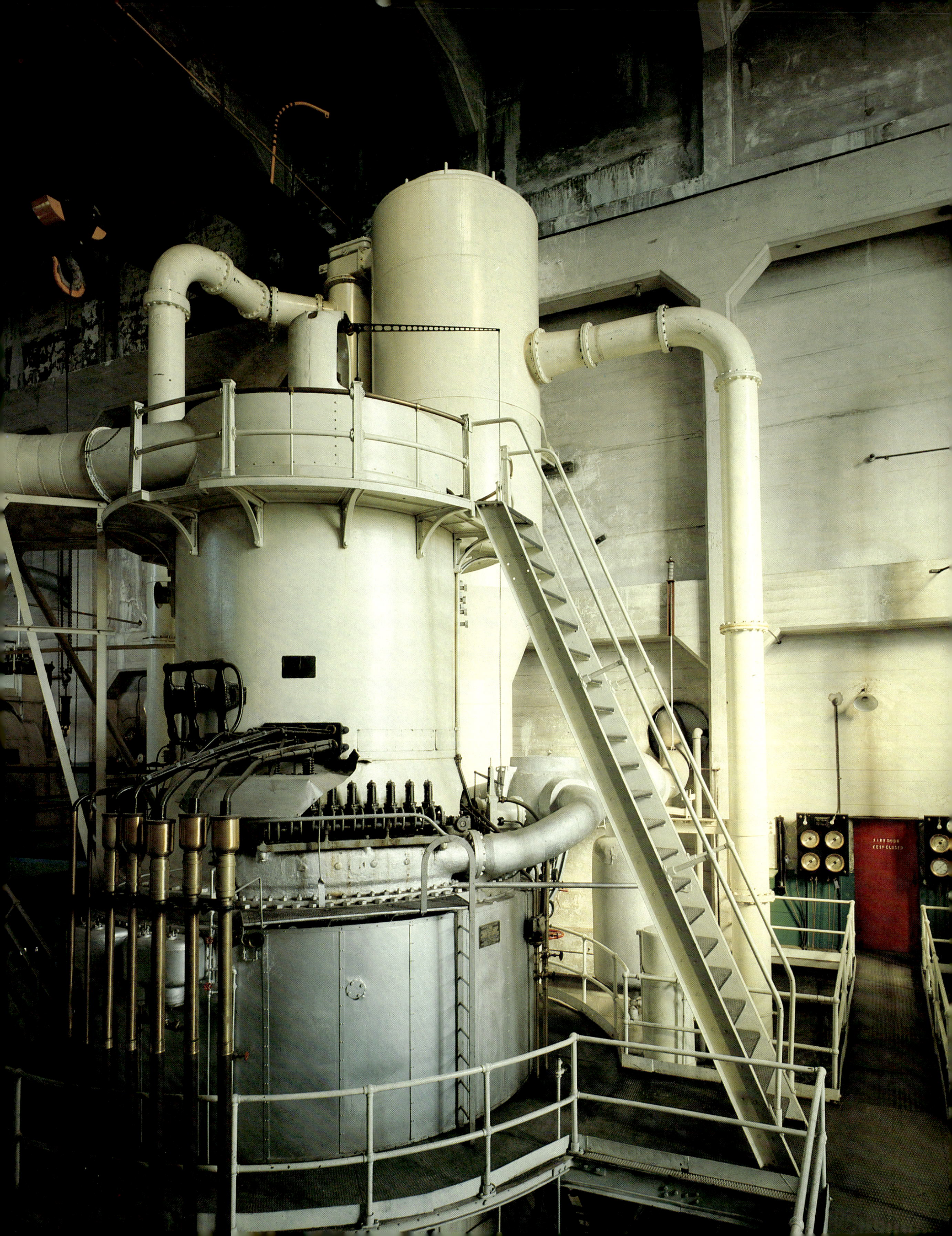
FIRE DOOR
KEEP CLOSED

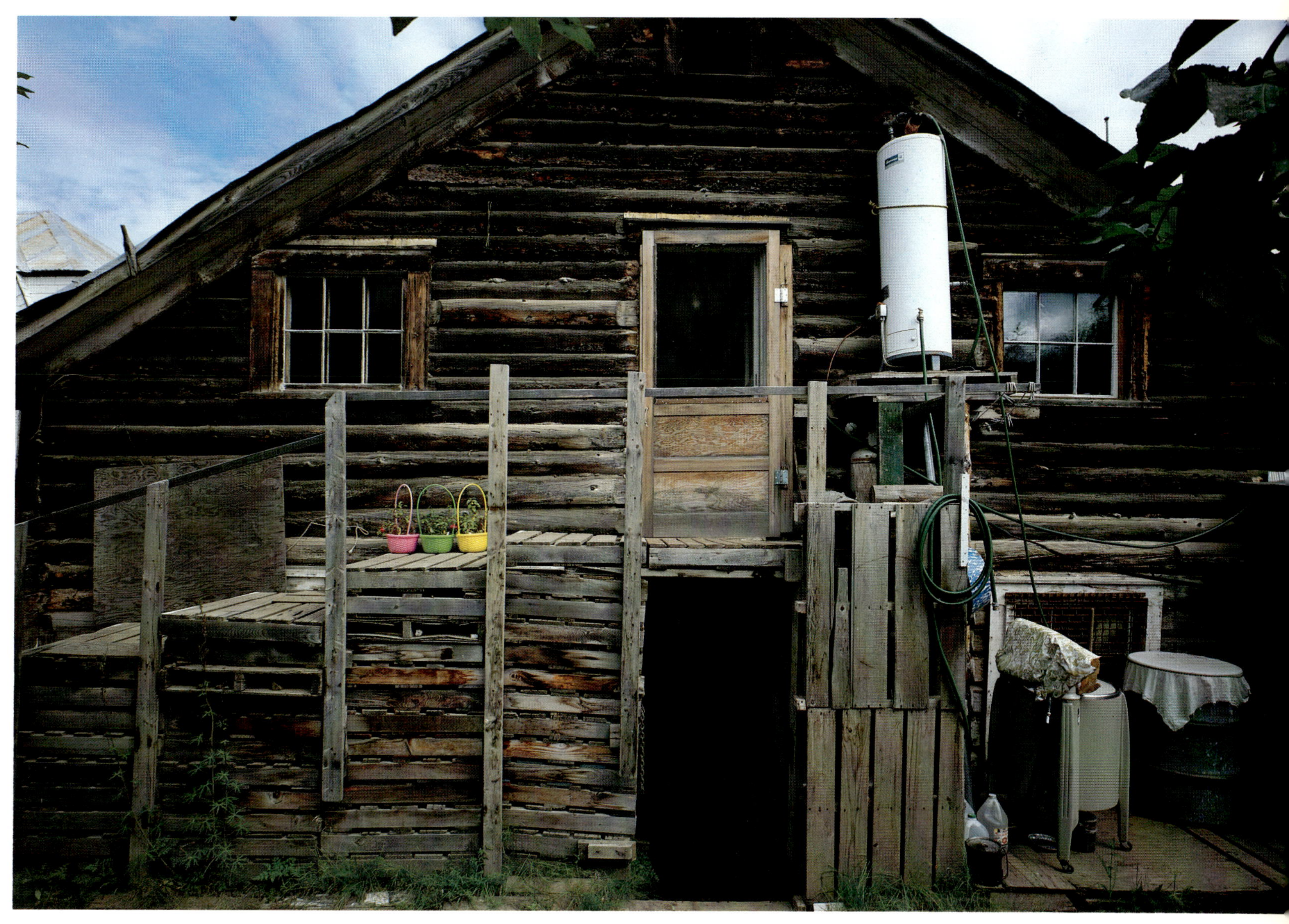

GEORGETOWN STEAM PLANT

Opposite. *Steam turbine and generator used to supply electricity to Seattle, installed in 1908. The barometric condenser in the background converted exhausted steam into water. The plant shut down in 1977.*

NORTHERN COMMERCIAL COMPANY

Above. *Hot water heater, Eagle, Alaska. The company took over from the Russian-American Company in 1867 and about 1898 built this false-front log structure as a dry goods store. It is now a residence.*

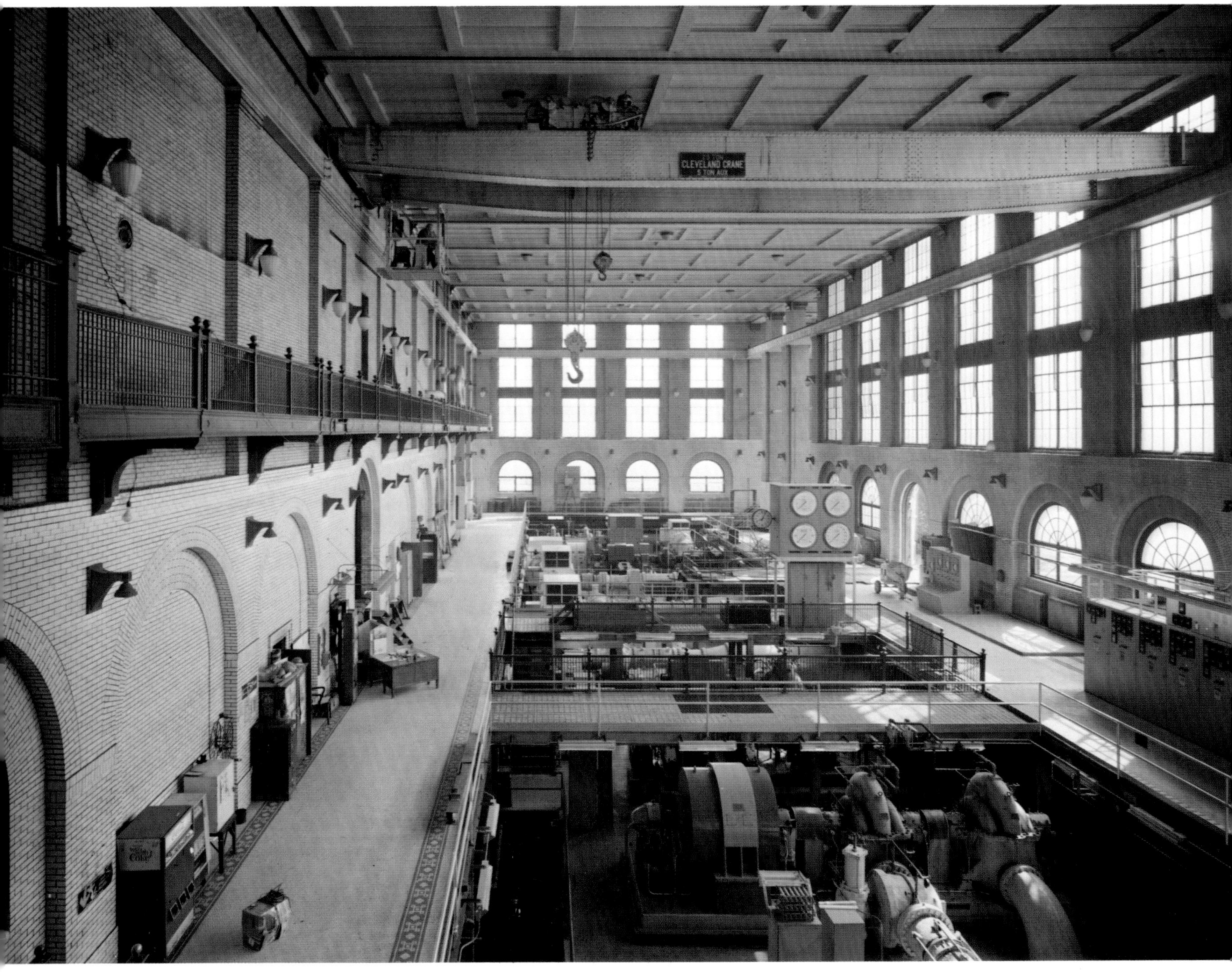

DIVISION AVENUE PUMPING STATION

Above. *Interior of the steam-powered pumping station, Cleveland, built 1914–18. Three generations of pumping stations have occupied this site since the 1850s, drawing from Lake Erie to provide the city's water supply.*

LAKE LYNN HYDROELECTRIC PLANT

Opposite. *On the Cheat River, near Morgantown, W. Va. Built into the Lake Lynn Dam in two stages, 1913–14 and 1925–26, the power plant's generators provide electricity for a number of towns in the region.*

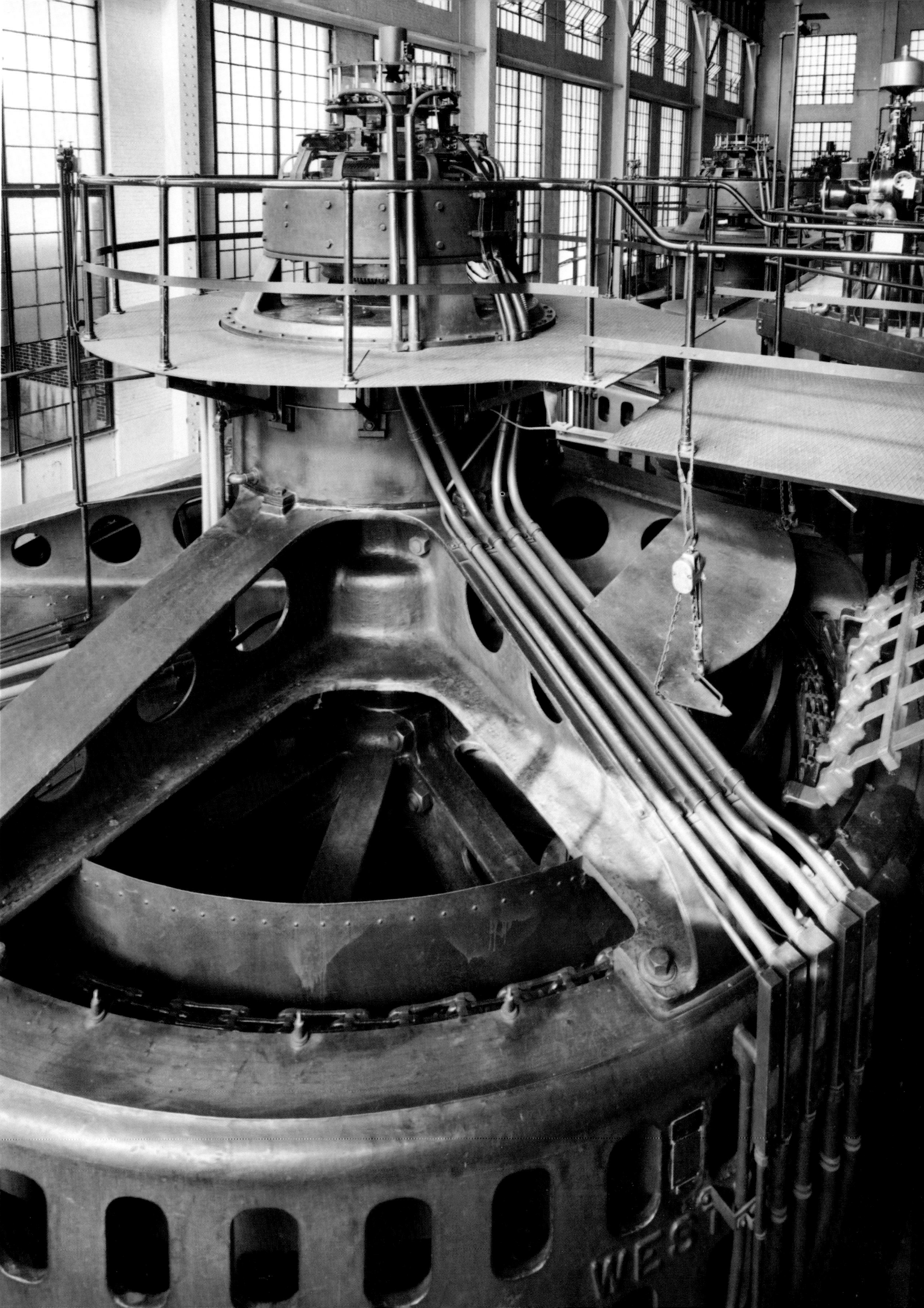
WES

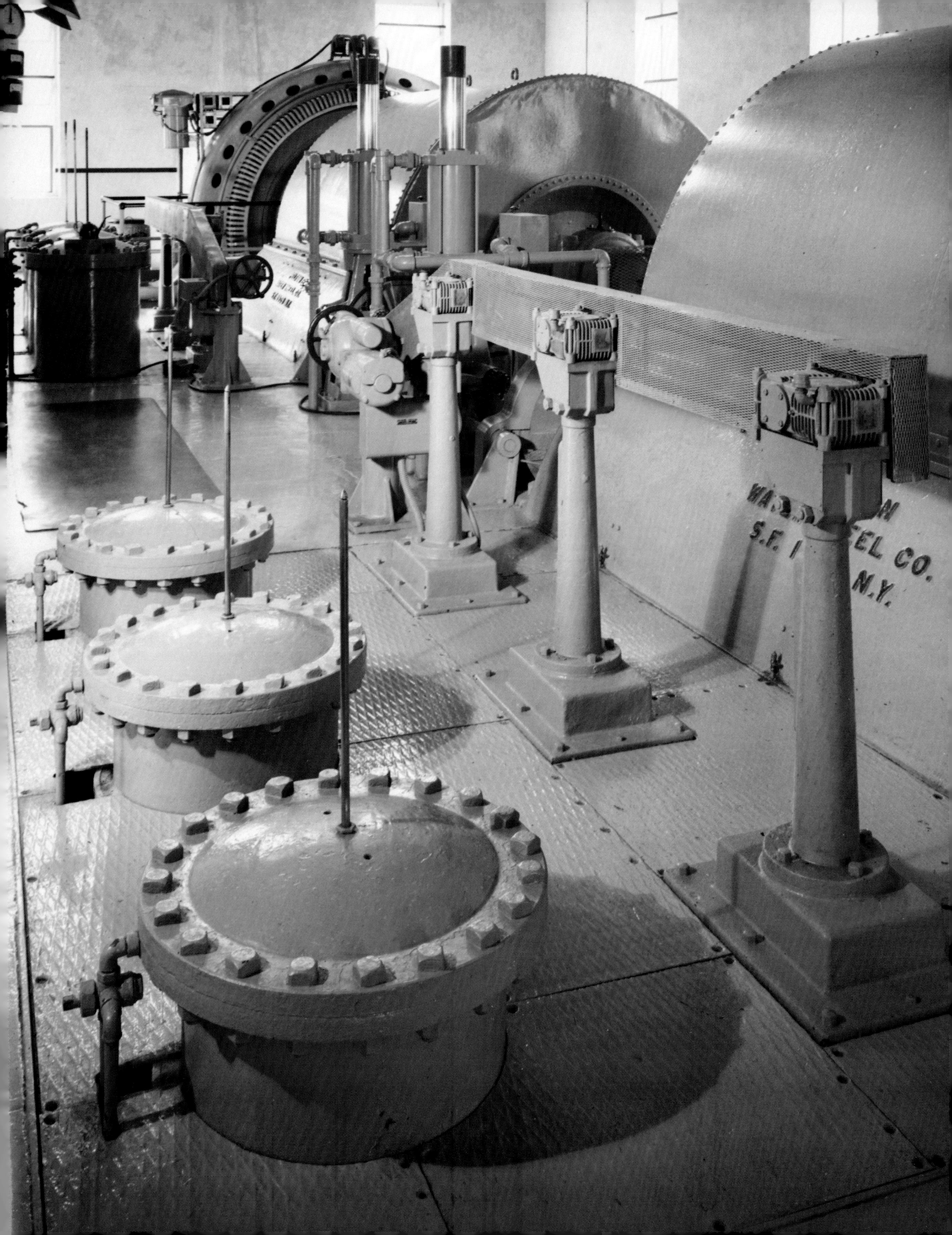

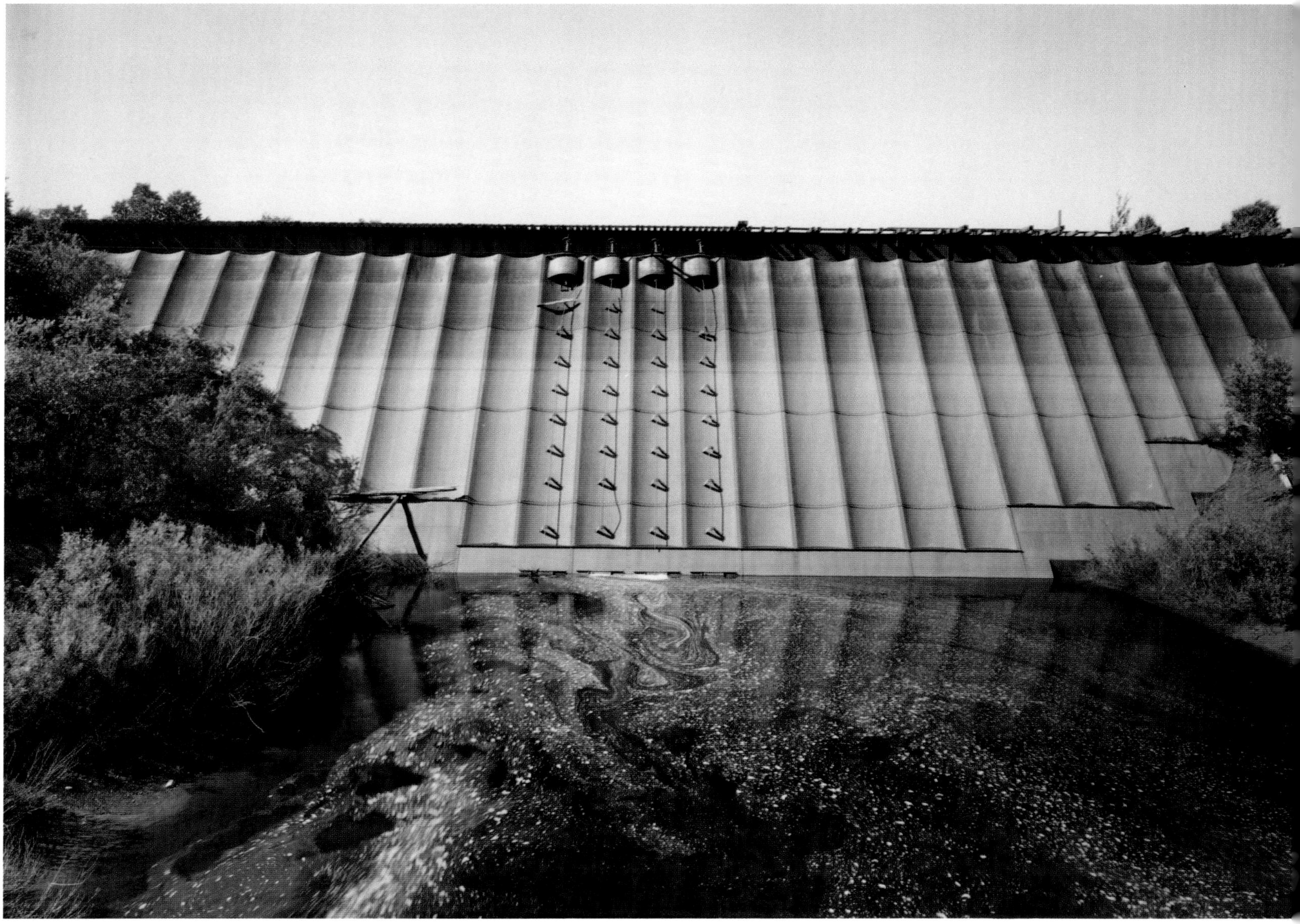

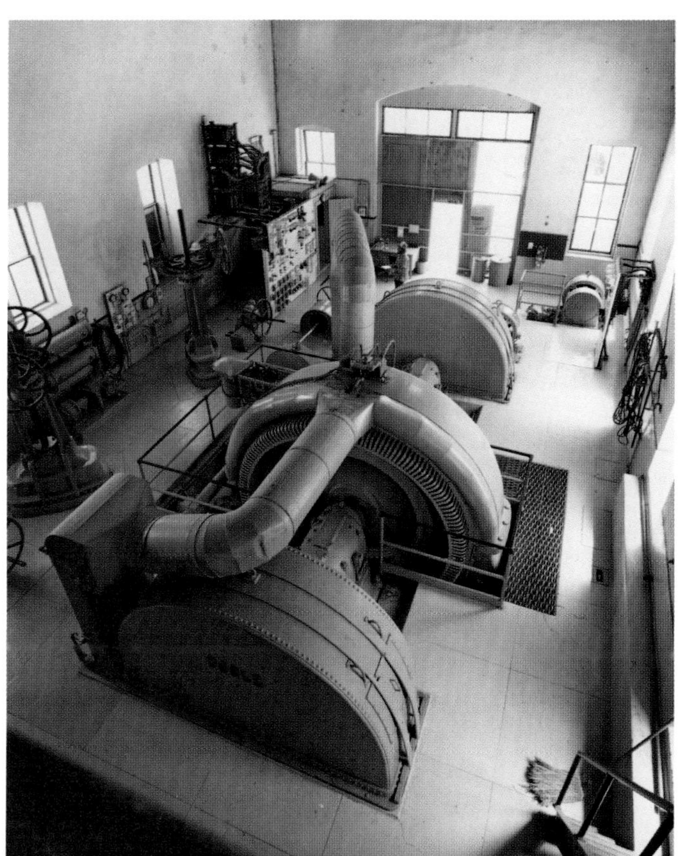

BATTLE CREEK HYDROELECTRIC

Opposite. *Generator room valves and controls in the Inskip Powerhouse, near Red Bluff, Calif. Built in 1910, this is one of four early 20th-century powerhouses along Battle Creek in the Sierra Nevadas.*

Left. *South Powerhouse generator with dual waterwheels and cool-air ducts, constructed in 1910.*

REDRIDGE DAM

Above. *On the Salmon Trout River, near Beacon Hill, on Michigan's Upper Peninsula. When completed in 1901, Redridge was the first steel gravity dam of any significant size in the United States.*

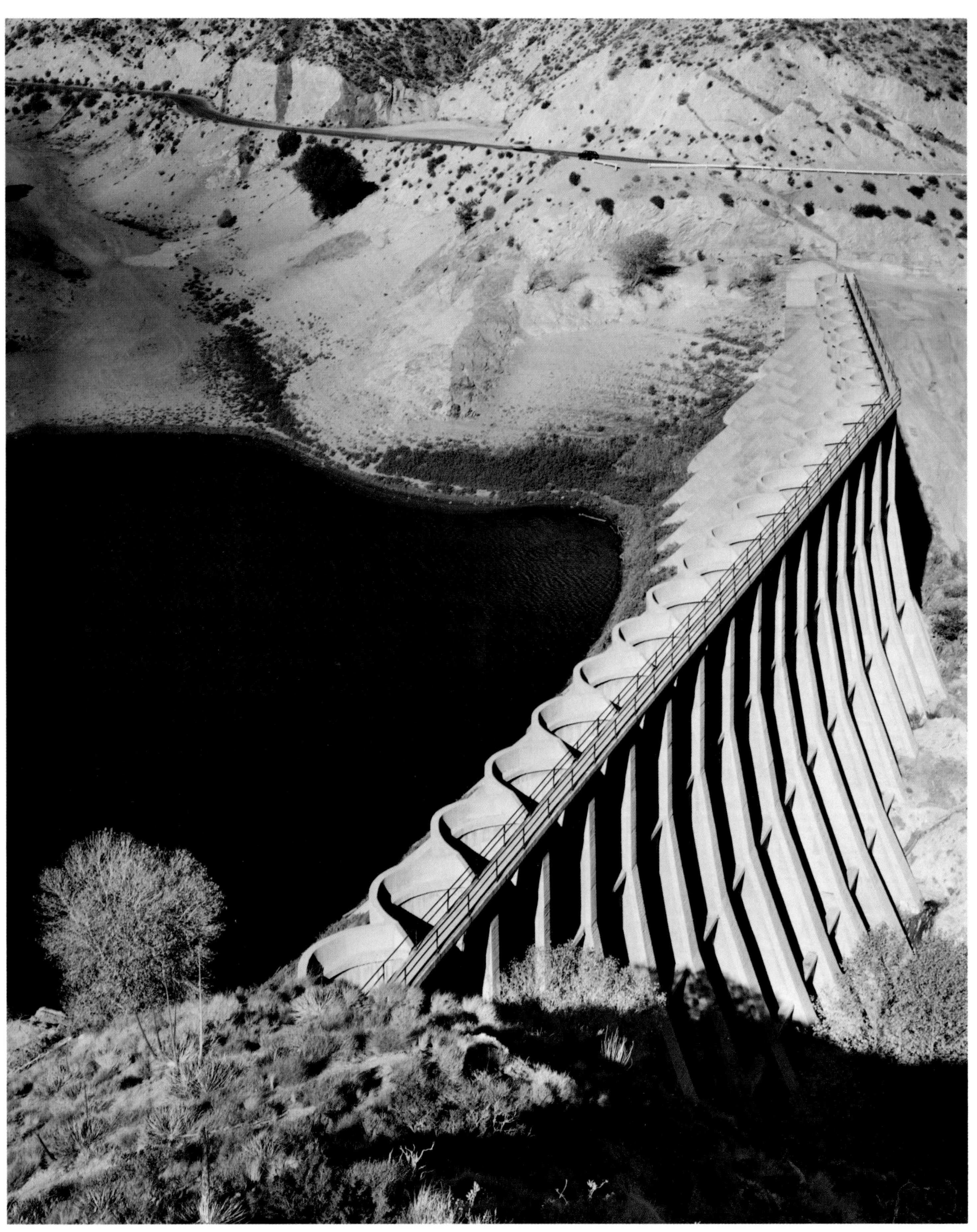

LITTLE ROCK DAM

Opposite. *Reinforced concrete, multiple-arch dam on Little Rock Creek in California's San Gabriel Mountains. Used for irrigation, the dam was designed by John S. Eastwood and built 1922–24.*

Below. *Upstream face of the dam showing the incline of the arches. By using the arch design, Eastwood devised a structure that was economically superior to the more common concrete gravity dams as well as being highly sculptural.*

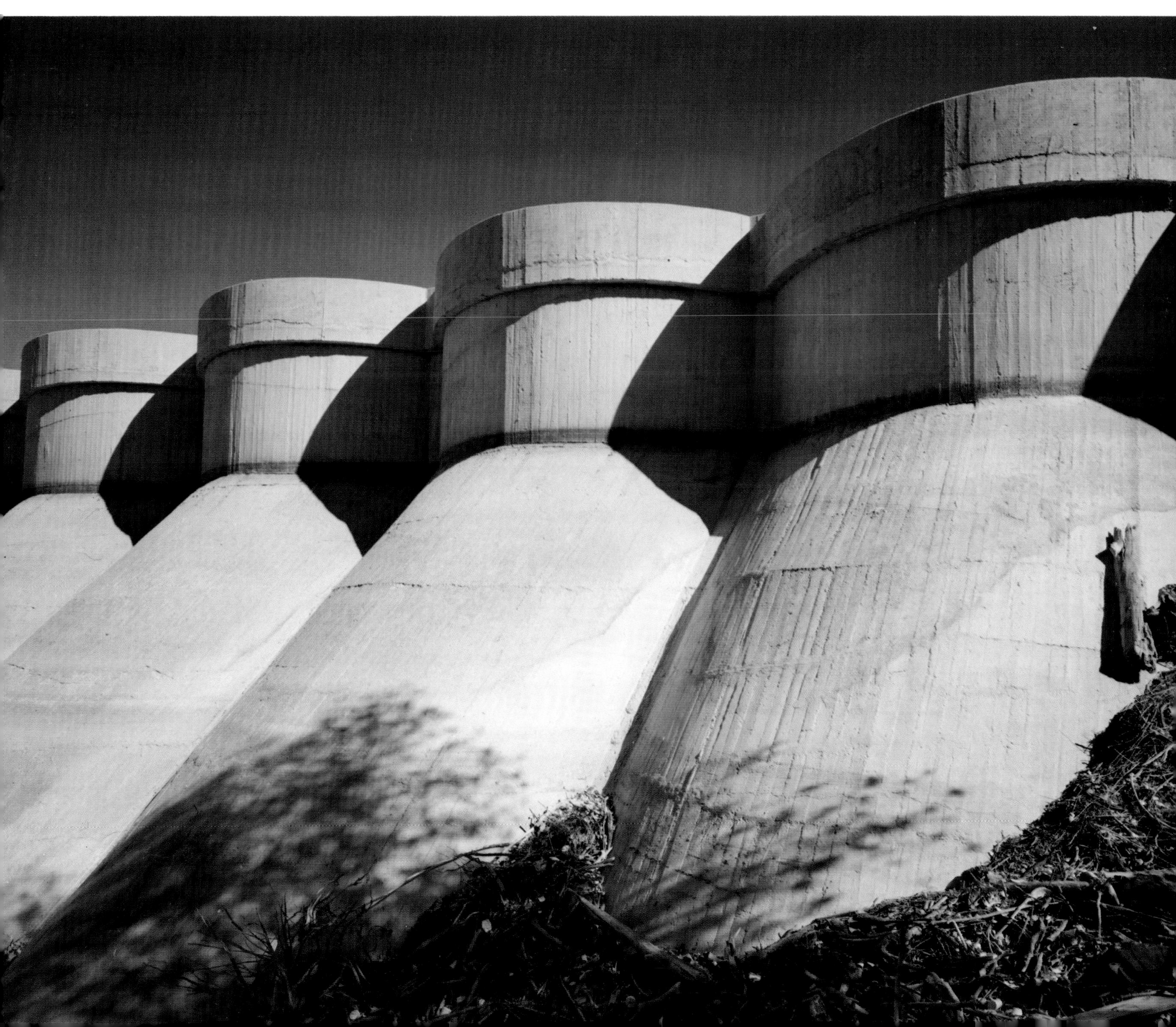

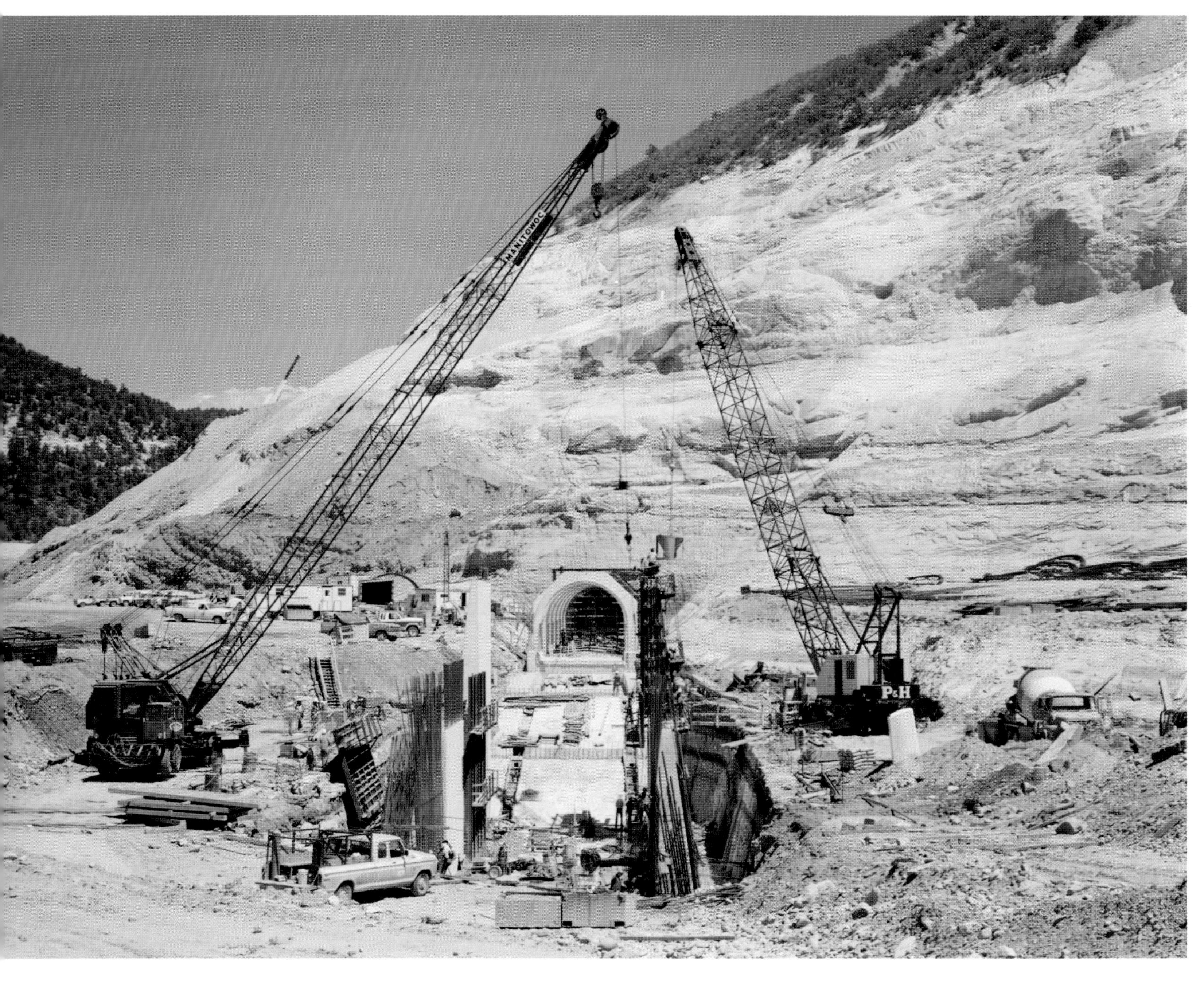

MONTEZUMA VALLEY
IRRIGATION PROJECT

Above. *Construction of the tailrace running to the Delores River Powerhouse, Cortez, Colo., in 1980. The Bureau of Reclamation designed this hydroelectric system solely to operate the irrigation project.*

MILK RIVER
IRRIGATION PROJECT

Opposite. *Bridge and penstocks crossing the St. Mary River near Babb, Mont. Installed in 1915, the penstocks divert irrigation water from the St. Mary River into the Milk River watershed system.*

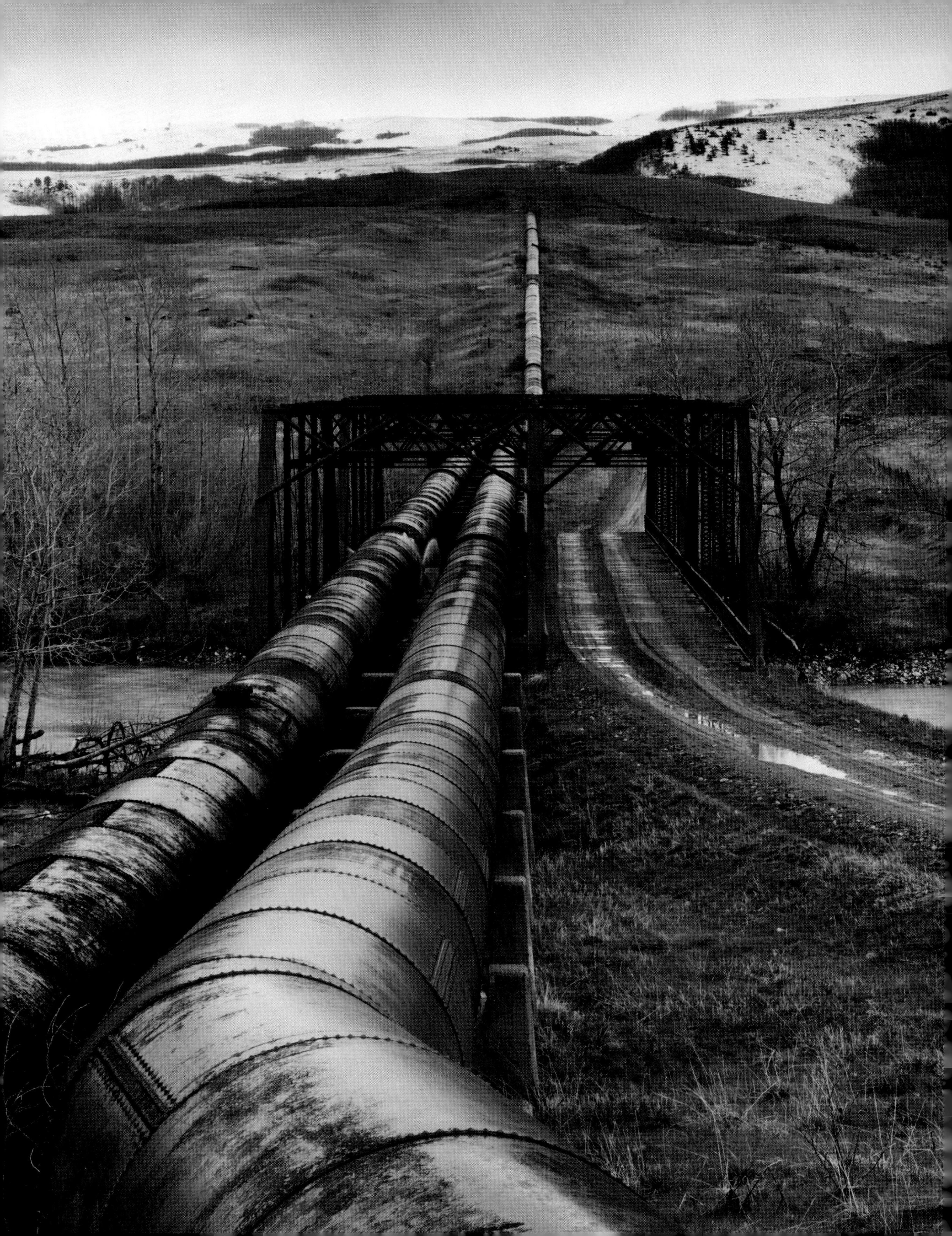

LIBERTY

. . . and we should have
such an empire for liberty
as she has never surveyed
since the creation. . . .

THOMAS JEFFERSON
Letter to James Madison

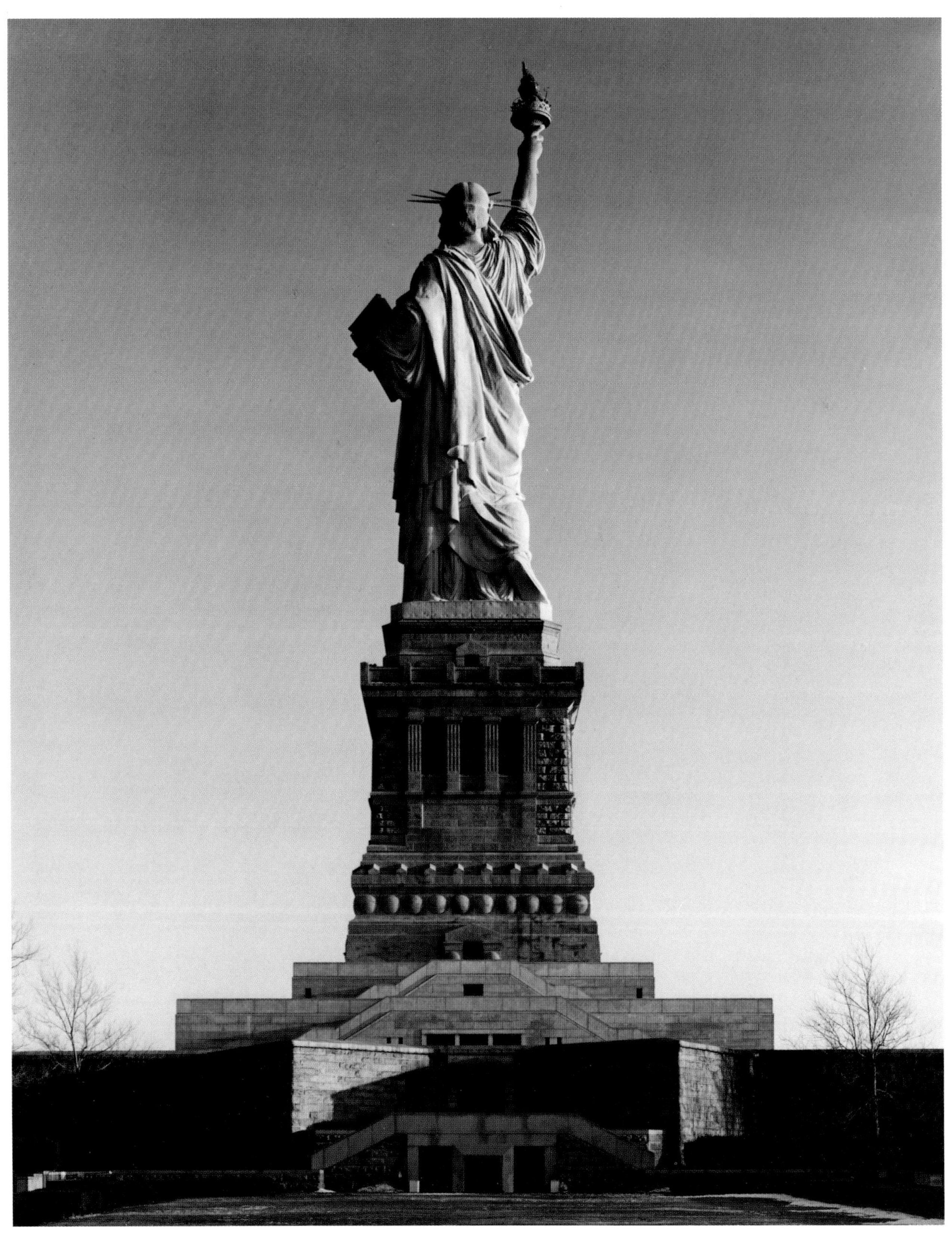

LIBERTY, FEBRUARY 1984

North side of Frédéric-Auguste Bartholdi's masterpiece before restoration took place from 1984 to 1986. The goal was to repair a century of deterioration and alterations made to the statue.

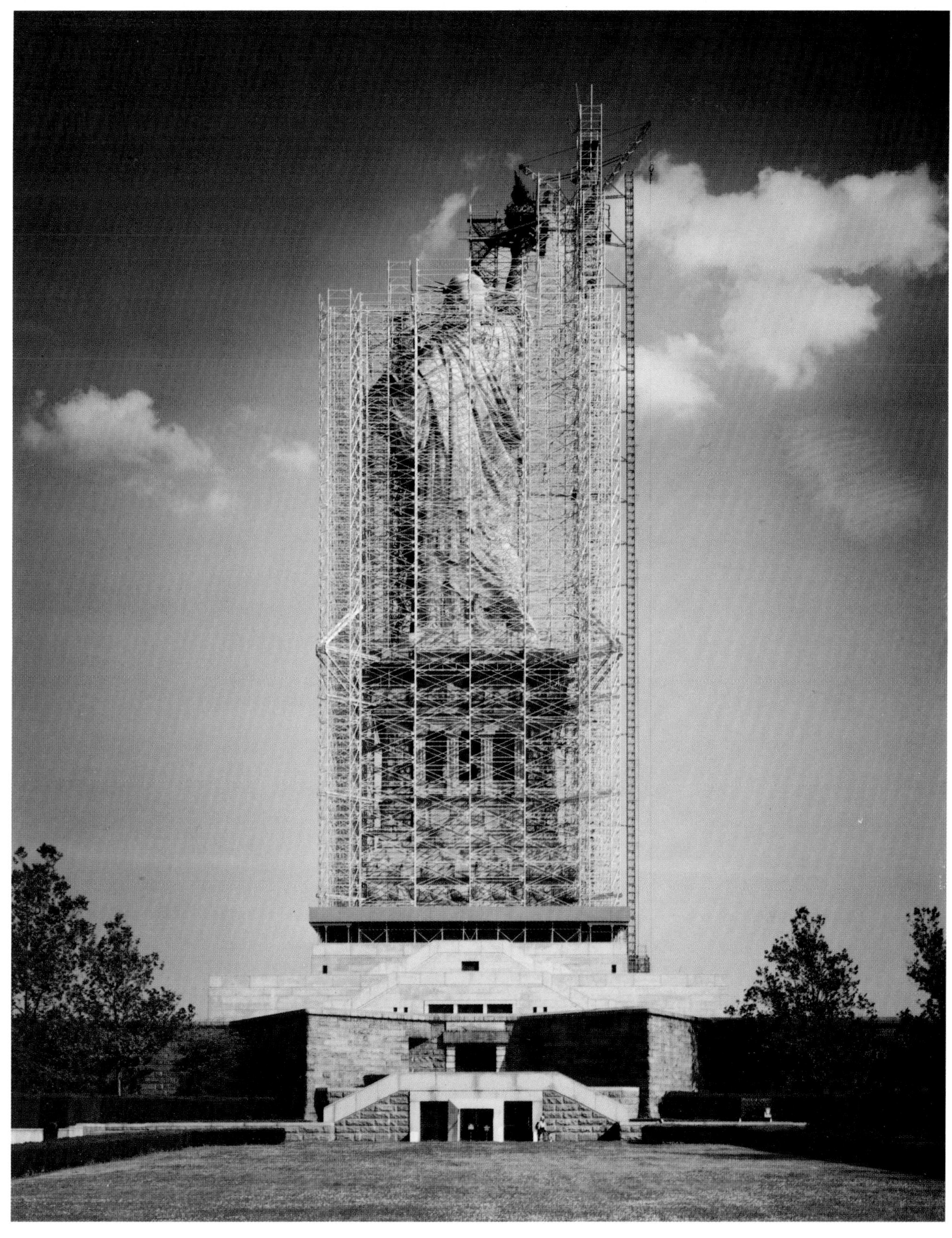

LIBERTY, MAY 1984

Dressed in scaffolding whose engineering complexity almost rivaled the landmark's own. The $2 million prefabricated aluminum structure could withstand 100-mile-an-hour winds.

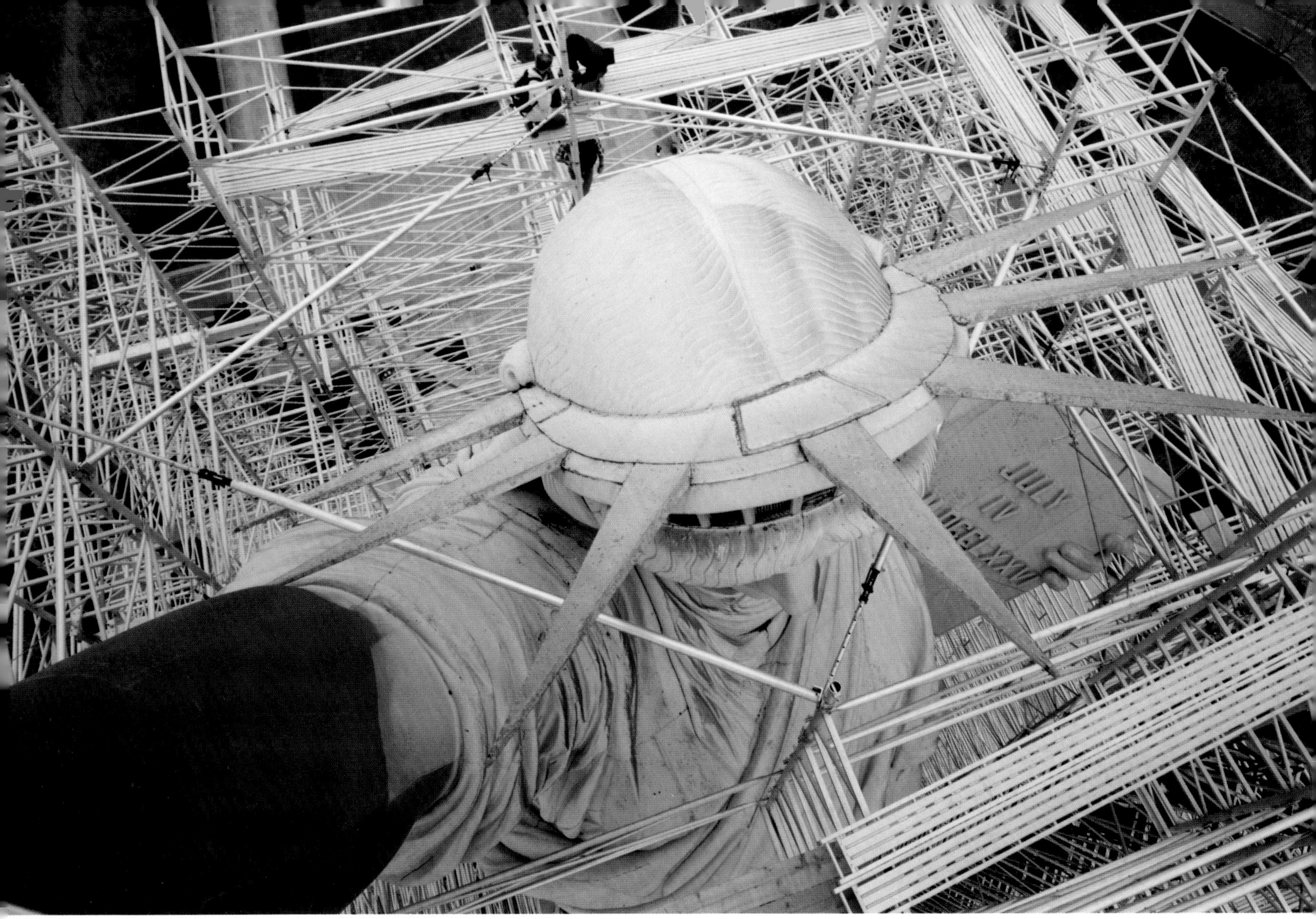

HEAD AND CROWN

Above. *Crown with its bronze and brass spikes, which had blackened from periodic bolts of lightning. Each represents one of the seven seas.*

Right. *Structural frame of the head, designed by French architect Eugène Viollet-le-Duc. Following Viollet-le-Duc's death in 1879, Alexandre-Gustave Eiffel was called in to complete the statue's iron frame.*

Opposite. *Back of the head before restoration. Liberty's waves cover the 30-foot head with some of the 310 copper plates used to construct the statue.*

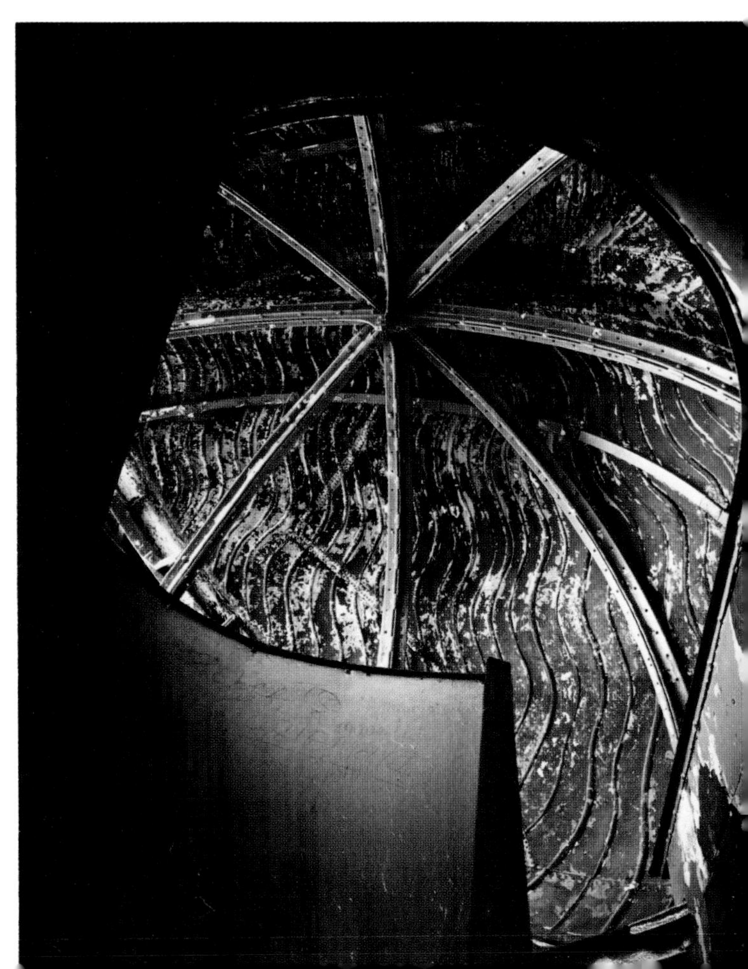

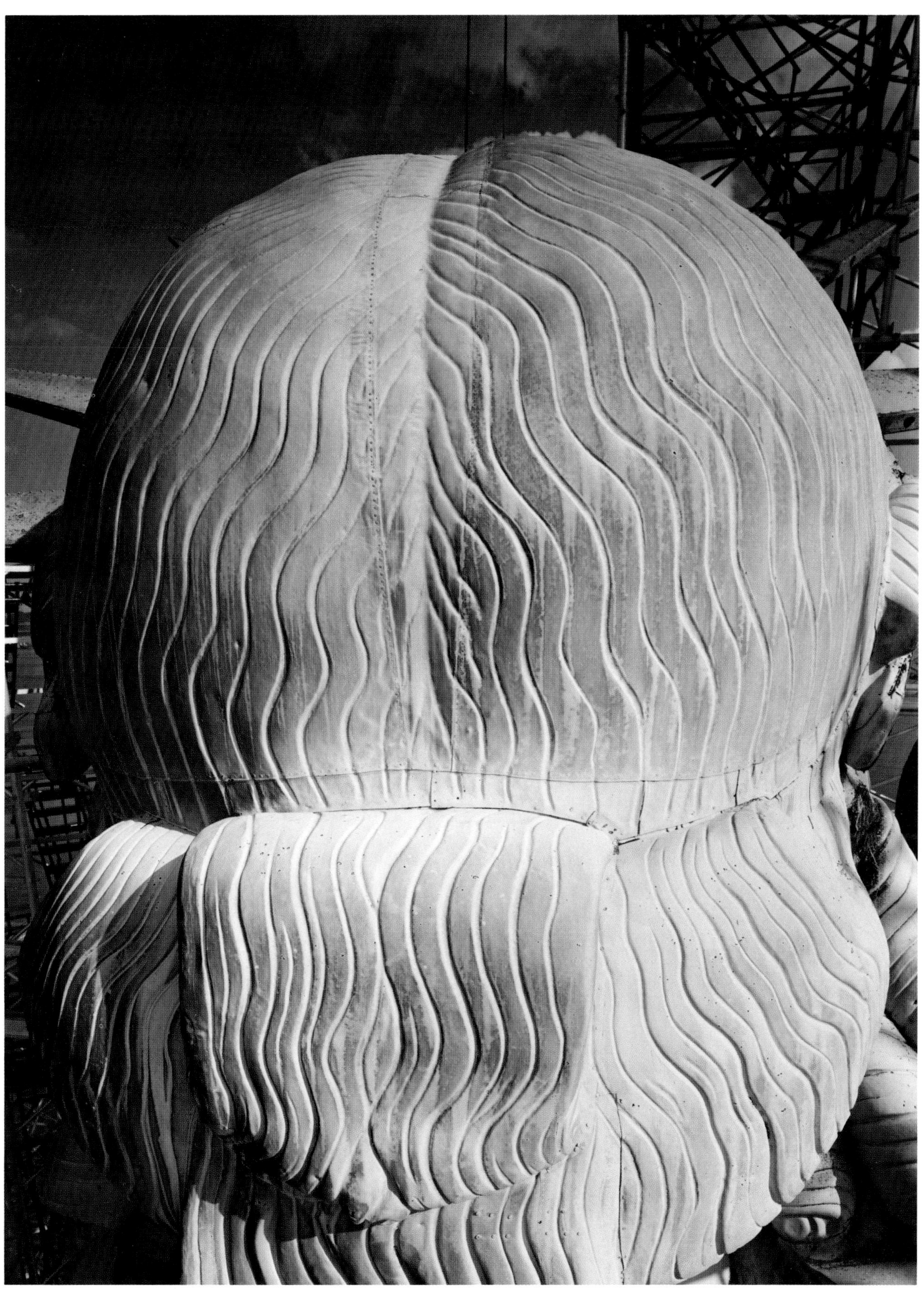

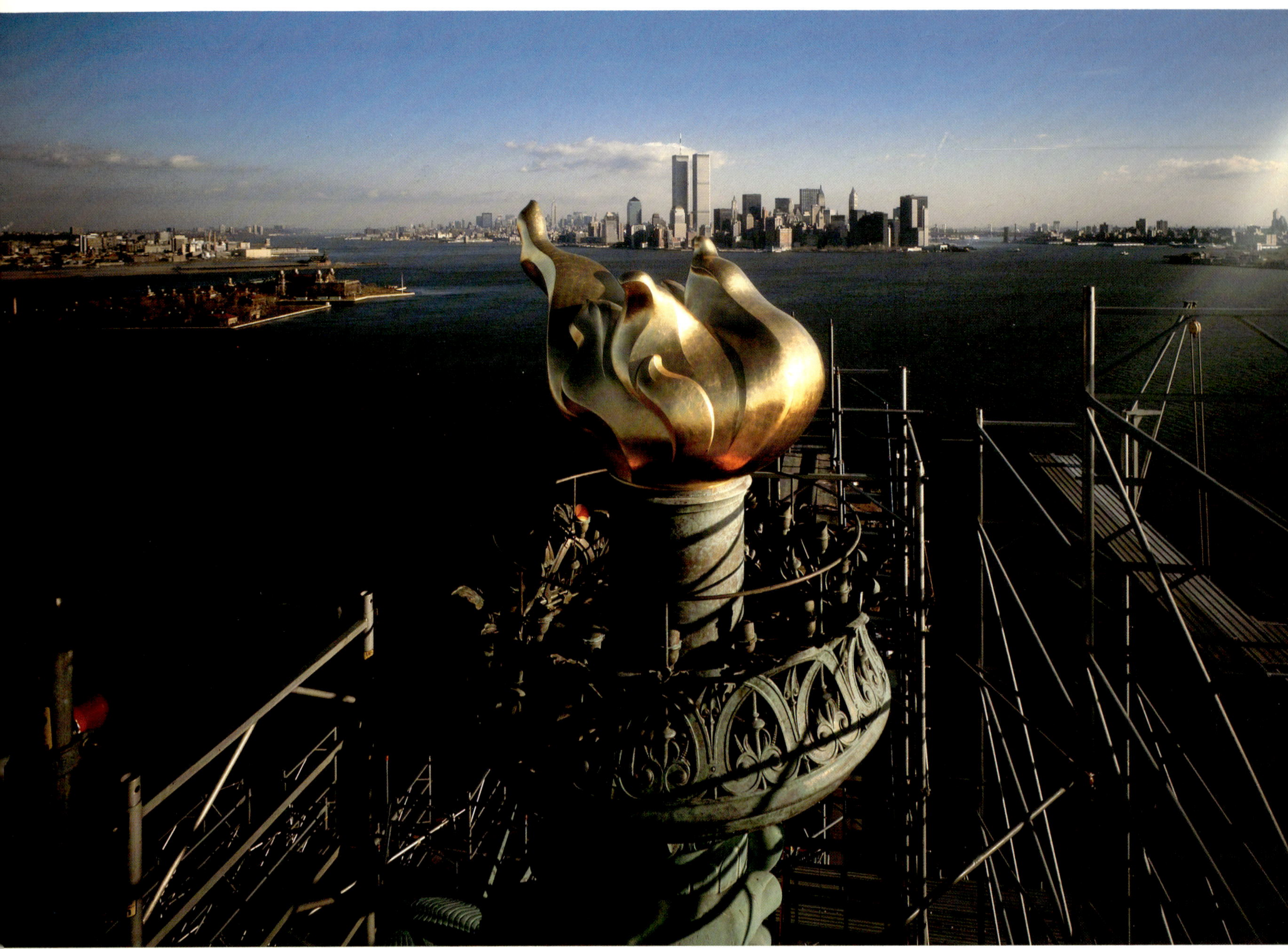

TORCH

Above. *New golden flame, crafted in copper and gold leaf to follow Bartholdi's original design.*

SCAFFOLDING

Opposite. *Robe encased in scaffolding, designed to allow restoration craftsmen access to every inch of the statue's copper skin.*

STRUCTURAL FRAME

Overleaf. *Eiffel's innovative framework, composed of a vertical truss, triangulated secondary framing and an armature conforming to the copper skin.*

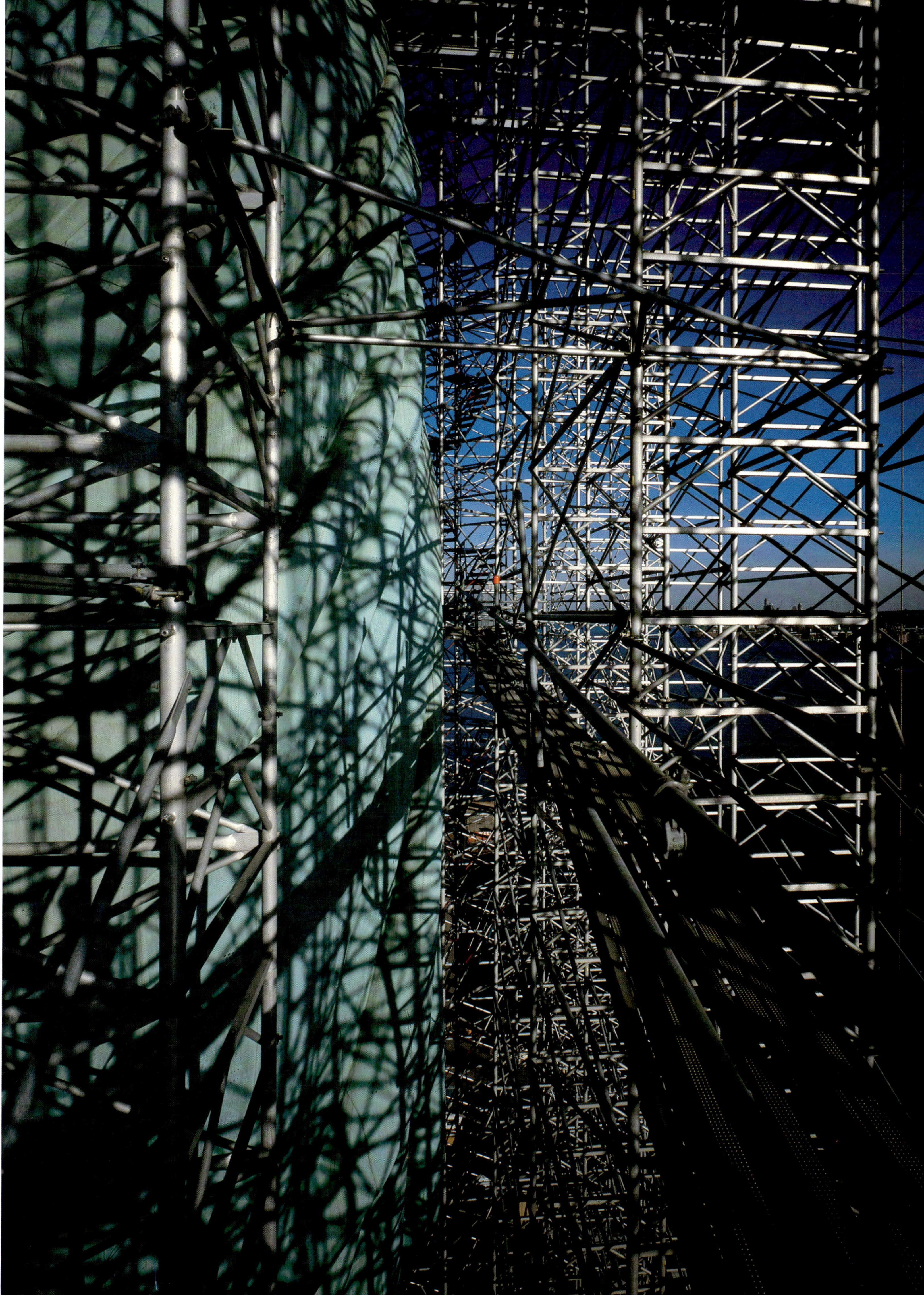

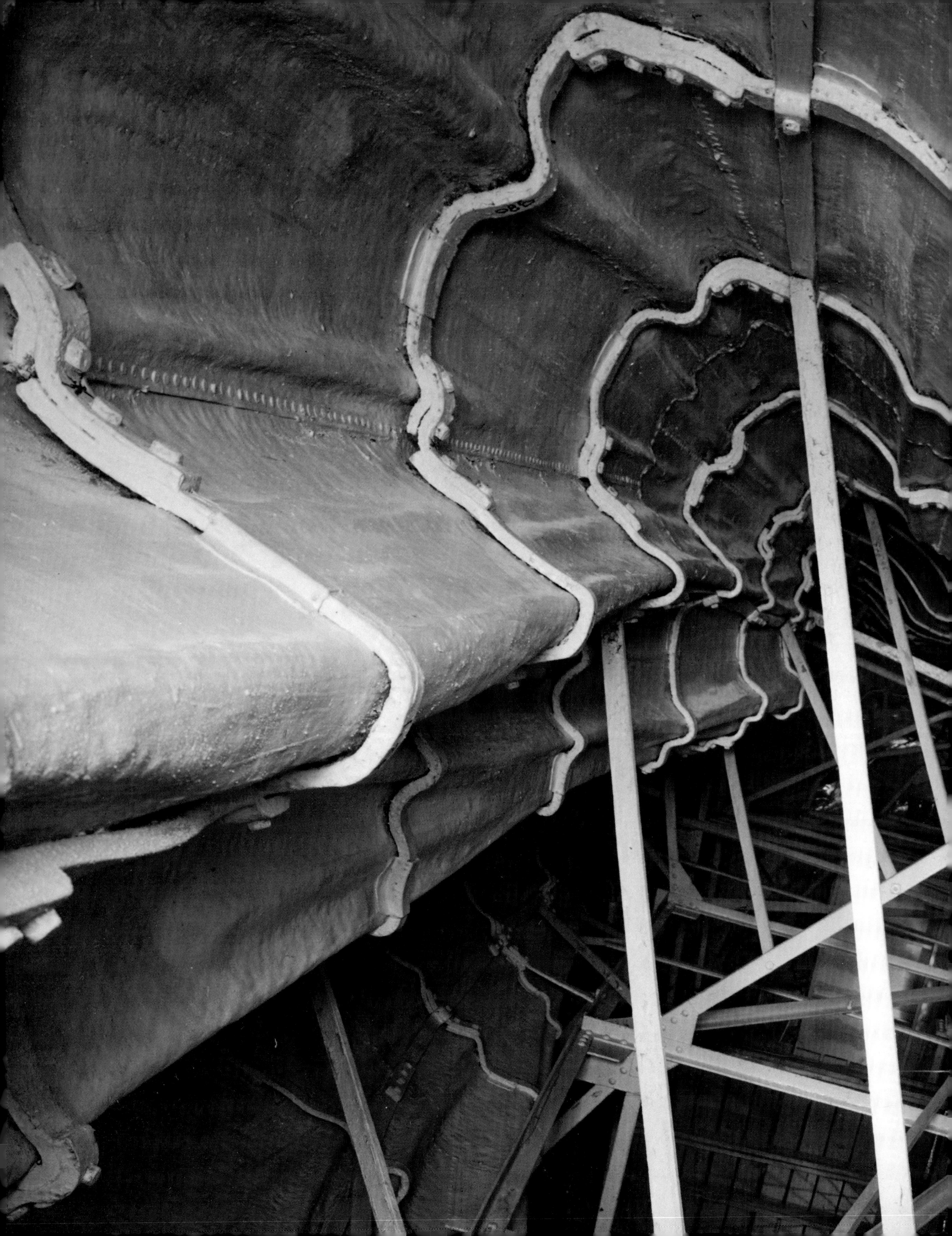

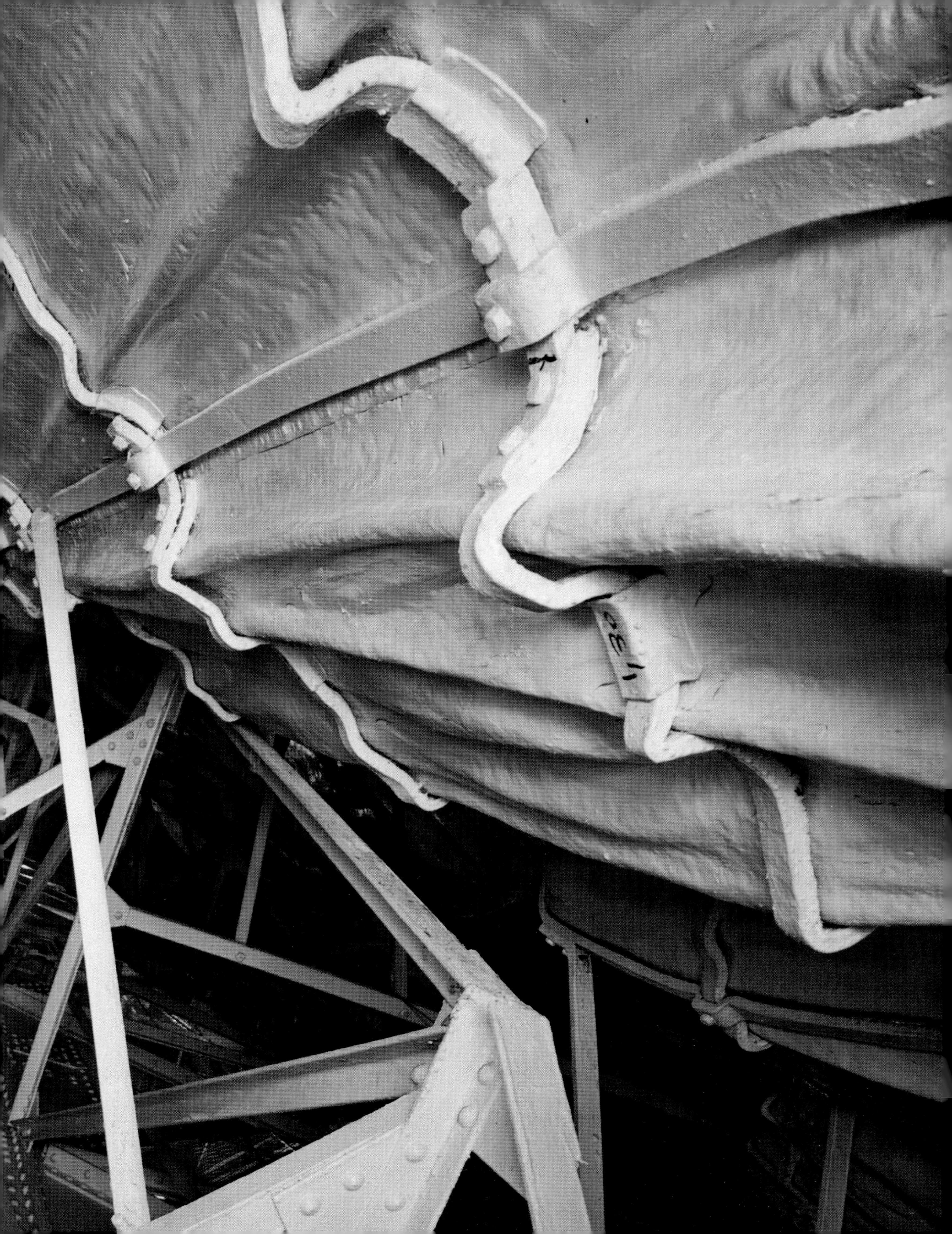

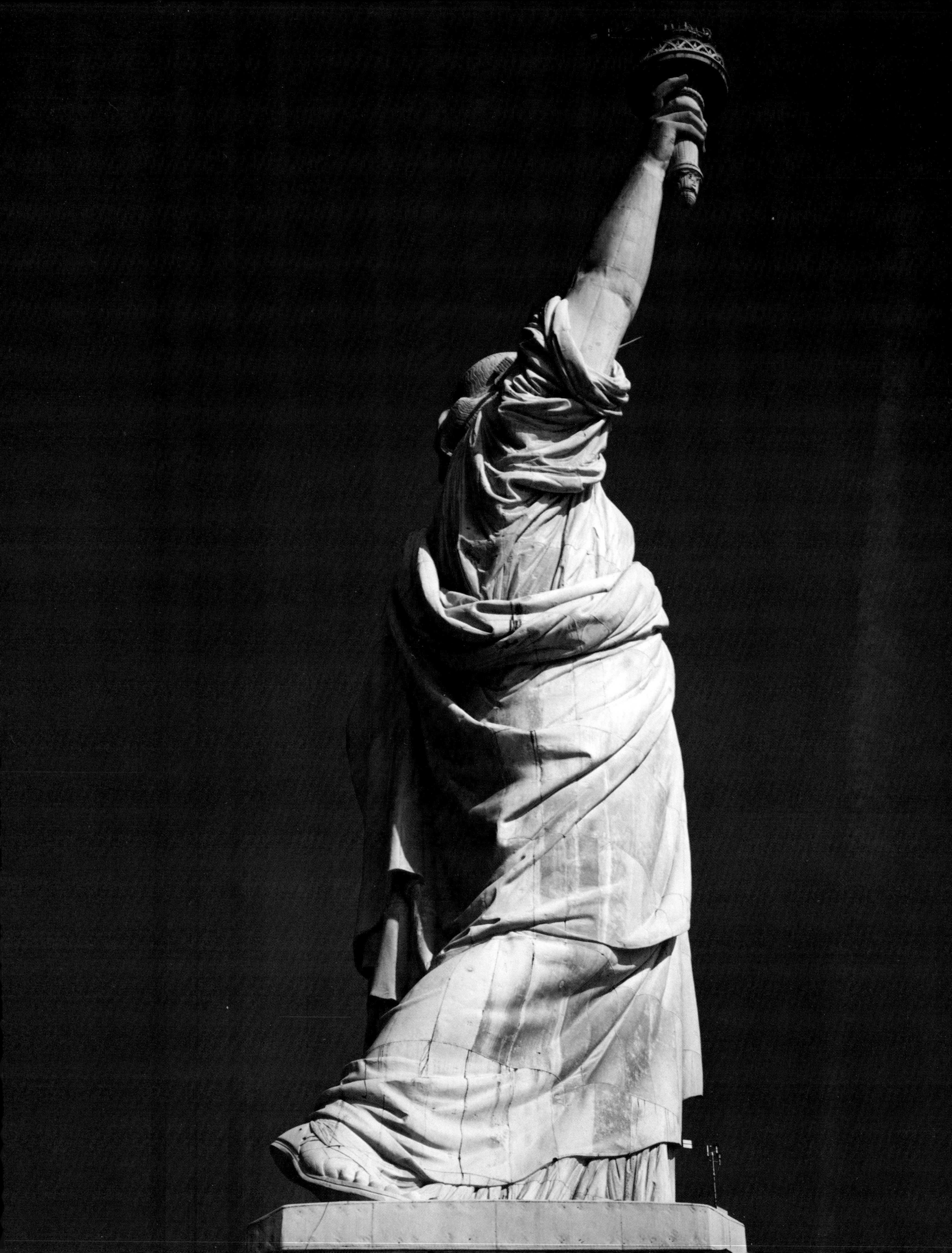

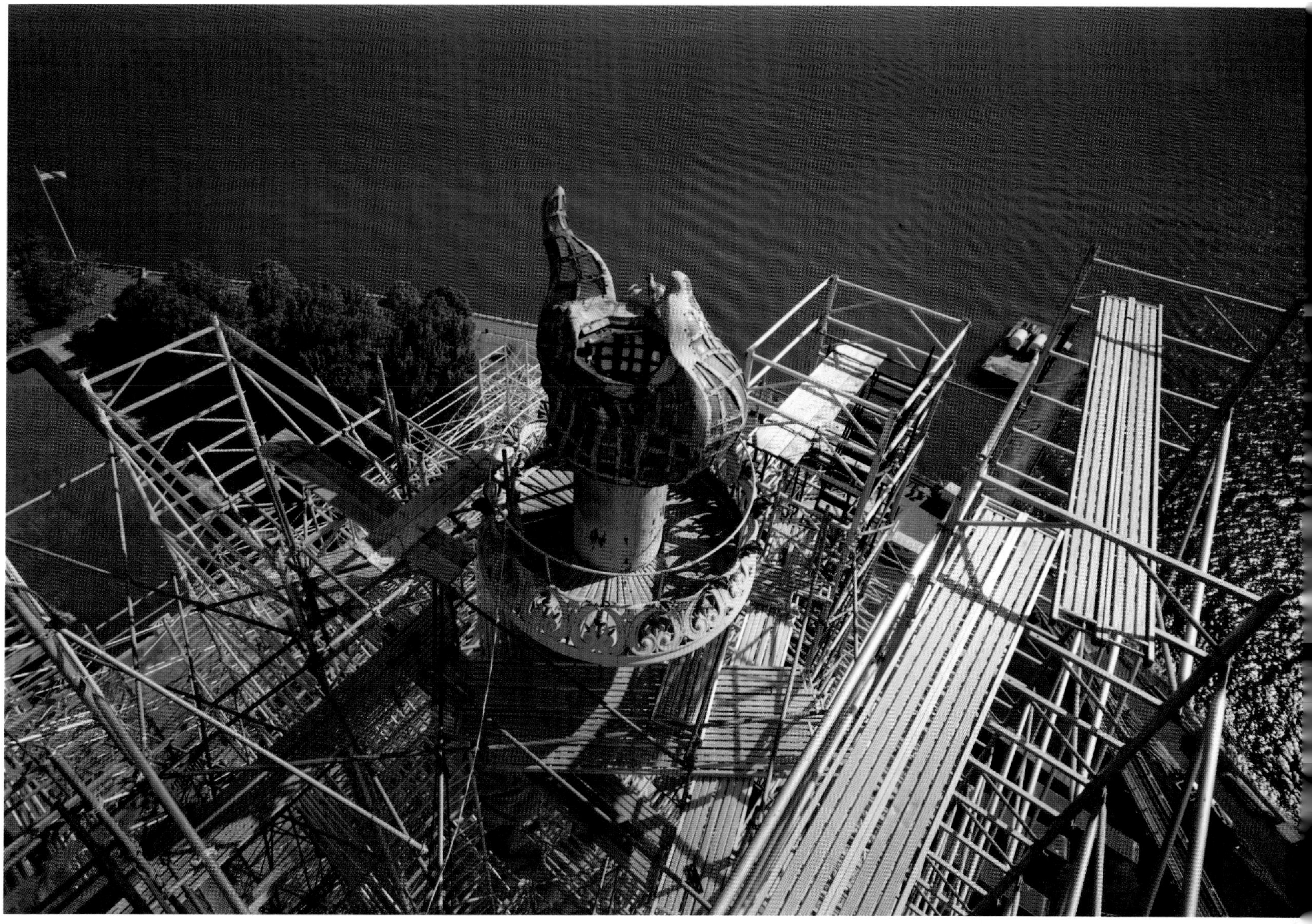

TORCH

Opposite. *Liberty carrying the torch of freedom before the scaffolding was erected.*

Above. *Old torch a few days before its removal. The flame known to generations of Americans was not the original but was actually resculpted into a lantern of amber glass by Gutzon Borglum in 1916.*

Right. *New location for the old torch, at the ground-floor museum in the pedestal.*

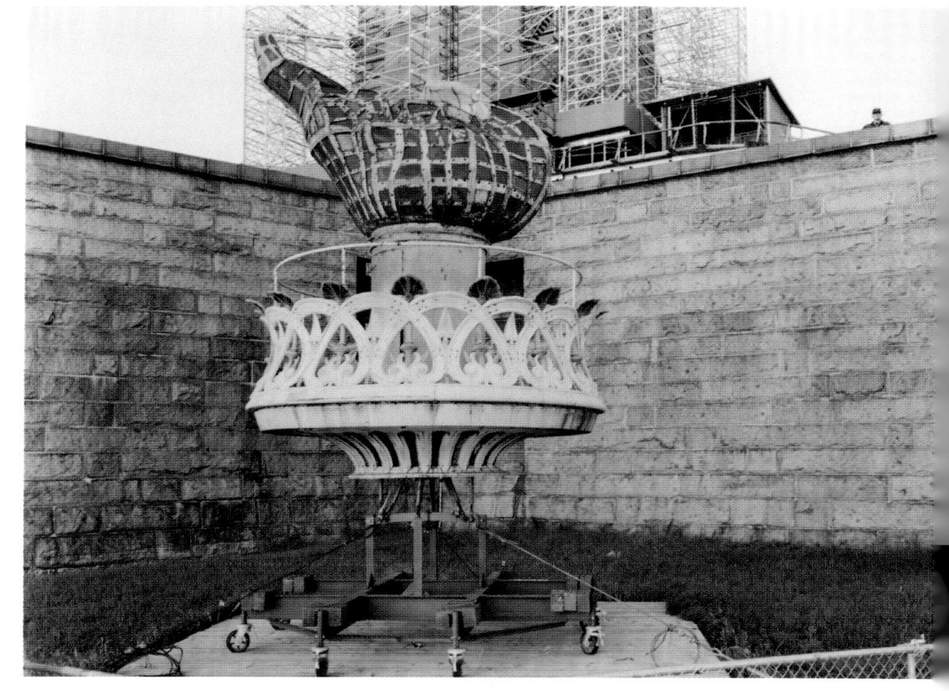

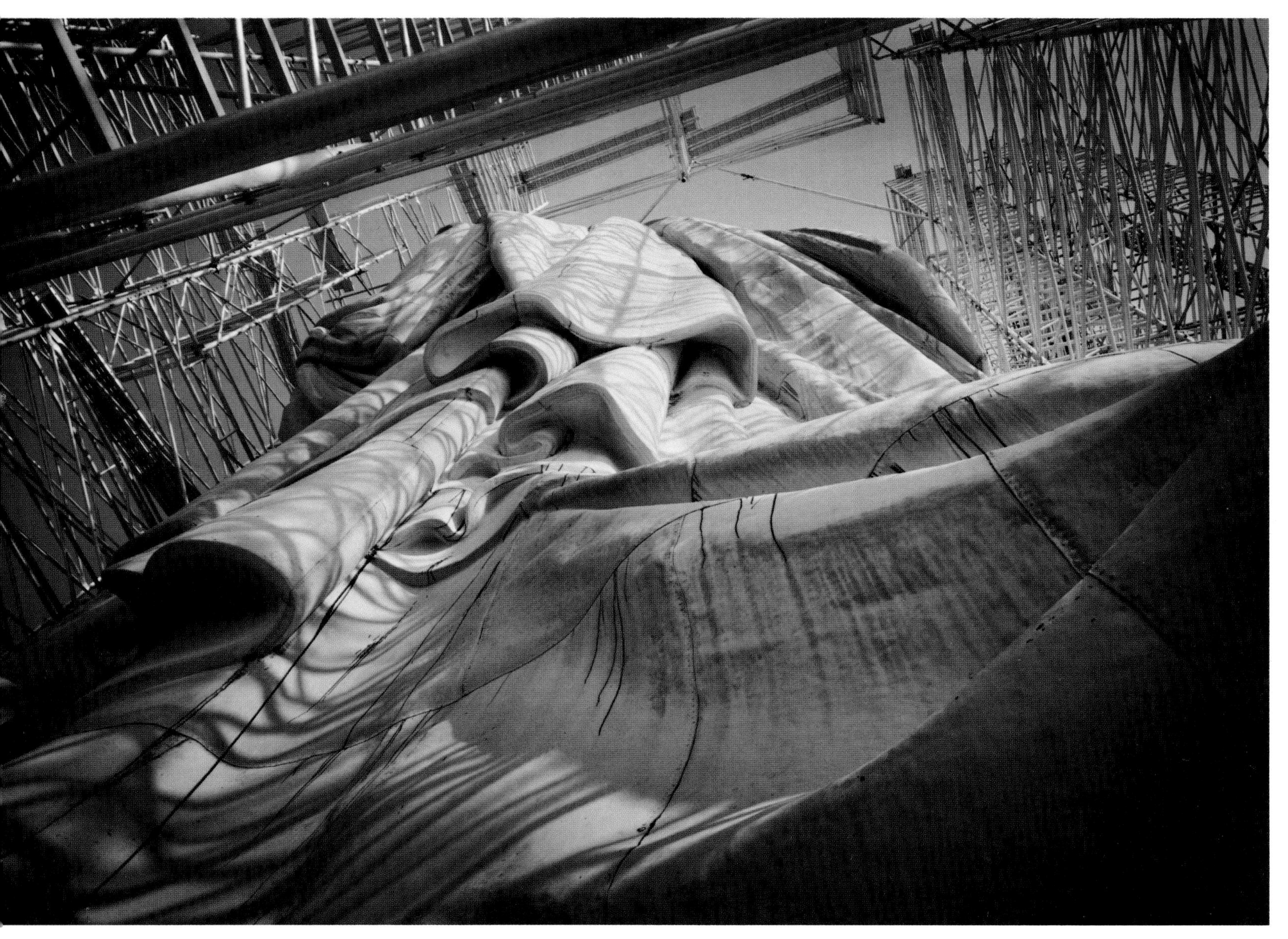

ROBE

Above. *Folds of the classically draped robe rising above the pedestal, which was designed by Richard Morris Hunt.*

Opposite. *Iron frame supporting the statue's armature, connected with riveted gusset plates. Iron straps hold up the copper sheets of the robe.*

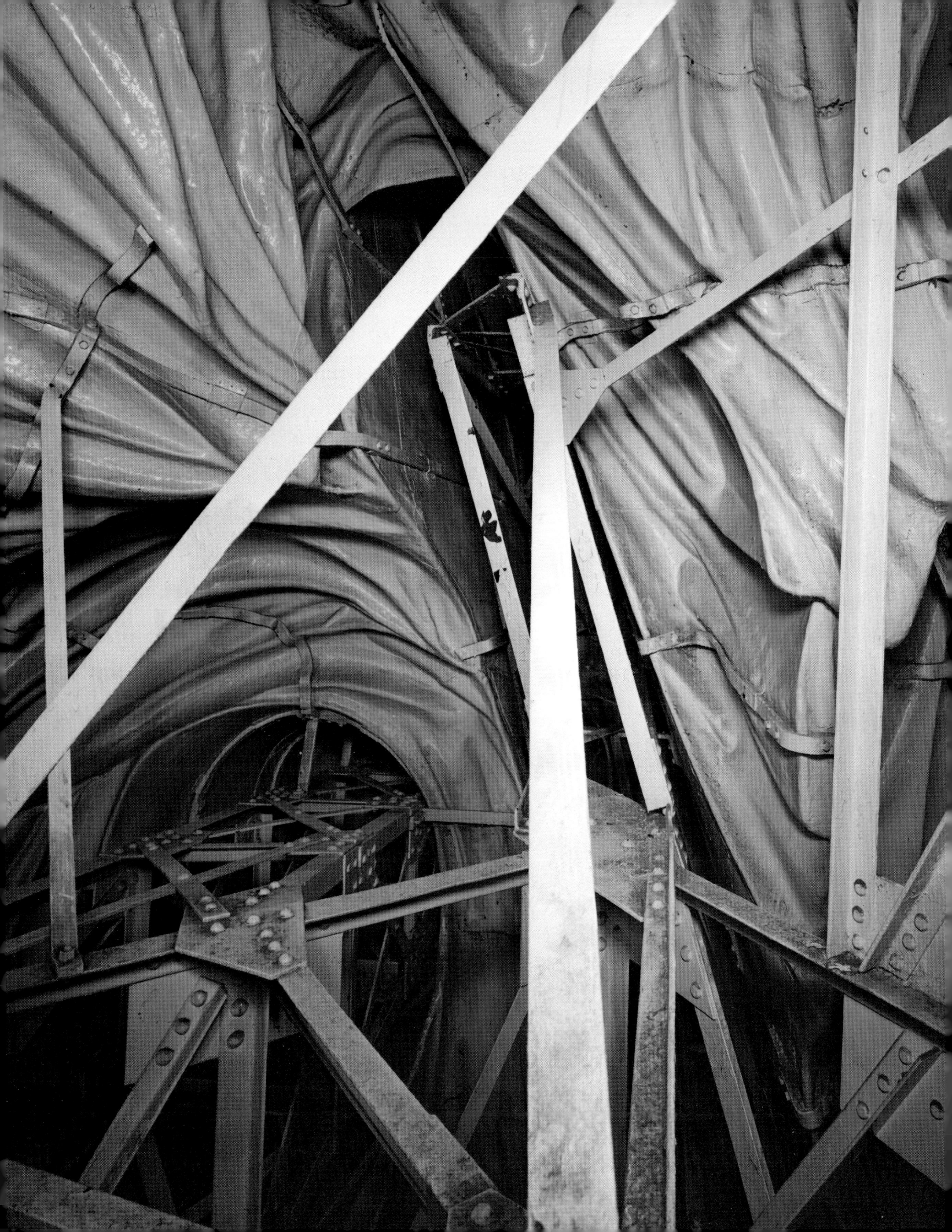

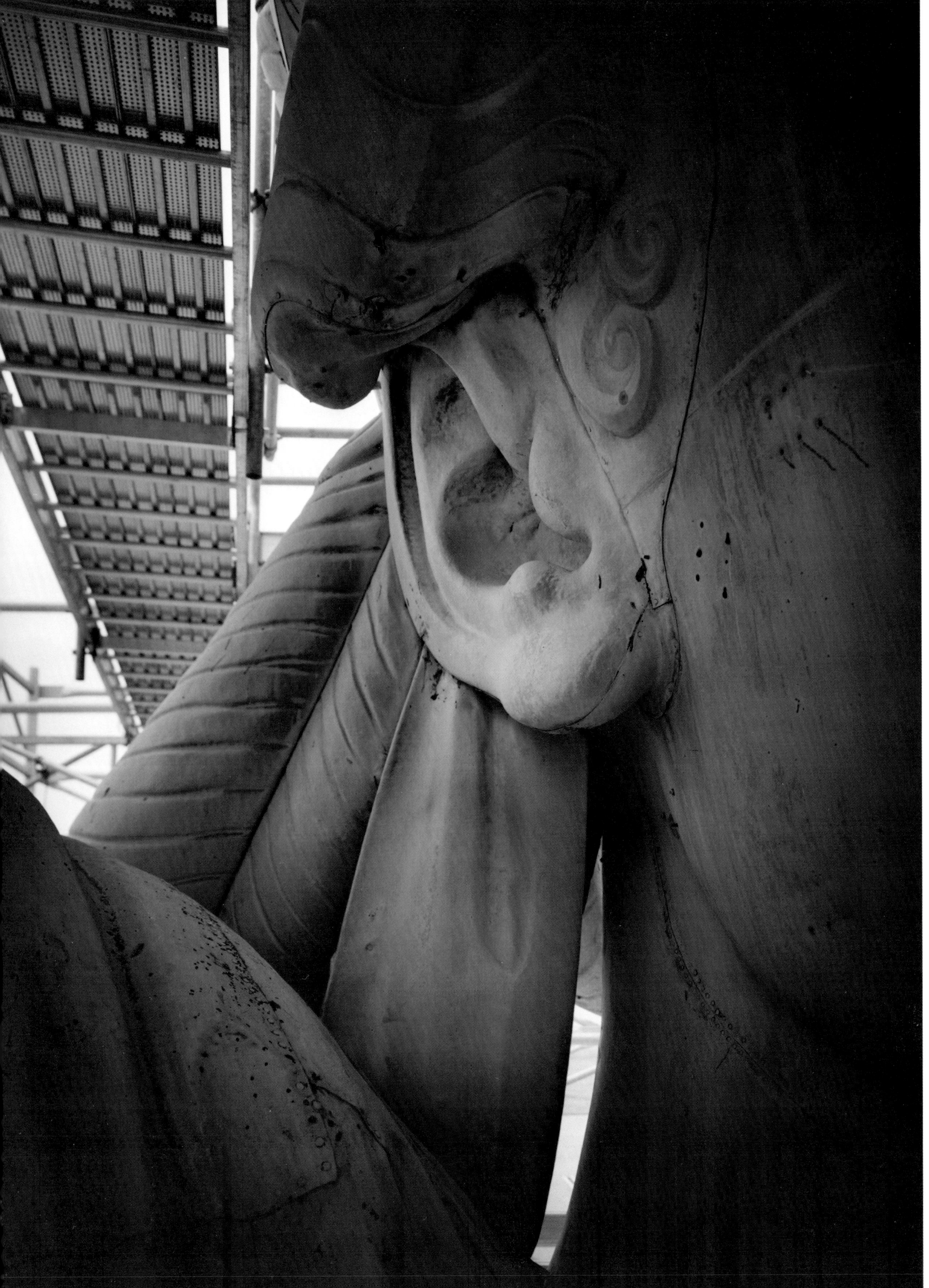

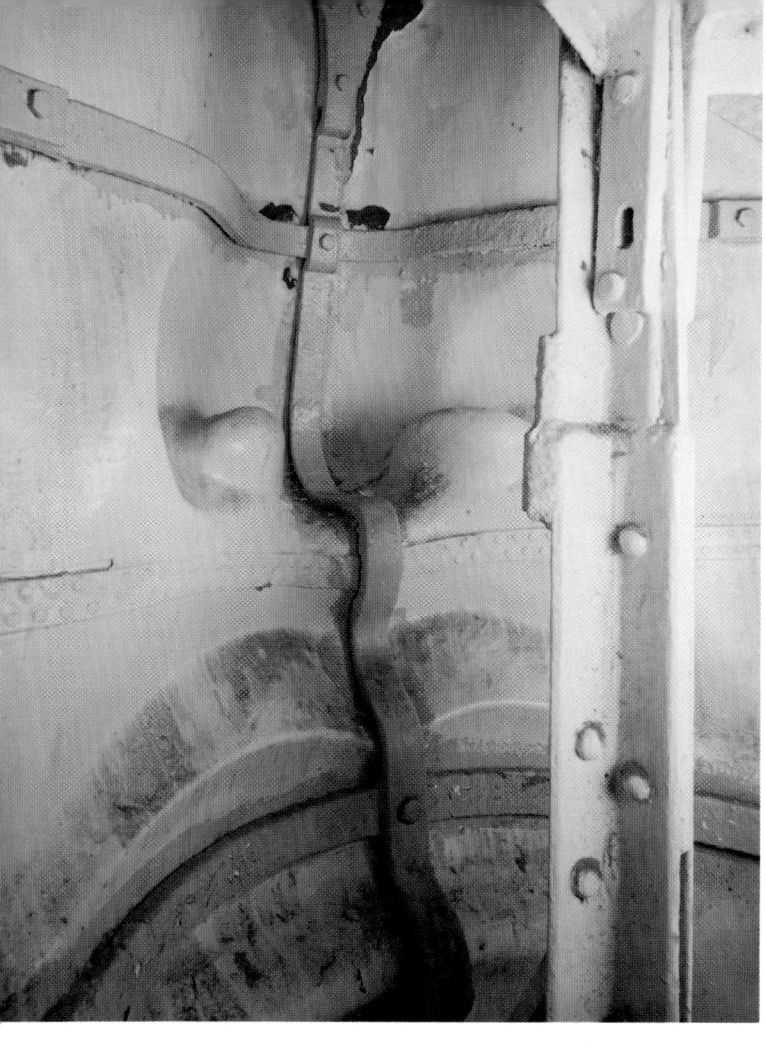

HEAD TO FOOT

Opposite. *Right ear and cheek before restoration, showing where rivets had come off the deteriorated interior iron straps that kept the copper skin in place.*

Left. *Mouth and nose, each about three feet in size. Cracks in these features were repaired during the restoration.*

Below. *Left foot, placed on a symbolically broken chain.*

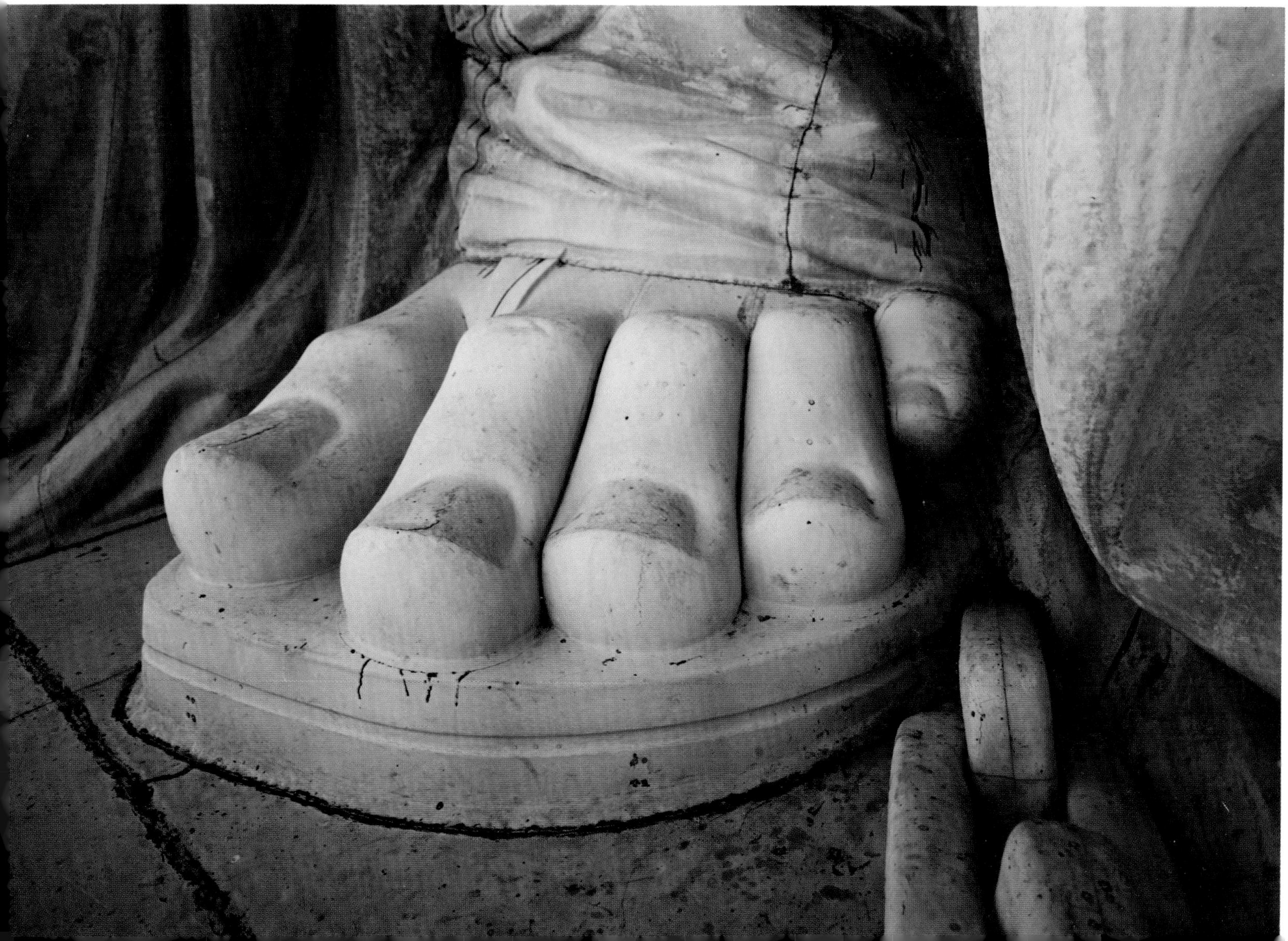

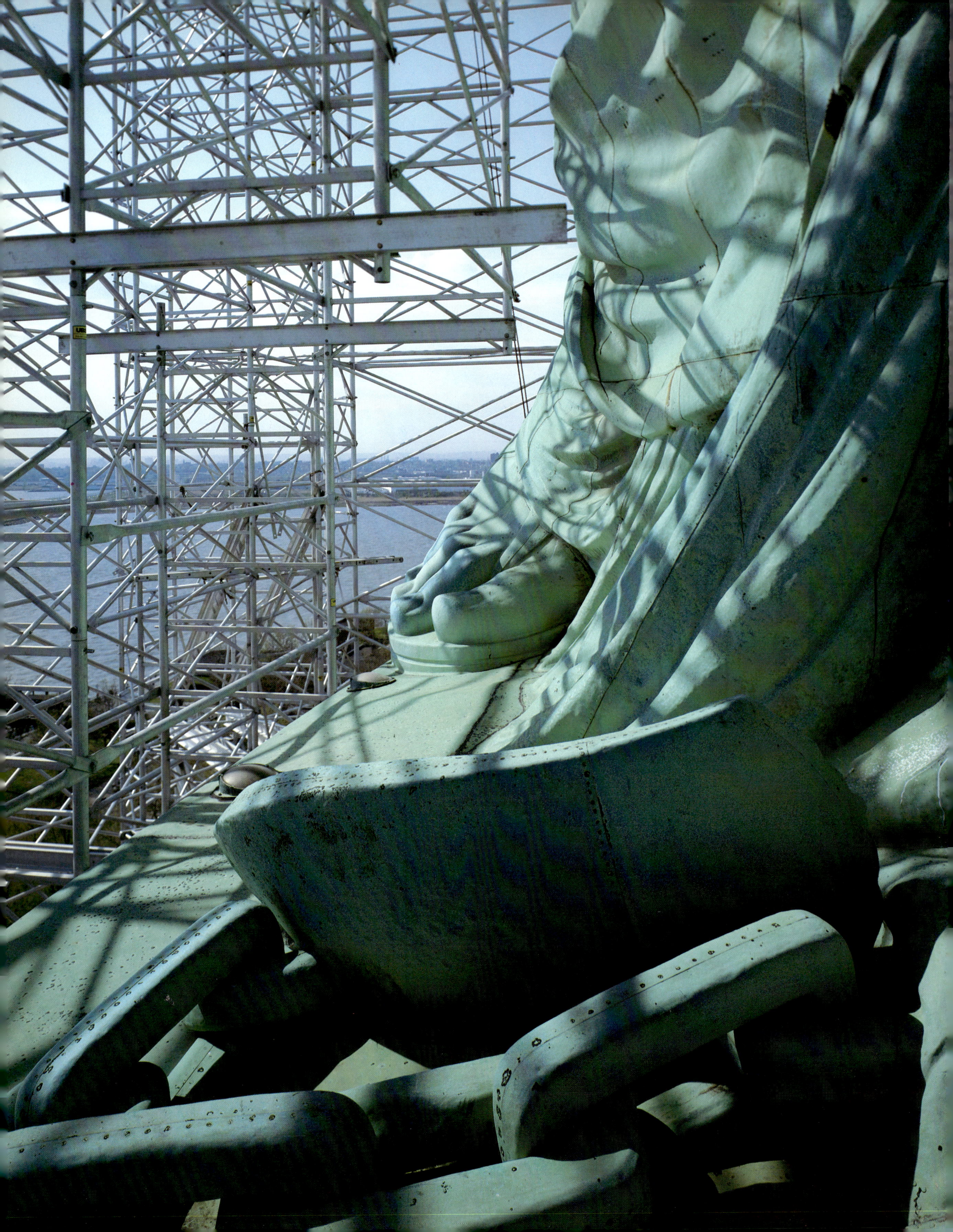

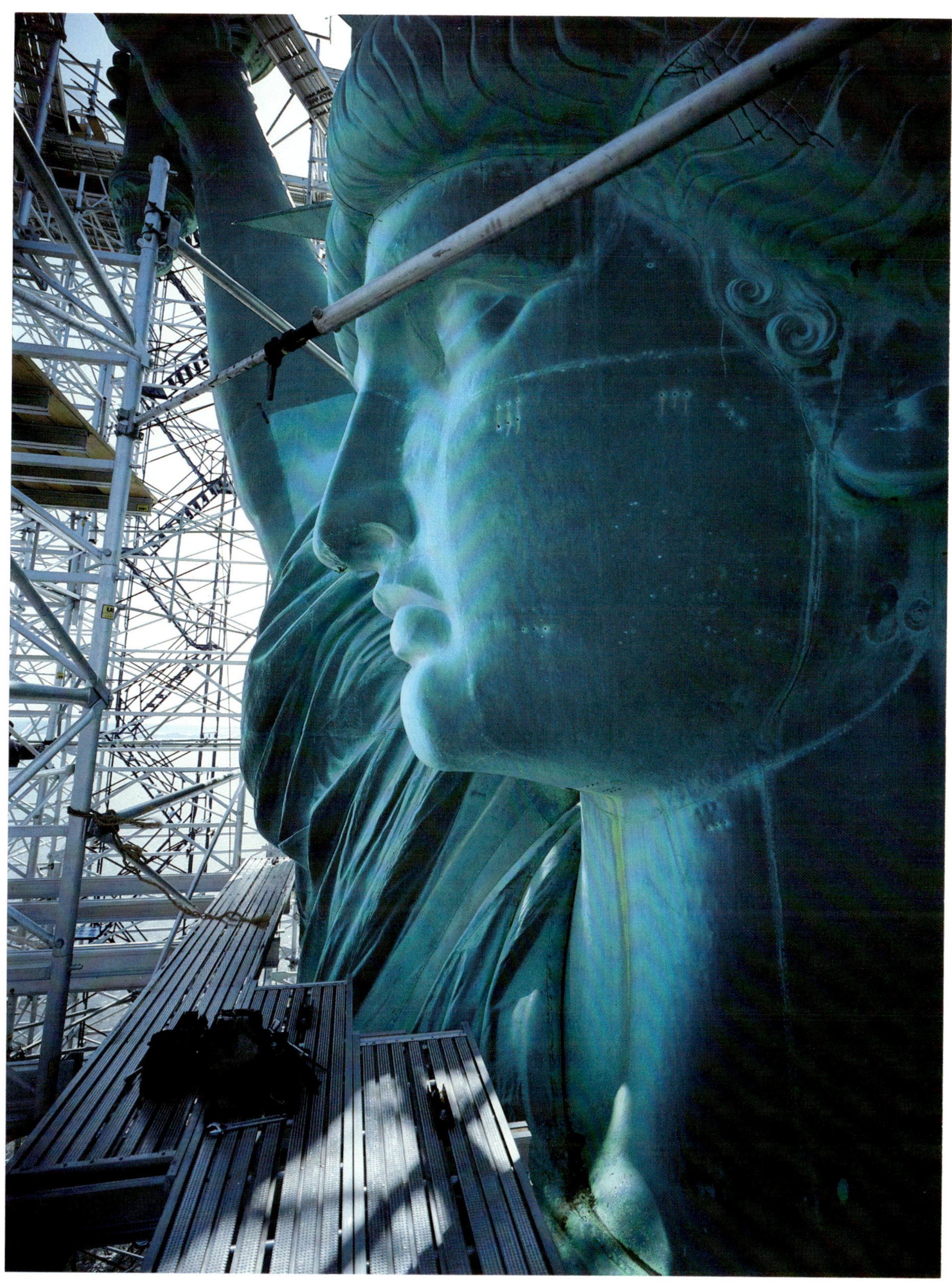

REBIRTH

Opposite. *Leg with the chain and shackle from which Liberty has been freed.*

Above. *Profile of the statue before the restoration and centennial rededication.*

THE PHOTOGRAPHS

All the photographs in this book were made with either a 4-by-5 or a 5-by-7-inch Toyo 57G camera. The focal length of the lenses ranged from 75-millimeter to 480-millimeter, but I find myself using the 75-millimeter or 121-millimeter wide-angle lenses almost exclusively.

My lighting system is quite simple, relying on an open shutter while often moving around in the picture sequentially firing off the old Sylvania Type 3 flash bulbs. In recent years I have taken to using a Norman 200B electronic flash unit in smaller spaces while employing it in the same manner as I do the large flash bulbs. Flash engineers have yet to come up with a portable electronic flash system that can compare with the light output of the old bulbs. They are still unmatched for what I call "unavailable-light interiors" in these old structures, with their inherent light-absorbing qualities.

The films I tend to use are Kodak Plus-X and Royal Pan in 4-by-5 and 5-by-7-inch sizes. For color, Ektachrome daylight film is about all that is available in these large sizes.

I developed all the black-and-white photographs in this book myself. For views such as steel plants where the lighting is dim, I chose Acufine developer to double the emulsion speed. For normal lighting, Kodak Microdol-X works well for most sites. I use a zone processing system, printing on a wide range of papers based on the contrast ranges of the negatives.

JET LOWE

THE HAER ARCHIVES

The photographs, measured drawings and historical information that form the collection of the Historic American Engineering Record are housed in the Prints and Photographs Division (Architecture, Design and Engineering Collections) of the Library of Congress in Washington, D.C. The division's reading room is open to visitors and researchers. The records, which may be researched using a printed checklist, card catalog and subject card index, are arranged in geographical order by state, county, city or vicinity and building or project name. Researchers may consult captioned black-and-white photographs, written histories and photocopies of measured drawings (not all buildings are recorded in all three forms of documentation). In 1985 a computerized checklist of the HAER collection was published covering the years 1969 to 1985.

Copies of all HAER materials in the Library of Congress, including the black-and-white photographs published in this book, may be ordered from the Photoduplication Service. Those making such requests should provide the names and locations of the buildings and type of documentation desired to the Photoduplication Service, Library of Congress, Washington, D.C. 20540. The library will respond with complete ordering and price information. (Some recent projects may not yet have been transmitted.)

FURTHER READING

American Society of Civil Engineers. *ASCE Guide to History and Heritage Programs.* New York: ASCE, 1984.

American Society of Mechanical Engineers. *ASME Guide to History and Heritage.* New York: ASME, 1979.

Baker, T. Lindsay. *A Field Guide to American Windmills.* Norman: University of Oklahoma Press, 1985.

Billington, David. *The Tower and the Bridge: The Art of Structural Engineering.* New York: Basic Books, 1983.

Chamberlin, William P. *Historic Bridges: Criteria for Decision Making.* Washington, D.C.: National Academy of Sciences, 1983.

DeLony, Eric N., et al. *HAER Checklist: 1969–1985.* Washington, D.C.: National Park Service, 1985. Pub. No. 174661/AS, National Technical Information Service, Springfield, Va. 22161.

Greenhill, Ralph. *Engineer's Witness.* Boston: David Godine, 1985.

Hartenberg, Richard S., ed. *National Historic Mechanical Engineering Landmarks.* New York: ASME, 1979.

Hefner, Robert J. *Windmills of Long Island.* New York: W. W. Norton, 1984.

Historic American Buildings Survey — Historic American Engineering Record. *Historic America: Buildings, Structures, and Sites.* Washington, D.C.: Library of Congress, 1983.

Hudson, Kenneth. *The Archaeology of Industry.* New York: Scribner's, 1976.

IA: The Journal of the Society for Industrial Archeology (National Museum of American History, Room 5020, Washington, D.C. 20560). Annual.

Kemp, Emory L., and Theodore Anton Sande, eds. *Historic Preservation of Engineering Works.* New York: ASCE, 1981.

Kidney, Walter C. *Working Places: The Adaptive Use of Industrial Buildings.* Pittsburgh: Ober Park Associates, 1976.

Macaulay, David. *Mill.* Boston: Houghton Mifflin, 1983.

McCullough, David. *The Great Bridge.* New York: Simon and Schuster, 1972.

Moffett, Marian, and Lawrence Wodehouse. *Built for the People of the United States: Fifty Years of TVA Architecture.* Knoxville: School of Architecture, University of Tennessee, 1983.

Plowden, David. *Bridges: The Spans of North America.* 1974. New York: W. W. Norton, 1984.

Sande, Theodore Anton. *Industrial Archeology: A New Look at the American Heritage.* Brattleboro, Vt.: Stephen Greene Press, 1976.

SIA Newsletter. Society for Industrial Archeology. Quarterly.

Starbuck, David, ed. *An Introductory Bibliography in Industrial Archeology.* Washington, D.C.: Society for Industrial Archeology, 1983.

Weitzman, David. *Traces of the Past: A Field Guide to American Industrial Archeology.* New York: Scribner's, 1980.

______. *Windmills, Bridges and Old Machines: Discovering Our Industrial Past.* New York: Scribner's, 1982.

THE PRESERVATION PRESS

National Trust for Historic Preservation
1785 Massachusetts Avenue, N.W.
Washington, D.C. 20036

The National Trust for Historic Preservation is the only private, nonprofit national organization chartered by Congress to encourage public participation in the preservation of sites, buildings and objects significant in American history and culture. Support is provided by membership dues, endowment funds, contributions and grants from federal agencies, including the U.S. Department of the Interior, under provisions of the National Historic Preservation Act of 1986. Membership in the National Trust is open to all interested individuals, organizations, corporations and libraries; for further information, write to the above address.

Printed in the United States of America
90 89 88 87 86 5 4 3 2 1

Library of Congress Cataloging in Publication Data

Lowe, Jet.
Industrial eye.
Bibliography: p. 127
1. Photography, Industrial – United States. 2. Industrial archaeology – United States. I. Maddex, Diane. II. Historic American Engineering Record. III. Title.
TR706.L69 1986 779'.96'0973 86-25269
ISBN 0-89133-124-7

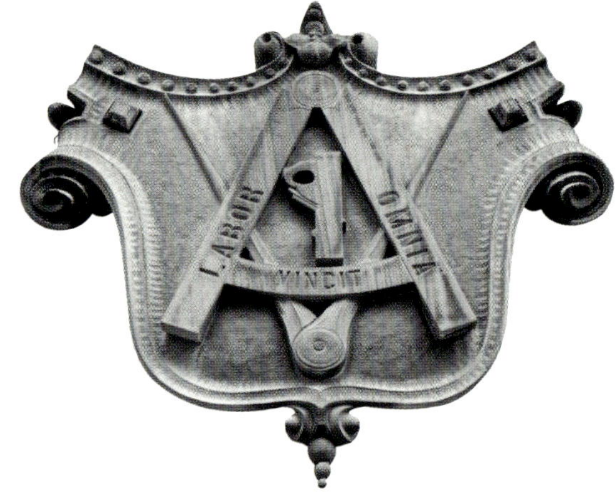

Designed by Marc Alain Meadows and Robert Wiser, Meadows & Wiser, Washington, D.C.

Developed and edited by Diane Maddex, editor, The Preservation Press, Washington, D.C.

Composed in Bodoni by General Typographers, Inc., Washington, D.C.

Printed on 100-pound Potlatch Eloquence stock by Wolk Press, Woodlawn, Md.

Bound in Record Buckram Natural Finish cloth with 80-pound Strathmore Grandee Marina Teal endpapers by American Trade Bindery, Columbia, Md.

The Preservation Press wishes to thank the following persons for their generous assistance with the preparation of this book: Robert J. Kapsch, chief, Historic American Buildings Survey – Historic American Engineering Record; Sally K. Tompkins, deputy chief; Jet Lowe, photographer; Gray Fitzsimons, historian; Eric N. DeLony, architect; Marlene Bergstrom, photographic services assistant; Mary Ison, Joyce Nalewajk and Phillip Seitz, Prints and Photographs Division, Library of Congress; and Terri Brand, Meadows & Wiser.

Dust jacket cover photograph. *Carding machine at Watkins Mill, a woolen mill in Lawson, Mo., built in 1861.*

Frontispiece. *View over the Republic Steel Company plant from the Clark Avenue Bridge, Cleveland.*

Colophon. *Keystone on Carpenters Union Hall, Butte, Mont.*

Dust jacket flap photograph. *Jet Lowe recording a cable car in the powerhouse and barn operated by United Railroads of San Francisco. Photograph by Dick Freer, National Park Service.*